אֶסְתֵּר

ים, עַל-סֵפֶר דִּבְרֵי הַיָּמִים, לְמַלְכֵי, מָדַי וּפָרָס
halo-hem ketuvim, al-sefer divrei hayamim, le
are they not written in the book of the chronicles of th

כִּי מָרְדֳּכַי הַיְּהוּדִי, מִשְׁנֶה לַמֶּלֶךְ אֲחַשְׁוֵרוֹשׁ, וְגָדוֹל לַיְּהוּדִים
ki mordechai hayehudi, mishneh lammelech achashverosh, vegadol layehudim
For Mordecai the Jew was next unto king Ahasuerus, and great among the Jews,

וְרָצוּי לְרֹב אֶחָיו--דֹּרֵשׁ טוֹב לְעַמּוֹ, וְדֹבֵר שָׁלוֹם לְכָל-זַרְעוֹ
veratzui lerov echav; doresh tov le'ammo, vedover shalom lechol-zar'o
and accepted of the multitude of his brethren; seeking the good of his people and speaking peace to all his seed.

אֶסְתֵּר

וִימֵי הַפּוּרִים הָאֵלֶּה, לֹא יַעַבְרוּ מִתּוֹךְ הַיְּהוּדִים, וְזִכְרָם, לֹא-יָסוּף מִזַּרְעָם
viymei happurim ha'elleh, lo ya'avru mittoch hayehudim, vezichram lo-yasuf mizzar'am
and that these days of Purim should not fail from among the Jews, nor the memorial of them perish from their seed.

וַתִּכְתֹּב אֶסְתֵּר הַמַּלְכָּה בַת-אֲבִיחַיִל, וּמָרְדֳּכַי הַיְּהוּדִי--אֶת-כָּל-תֹּקֶף
vattichtov ester hammalkah vat-'avichayil umordechai hayehudi et-kol-tokef
Then Esther the queen, the daughter of Abihail, and Mordecai the Jew, wrote down all the acts of power,

לְקַיֵּם, אֵת אִגֶּרֶת הַפֻּרִים הַזֹּאת--הַשֵּׁנִית
lekayem, et iggeret happurim hazzot hashenit
to confirm this second letter of Purim.

וַיִּשְׁלַח סְפָרִים אֶל-כָּל-הַיְּהוּדִים, אֶל-שֶׁבַע וְעֶשְׂרִים וּמֵאָה מְדִינָה
vayishlach sefarim el-kol-hayehudim, el-sheva ve'esrim ume'ah medinah
And he sent letters unto all the Jews, to the hundred twenty and seven provinces

מַלְכוּת, אֲחַשְׁוֵרוֹשׁ: דִּבְרֵי שָׁלוֹם, וֶאֱמֶת
malchut achashverosh; divrei shalom ve'emet
of the kingdom of Ahasuerus, with words of peace and truth,

לְקַיֵּם אֶת-יְמֵי הַפֻּרִים הָאֵלֶּה בִּזְמַנֵּיהֶם
lekayem et-yemei happurim ha'elleh bizmanneihem
to confirm these days of Purim in their appointed times,

כַּאֲשֶׁר קִיַּם עֲלֵיהֶם מָרְדֳּכַי הַיְּהוּדִי וְאֶסְתֵּר הַמַּלְכָּה
ka'asher kiyam aleihem mordechai hayehudi ve'ester hammalkah
according as Mordecai the Jew and Esther the queen had enjoined them,

וְכַאֲשֶׁר קִיְּמוּ עַל-נַפְשָׁם, וְעַל-זַרְעָם: דִּבְרֵי הַצּוֹמוֹת, וְזַעֲקָתָם
vecha'asher kiyemu al-nafsham ve'al-zar'am; divrei hatzomot veza'akatam
and as they had ordained for themselves and for their seed, the matters of the fastings and their cry.

וּמַאֲמַר אֶסְתֵּר--קִיַּם, דִּבְרֵי הַפֻּרִים הָאֵלֶּה; וְנִכְתָּב, בַּסֵּפֶר
uma'amar ester, kiyam divrei happurim ha'elleh; venichtav bassefer
And the commandment of Esther confirmed these matters of Purim; and it was written in the book.

וַיָּשֶׂם הַמֶּלֶךְ אֲחַשְׁוֵרֹשׁ מַס עַל-הָאָרֶץ, וְאִיֵּי הַיָּם
Vayasem hammelech achashverosh mas al-ha'aretz ve'iyei hayam
And the king Ahasuerus laid a tribute upon the land, and upon the isles of the sea.

וְכָל-מַעֲשֵׂה תָקְפּוֹ, וּגְבוּרָתוֹ, וּפָרָשַׁת גְּדֻלַּת מָרְדֳּכַי, אֲשֶׁר גִּדְּלוֹ הַמֶּלֶךְ
vechol-ma'aseh tokpo ugevurato, ufarashat gedullat mordechai, asher giddelo hammelech
And all the acts of his power and of his might, and the full account of the greatness of Mordecai, how the king advanced him,

אֶסְתֵּר

כִּי הָמָן בֶּן-הַמְּדָתָא הָאֲגָגִי, צֹרֵר כָּל-הַיְּהוּדִים
ki haman ben-hammedata ha'agagi, tzorer kol-hayehudim
because Haman the son of Hammedatha, the Agagite, the enemy of all the Jews,

חָשַׁב עַל-הַיְּהוּדִים, לְאַבְּדָם; וְהִפִּל פּוּר הוּא הַגּוֹרָל, לְהֻמָּם וּלְאַבְּדָם
chashav al-hayehudim le'abbedam; vehippil pur hu haggoral, lehummam ule'abbedam
had devised against the Jews to destroy them, and had cast pur, that is, the lot, to discomfit them, and to destroy them;

וּבְבֹאָהּ, לִפְנֵי הַמֶּלֶךְ, אָמַר עִם-הַסֵּפֶר, יָשׁוּב מַחֲשַׁבְתּוֹ הָרָעָה
uvevo'ah lifnei hammelech amar im-hassefer, yashuv machashavto hara'ah
but when she came before the king, he commanded by letters that his wicked device,

אֲשֶׁר-חָשַׁב עַל-הַיְּהוּדִים עַל-רֹאשׁוֹ
asher-chashav al-hayehudim al-rosho
which he had devised against the Jews, should return upon his own head;

וְתָלוּ אֹתוֹ וְאֶת-בָּנָיו, עַל-הָעֵץ
vetalu oto ve'et-banav al-ha'etz
and that he and his sons should be hanged on the gallows.

עַל-כֵּן קָרְאוּ לַיָּמִים הָאֵלֶּה פוּרִים, עַל-שֵׁם הַפּוּר--עַל-כֵּן, עַל-כָּל-דִּבְרֵי הָאִגֶּרֶת הַזֹּאת
'al-ken kare'u layamim ha'elleh furim al-shem happur, al-ken al-kol-divrei ha'iggeret hazzot
Wherefore they called these days Purim, after the name of pur. Therefore because of all the words of this letter,

וּמָה-רָאוּ עַל-כָּכָה, וּמָה הִגִּיעַ אֲלֵיהֶם
umah-ra'u al-kachah, umah higgia aleihem
and of that which they had seen concerning this matter, and that which had come unto them,

קִיְּמוּ וְקִבְּלוּ הַיְּהוּדִים עֲלֵיהֶם וְעַל-זַרְעָם וְעַל כָּל-הַנִּלְוִים עֲלֵיהֶם
kiyemu vekibbelu hayehudim aleihem ve'al-zar'am ve'al kol-hannilvim aleihem
the Jews ordained, and took upon them, and upon their seed, and upon all such as joined themselves unto them,

וְלֹא יַעֲבוֹר--לִהְיוֹת עֹשִׂים אֵת שְׁנֵי הַיָּמִים הָאֵלֶּה, כִּכְתָבָם
velo ya'avor, lihyot osim, et shenei hayamim ha'elleh, kichtavam
so as it should not fail, that they would keep these two days according to the writing thereof,

וְכִזְמַנָּם: בְּכָל-שָׁנָה, וְשָׁנָה
vechizmannam; bechol-shanah veshanah
and according to the appointed time thereof, every year;

וְהַיָּמִים הָאֵלֶּה נִזְכָּרִים וְנַעֲשִׂים בְּכָל-דּוֹר וָדוֹר
vehayamim ha'elleh nizkarim vena'asim bechol-dor vador
and that these days should be remembered and kept throughout every generation,

מִשְׁפָּחָה וּמִשְׁפָּחָה, מְדִינָה וּמְדִינָה, וְעִיר וָעִיר
mishpachah umishpachah, medinah umedinah ve'ir va'ir;
every family, every province, and every city;

אֶסְתֵּר

וְנוֹחַ, בְּאַרְבָּעָה עָשָׂר בּוֹ, וְעָשֹׂה אֹתוֹ, יוֹם מִשְׁתֶּה וְשִׂמְחָה
venoach, be'arba'ah asar bo, ve'asoh oto, yom mishteh vesimchah
and on the fourteenth day of the same they rested, and made it a day of feasting and gladness.

וְהַיְּהוּדִים אֲשֶׁר-בְּשׁוּשָׁן, נִקְהֲלוּ בִּשְׁלוֹשָׁה עָשָׂר בּוֹ, וּבְאַרְבָּעָה עָשָׂר, בּוֹ
vehayehudim asher-beshushan, nik'halu bishloshah asar bo, uve'arba'ah asar bo
But the Jews that were in Shushan assembled together on the thirteenth day thereof, and on the fourteenth thereof;

וְנוֹחַ, בַּחֲמִשָּׁה עָשָׂר בּוֹ, וְעָשֹׂה אֹתוֹ, יוֹם מִשְׁתֶּה וְשִׂמְחָה
venoach, bachamishah asar bo, ve'asoh oto, yom mishteh vesimchah
and on the fifteenth day of the same they rested, and made it a day of feasting and gladness.

עַל-כֵּן הַיְּהוּדִים הַפְּרָזִים, הַיֹּשְׁבִים בְּעָרֵי הַפְּרָזוֹת--עֹשִׂים אֵת יוֹם אַרְבָּעָה עָשָׂר
'al-ken hayehudim happerazim, hayoshevim be'arei happerazot osim, et yom arba'ah asar
Therefore do the Jews of the villages, that dwell in the unwalled towns, make the fourteenth day

לְחֹדֶשׁ אֲדָר, שִׂמְחָה וּמִשְׁתֶּה וְיוֹם טוֹב; וּמִשְׁלוֹחַ מָנוֹת, אִישׁ לְרֵעֵהוּ
lechodesh adar, simchah umishteh veyom tov; umishloach manot ish lere'ehu
of the month Adar a day of gladness and feasting, and a good day, and of sending portions one to another.

וַיִּכְתֹּב מָרְדֳּכַי, אֶת-הַדְּבָרִים הָאֵלֶּה; וַיִּשְׁלַח סְפָרִים אֶל-כָּל-הַיְּהוּדִים
vayichtov mordechai, et-haddevarim ha'elleh; vayishlach sefarim el-kol-hayehudim
And Mordecai wrote these things, and sent letters unto all the Jews

אֲשֶׁר בְּכָל-מְדִינוֹת הַמֶּלֶךְ אֲחַשְׁוֵרוֹשׁ--הַקְּרוֹבִים, וְהָרְחוֹקִים
asher bechol-medinot hammelech achashverosh, hakkerovim veharechokim
that were in all the provinces of the king Ahasuerus, both nigh and far,

לְקַיֵּם, עֲלֵיהֶם--לִהְיוֹת עֹשִׂים אֵת יוֹם אַרְבָּעָה עָשָׂר לְחֹדֶשׁ אֲדָר, וְאֵת יוֹם-חֲמִשָּׁה עָשָׂר בּוֹ: בְּכָל-שָׁנָה, וְשָׁנָה
lekayem aleihem lihyot osim, et yom arba'ah asar lechodesh adar, ve'et yom-chamishah asar bo; bechol-shanah veshanah
to enjoin them that they should keep the fourteenth day of the month Adar, and the fifteenth day of the same, yearly,

כַּיָּמִים, אֲשֶׁר-נָחוּ בָהֶם הַיְּהוּדִים מֵאֹיְבֵיהֶם, וְהַחֹדֶשׁ אֲשֶׁר נֶהְפַּךְ לָהֶם מִיָּגוֹן לְשִׂמְחָה
kayamim, asher-nachu vahem hayehudim me'oyeveihem, vehachodesh, asher nehpach lahem miyagon lesimchah
the days wherein the Jews had rest from their enemies, and the month which was turned unto them from sorrow to gladness,

וּמֵאֵבֶל לְיוֹם טוֹב; לַעֲשׂוֹת אוֹתָם, יְמֵי מִשְׁתֶּה וְשִׂמְחָה
ume'evel leyom tov; la'asot otam, yemei mishteh vesimchah
and from mourning into a good day; that they should make them days of feasting and gladness,

וּמִשְׁלוֹחַ מָנוֹת אִישׁ לְרֵעֵהוּ, וּמַתָּנוֹת לָאֶבְיוֹנִים
umishloach manot ish lere'ehu, umattanot la'evyonim
and of sending portions one to another, and gifts to the poor.

וְקִבֵּל, הַיְּהוּדִים, אֵת אֲשֶׁר-הֵחֵלּוּ, לַעֲשׂוֹת; וְאֵת אֲשֶׁר-כָּתַב מָרְדֳּכַי אֲלֵיהֶם
vekibbel hayehudim, et asher-hechellu la'asot; ve'et asher-katav mordechai aleihem
And the Jews took upon them to do as they had begun, and as Mordecai had written unto them;

אֶסְתֵּר

וַיֹּאמֶר הַמֶּלֶךְ לְאֶסְתֵּר הַמַּלְכָּה, בְּשׁוּשַׁן הַבִּירָה הָרְגוּ הַיְּהוּדִים וְאַבֵּד חֲמֵשׁ מֵאוֹת אִישׁ
vayomer hammelech le'ester hammalkah, beshushan habbirah haregu hayehudim ve'abbed chamesh me'ot ish,
And the king said unto Esther the queen: 'The Jews have slain and destroyed five hundred men in Shushan the castle,

וְאֵת עֲשֶׂרֶת בְּנֵי-הָמָן--בִּשְׁאָר מְדִינוֹת הַמֶּלֶךְ, מֶה עָשׂוּ
ve'et aseret benei-haman, bish'ar medinot hammelech meh asu
and the ten sons of Haman; what then have they done in the rest of the king's provinces!

וּמַה-שְּׁאֵלָתֵךְ וְיִנָּתֵן לָךְ, וּמַה-בַּקָּשָׁתֵךְ עוֹד וְתֵעָשׂ
umah-she'elatech veyinnaten lach, umah-bakkashatech od vete'as
Now whatever thy petition, it shall be granted thee; and whatever thy request further, it shall be done.'

וַתֹּאמֶר אֶסְתֵּר, אִם-עַל-הַמֶּלֶךְ טוֹב--יִנָּתֵן גַּם-מָחָר לַיְּהוּדִים אֲשֶׁר בְּשׁוּשָׁן, לַעֲשׂוֹת
vattomer ester im-'al-hammelech tov, yinnaten gam-machar, layehudim asher beshushan, la'asot
Then said Esther: 'If it please the king, let it be granted to the Jews that are in Shushan to do to-morrow

כְּדָת הַיּוֹם; וְאֵת עֲשֶׂרֶת בְּנֵי-הָמָן, יִתְלוּ עַל-הָעֵץ
kedat hayom; ve'et aseret benei-haman yitlu al-ha'etz
also according unto this day's decree, and let Haman's ten sons be hanged upon the gallows.'

וַיֹּאמֶר הַמֶּלֶךְ לְהֵעָשׂוֹת כֵּן, וַתִּנָּתֵן דָּת בְּשׁוּשָׁן; וְאֵת עֲשֶׂרֶת בְּנֵי-הָמָן, תָּלוּ
vayomer hammelech lehe'asot ken, vattinnaten dat beshushan; ve'et aseret benei-haman talu
And the king commanded it so to be done; and a decree was given out in Shushan; and they hanged Haman's ten sons.

וַיִּקָּהֲלוּ הַיְּהוּדִים אֲשֶׁר-בְּשׁוּשָׁן, גַּם בְּיוֹם אַרְבָּעָה עָשָׂר לְחֹדֶשׁ אֲדָר
vayikkahalu hayehudim asher-beshushan, gam beyom arba'ah asar lechodesh adar
And the Jews that were in Shushan gathered themselves together on the fourteenth day also of the month Adar,

וַיַּהַרְגוּ בְשׁוּשָׁן, שְׁלֹשׁ מֵאוֹת אִישׁ; וּבַבִּזָּה--לֹא שָׁלְחוּ, אֶת-יָדָם
vayahargu veshushan, shelosh me'ot ish; uvabbizzah, lo shalechu et-yadam
and slew three hundred men in Shushan; but on the spoil they laid not their hand.

וּשְׁאָר הַיְּהוּדִים אֲשֶׁר בִּמְדִינוֹת הַמֶּלֶךְ נִקְהֲלוּ
ushe'ar hayehudim asher bimdinot hammelech nik'halu
And the other Jews that were in the king's provinces gathered themselves together,

וְעָמֹד עַל-נַפְשָׁם, וְנוֹחַ מֵאֹיְבֵיהֶם
ve'amod al-nafsham, venoach me'oyeveihem
and stood for their lives, and had rest from their enemies,

וְהָרוֹג בְּשֹׂנְאֵיהֶם, חֲמִשָּׁה וְשִׁבְעִים אָלֶף; וּבַבִּזָּה--לֹא שָׁלְחוּ, אֶת-יָדָם
veharog besone'eihem, chamishah veshiv'im alef; uvabbizzah, lo shalechu et-yadam
and slew of them that hated them seventy and five thousand--but on the spoil they laid not their hand--

בְּיוֹם-שְׁלוֹשָׁה עָשָׂר, לְחֹדֶשׁ אֲדָר
beyom-sheloshah asar lechodesh adar
on the thirteenth day of the month Adar,

אֶסְתֵּר

וְכָל-שָׂרֵי הַמְּדִינוֹת וְהָאֲחַשְׁדַּרְפְּנִים וְהַפַּחוֹת, וְעֹשֵׂי הַמְּלָאכָה אֲשֶׁר לַמֶּלֶךְ
vechol-sarei hammedinot veha'achashdarpenim vehappachot, ve'osei hammelachah asher lammelech
And all the princes of the provinces, and the satraps, and the governors, and they that did the king's business,

מְנַשְּׂאִים, אֶת-הַיְּהוּדִים: כִּי-נָפַל פַּחַד-מָרְדֳּכַי, עֲלֵיהֶם
menasse'im et-hayehudim; ki-nafal pachad-mordechai aleihem
helped the Jews; because the fear of Mordecai was fallen upon them.

כִּי-גָדוֹל מָרְדֳּכַי בְּבֵית הַמֶּלֶךְ, וְשָׁמְעוֹ הוֹלֵךְ בְּכָל-הַמְּדִינוֹת
ki-gadol mordechai beveit hammelech, veshom'o holech bechol-hammedinot
For Mordecai was great in the king's house, and his fame went forth throughout all the provinces;

כִּי-הָאִישׁ מָרְדֳּכַי, הוֹלֵךְ וְגָדוֹל
ki-ha'ish mordechai holech vegadol
for the man Mordecai waxed greater and greater.

וַיַּכּוּ הַיְּהוּדִים בְּכָל-אֹיְבֵיהֶם, מַכַּת-חֶרֶב
vayakku hayehudim bechol-'oyeveihem, makkat-cherev
And the Jews smote all their enemies with the stroke of the sword,

וְהֶרֶג וְאַבְדָן; וַיַּעֲשׂוּ בְשֹׂנְאֵיהֶם, כִּרְצוֹנָם
vehereg ve'avdan; vaya'asu vesone'eihem kirtzonam
and with slaughter and destruction, and did what they would unto them that hated them.

וּבְשׁוּשַׁן הַבִּירָה, הָרְגוּ הַיְּהוּדִים וְאַבֵּד--חֲמֵשׁ מֵאוֹת, אִישׁ.
uveshushan habbirah, haregu hayehudim ve'abbed, chamesh me'ot ish
And in Shushan the castle the Jews slew and destroyed five hundred men.

וְאֵת פַּרְשַׁנְדָּתָא וְאֵת דַּלְפוֹן, וְאֵת אַסְפָּתָא
ve'et parshandata ve'et dalfon ve'et aspata
And Parshandatha, and Dalphon, and Aspatha,

וְאֵת פּוֹרָתָא וְאֵת אֲדַלְיָא, וְאֵת אֲרִידָתָא
ve'et porata ve'et adalya ve'et aridata
and Poratha, and Adalia, and Aridatha,

וְאֵת פַּרְמַשְׁתָּא וְאֵת אֲרִיסַי, וְאֵת אֲרִידַי וְאֵת וַיְזָתָא
ve'et parmashta ve'et arisai, ve'et aridai ve'et vayzata
and Parmashta, and Arisai, and Aridai, and Vaizatha,

עֲשֶׂרֶת בְּנֵי הָמָן בֶּן-הַמְּדָתָא, צֹרֵר הַיְּהוּדִים--הָרָגוּ; וּבַבִּזָּה--לֹא שָׁלְחוּ, אֶת-יָדָם
'aseret benei haman ben-hammedata tzorer hayehudim haragu; uvabbizzah, lo shalechu et-yadam
the ten sons of Haman the son of Hammedatha, the Jews' enemy, slew they; but on the spoil they laid not their hand.

בַּיּוֹם הַהוּא, בָּא מִסְפַּר הַהֲרוּגִים בְּשׁוּשַׁן הַבִּירָה--לִפְנֵי הַמֶּלֶךְ
bayom hahu, ba mispar haharugim beshushan habbirah lifnei hammelech
On that day the number of those that were slain in Shushan the castle was brought before the king.

אֶסְתֵּר

וְתַכְרִיךְ בּוּץ וְאַרְגָּמָן; וְהָעִיר שׁוּשָׁן, צָהֲלָה וְשָׂמֵחָה
vetachrich butz ve'argaman; veha'ir shushan, tzahalah vesamechah
and with a robe of fine linen and purple; and the city of Shushan shouted and was glad.

לַיְּהוּדִים, הָיְתָה אוֹרָה וְשִׂמְחָה, וְשָׂשֹׂן, וִיקָר
layehudim hayetah orah vesimchah; vesason viykar
The Jews had light and gladness, and joy and honour.

וּבְכָל-מְדִינָה וּמְדִינָה וּבְכָל-עִיר וָעִיר, מְקוֹם אֲשֶׁר דְּבַר-הַמֶּלֶךְ וְדָתוֹ מַגִּיעַ
uvechol-medinah umedinah uvechol-'ir va'ir, mekom asher devar-hammelech vedato maggia'
And in every province, and in every city, whithersoever the king's commandment and his decree came,

שִׂמְחָה וְשָׂשֹׂן לַיְּהוּדִים, מִשְׁתֶּה וְיוֹם טוֹב
simchah vesason layehudim, mishteh veyom tov
the Jews had gladness and joy, a feast and a good day.

וְרַבִּים מֵעַמֵּי הָאָרֶץ, מִתְיַהֲדִים--כִּי-נָפַל פַּחַד-הַיְּהוּדִים, עֲלֵיהֶם
verabbim me'ammei ha'aretz mityahadim, ki-nafal pachad-hayehudim aleihem
And many from among the peoples of the land became Jews; for the fear of the Jews was fallen upon them.

ט

וּבִשְׁנֵים עָשָׂר חֹדֶשׁ הוּא-חֹדֶשׁ אֲדָר, בִּשְׁלוֹשָׁה עָשָׂר יוֹם בּוֹ, אֲשֶׁר הִגִּיעַ דְּבַר-הַמֶּלֶךְ
Uvishneim asar chodesh hu-chodesh adar, bishloshah asar yom bo, asher higgia devar-hammelech
Now in the twelfth month, which is the month Adar, on the thirteenth day of the same, when the king's commandment

וְדָתוֹ, לְהֵעָשׂוֹת: בַּיּוֹם, אֲשֶׁר שִׂבְּרוּ אֹיְבֵי הַיְּהוּדִים לִשְׁלוֹט בָּהֶם
vedato lehe'asot; bayom, asher sibberu oyevei hayehudim lishlot bahem
and his decree drew near to be put in execution, in the day that the enemies of the Jews hoped to have rule over them;

וְנַהֲפוֹךְ הוּא, אֲשֶׁר יִשְׁלְטוּ הַיְּהוּדִים הֵמָּה בְּשֹׂנְאֵיהֶם
venahafoch hu, asher yishletu hayehudim hemmah besone'eihem
whereas it was turned to the contrary, that the Jews had rule over them that hated them;

נִקְהֲלוּ הַיְּהוּדִים בְּעָרֵיהֶם, בְּכָל-מְדִינוֹת הַמֶּלֶךְ אֲחַשְׁוֵרוֹשׁ
nik'halu hayehudim be'areihem, bechol-medinot hammelech ochashverosh
the Jews gathered themselves together in their cities throughout all the provinces of the king Ahasuerus,

לִשְׁלֹחַ יָד, בִּמְבַקְשֵׁי רָעָתָם; וְאִישׁ לֹא-עָמַד לִפְנֵיהֶם
lishloach yad, bimvakshei ra'atam; ve'ish lo-'amad lifneihem
to lay hand on such as sought their hurt; and no man could withstand them;

כִּי-נָפַל פַּחְדָּם עַל-כָּל-הָעַמִּים
ki-nafal pachdam al-kol-ha'ammim
for the fear of them was fallen upon all the peoples.

אֶסְתֵּר

וַיִּכְתֹּב, בְּשֵׁם הַמֶּלֶךְ אֲחַשְׁוֵרֹשׁ, וַיַּחְתֹּם, בְּטַבַּעַת הַמֶּלֶךְ; וַיִּשְׁלַח סְפָרִים בְּיַד הָרָצִים בַּסּוּסִים
vayichtov, beshem hammelech achashverosh, vayachtom betabba'at hammelech; vayishlach sefarim beyad haratzim bassusim
And they wrote in the name of king Ahasuerus, and sealed it with the king's ring, and sent letters by posts on horseback,

רֹכְבֵי הָרֶכֶשׁ, הָאֲחַשְׁתְּרָנִים--בְּנֵי, הָרַמָּכִים
rochevei harechesh ha'achashteranim, benei harammachim
riding on swift steeds that were used in the king's service, bred of the stud;

אֲשֶׁר נָתַן הַמֶּלֶךְ לַיְּהוּדִים אֲשֶׁר בְּכָל-עִיר-וָעִיר, לְהִקָּהֵל וְלַעֲמֹד עַל-נַפְשָׁם
'asher natan hammelech layehudim asher bechol-'ir-va'ir, lehikkahel vela'amod al-nafsham
that the king had granted the Jews that were in every city to gather themselves together, and to stand for their life,

לְהַשְׁמִיד וְלַהֲרֹג וּלְאַבֵּד אֶת-כָּל-חֵיל עַם וּמְדִינָה הַצָּרִים אֹתָם
lehashmid velaharog ule'abbed et-kol-cheil am umedinah hatzarim otam
to destroy, and to slay, and to cause to perish, all the forces of the people and province that would assault them,

טַף וְנָשִׁים; וּשְׁלָלָם, לָבוֹז
taf venashim; ushelalam lavoz
their little ones and women, and to take the spoil of them for a prey,

בְּיוֹם אֶחָד, בְּכָל-מְדִינוֹת הַמֶּלֶךְ אֲחַשְׁוֵרוֹשׁ
beyom echad, bechol-medinot hammelech achashverosh
upon one day in all the provinces of king Ahasuerus,

בִּשְׁלוֹשָׁה עָשָׂר לְחֹדֶשׁ שְׁנֵים-עָשָׂר, הוּא-חֹדֶשׁ אֲדָר
bishloshah asar lechodesh sheneim-'asar hu-chodesh adar
namely, upon the thirteenth day of the twelfth month, which is the month Adar.

פַּתְשֶׁגֶן הַכְּתָב, לְהִנָּתֵן דָּת בְּכָל-מְדִינָה וּמְדִינָה, גָּלוּי, לְכָל-הָעַמִּים
patshegen hakketav, lehinnaten dat bechol-medinah umedinah, galui lechol-ha'ammim
The copy of the writing, to be given out for a decree in every province, was to be published unto all the peoples,

וְלִהְיוֹת הַיְּהוּדִים עֲתִידִים לַיּוֹם הַזֶּה, לְהִנָּקֵם מֵאֹיְבֵיהֶם
velihyot hayehudim atidim layom hazzeh, lehinnakem me'oyeveihem
and that the Jews should be ready against that day to avenge themselves on their enemies.

הָרָצִים רֹכְבֵי הָרֶכֶשׁ, הָאֲחַשְׁתְּרָנִים, יָצְאוּ
haratzim rochevei harechesh ha'achashteranim, yatze'u
So the posts that rode upon swift steeds that were used in the king's service went out,

מְבֹהָלִים וּדְחוּפִים, בִּדְבַר הַמֶּלֶךְ; וְהַדָּת נִתְּנָה, בְּשׁוּשַׁן הַבִּירָה
mevohalim udechufim bidvar hammelech; vehaddat nittenah beshushan habbirah
being hastened and pressed on by the king's commandment; and the decree was given out in Shushan the castle.

וּמָרְדֳּכַי יָצָא מִלִּפְנֵי הַמֶּלֶךְ, בִּלְבוּשׁ מַלְכוּת תְּכֵלֶת וָחוּר, וַעֲטֶרֶת זָהָב גְּדוֹלָה
umordechai yatza millifnei hammelech, bilvush malchut techelet vachur, va'ateret zahav gedolah
And Mordecai went forth from the presence of the king in royal apparel of blue and white, and with a great crown of gold,

אֶסְתֵּר

כִּי אֵיכָכָה אוּכַל, וְרָאִיתִי, בָּרָעָה, אֲשֶׁר-יִמְצָא אֶת-עַמִּי
ki eichachah uchal vera'iti, bara'ah asher-yimtza et-'ammi
for how can I endure to see the evil that shall come unto my people?

וְאֵיכָכָה אוּכַל וְרָאִיתִי, בְּאָבְדַן מוֹלַדְתִּי
ve'eichachah uchal vera'iti, be'ovedan moladti
or how can I endure to see the destruction of my kindred?'

וַיֹּאמֶר הַמֶּלֶךְ אֲחַשְׁוֵרוֹשׁ לְאֶסְתֵּר הַמַּלְכָּה, וּלְמָרְדֳּכַי הַיְּהוּדִי
vayomer hammelech achashverosh le'ester hammalkah, ulemordechai hayehudi
Then the king Ahasuerus said unto Esther the queen and to Mordecai the Jew:

הִנֵּה בֵית-הָמָן נָתַתִּי לְאֶסְתֵּר, וְאֹתוֹ תָּלוּ עַל-הָעֵץ
hinneh veit-haman natatti le'ester, ve'oto talu al-ha'etz
'Behold, I have given Esther the house of Haman, and him they have hanged upon the gallows,

עַל אֲשֶׁר-שָׁלַח יָדוֹ, בַּיְּהוּדִים
al asher-shalach yado bayehudim
because he laid his hand upon the Jews.

וְאַתֶּם כִּתְבוּ עַל-הַיְּהוּדִים כַּטּוֹב בְּעֵינֵיכֶם, בְּשֵׁם הַמֶּלֶךְ, וְחִתְמוּ, בְּטַבַּעַת הַמֶּלֶךְ
ve'attem kitvu al-hayehudim kattov be'eineichem beshem hammelech, vechitmu betabba'at hammelech
Write ye also concerning the Jews, as it liketh you, in the king's name, and seal it with the king's ring;

כִּי-כְתָב אֲשֶׁר-נִכְתָּב בְּשֵׁם-הַמֶּלֶךְ, וְנַחְתּוֹם בְּטַבַּעַת הַמֶּלֶךְ--אֵין לְהָשִׁיב
ki-chetav asher-nichtav beshem-hammelech, venachtom betabba'at hammelech ein lehashiv
for the writing which is written in the king's name, and sealed with the king's ring, may no man reverse.'

וַיִּקָּרְאוּ סֹפְרֵי-הַמֶּלֶךְ בָּעֵת-הַהִיא בַּחֹדֶשׁ הַשְּׁלִישִׁי הוּא-חֹדֶשׁ סִיוָן
vayikkare'u soferei-hammelech ba'et-hahi bachodesh hashelishi hu-chodesh sivan
Then were the king's scribes called at that time, in the third month, which is the month Sivan,

בִּשְׁלוֹשָׁה וְעֶשְׂרִים בּוֹ, וַיִּכָּתֵב כְּכָל-אֲשֶׁר-צִוָּה מָרְדֳּכַי אֶל-הַיְּהוּדִים
bishloshah ve'esrim bo vayikkatev kechol-'asher-tzivvah mordechai el-hayehudim
on the three and twentieth day thereof; and it was written according to all that Mordecai commanded concerning the Jews,

וְאֶל הָאֲחַשְׁדַּרְפְּנִים-וְהַפַּחוֹת וְשָׂרֵי הַמְּדִינוֹת אֲשֶׁר מֵהֹדּוּ וְעַד-כּוּשׁ
ve'el ha'achashdarpenim-vehappachot vesarei hammedinot asher mehoddu ve'ad-kush
even to the satraps, and the governors and princes of the provinces which are from India unto Ethiopia,

שֶׁבַע וְעֶשְׂרִים וּמֵאָה מְדִינָה, מְדִינָה וּמְדִינָה כִּכְתָבָהּ
sheva ve'esrim ume'ah medinah, medinah umedinah kichtavah
a hundred twenty and seven provinces, unto every province according to the writing thereof,

וְעַם וָעָם כִּלְשֹׁנוֹ; וְאֶל-הַיְּהוּדִים--כִּכְתָבָם, וְכִלְשׁוֹנָם
ve'am va'am kilshono; ve'el-hayehudim, kichtavam vechilshonam
and unto every people after their language, and to the Jews according to their writing, and according to their language.

אֶסְתֵּר

וַיִּתְלוּ, אֶת-הָמָן, עַל-הָעֵץ, אֲשֶׁר-הֵכִין לְמָרְדֳּכָי; וַחֲמַת הַמֶּלֶךְ, שָׁכָכָה
vayitlu et-haman, al-ha'etz asher-hechin lemordechai; vachamat hammelech shachachah
So they hanged Haman on the gallows that he had prepared for Mordecai. Then was the king's wrath assuaged.

ח

בַּיּוֹם הַהוּא, נָתַן הַמֶּלֶךְ אֲחַשְׁוֵרוֹשׁ לְאֶסְתֵּר הַמַּלְכָּה, אֶת-בֵּית הָמָן, צֹרֵר הַיְּהוּדִים
Bayom hahu, natan hammelech achashverosh le'ester hammalkah, et-beit haman tzorer hayehudim
On that day did the king Ahasuerus give the house of Haman the Jews' enemy unto Esther the queen.

וּמָרְדֳּכַי, בָּא לִפְנֵי הַמֶּלֶךְ--כִּי-הִגִּידָה אֶסְתֵּר, מַה הוּא-לָהּ
umordechai, ba lifnei hammelech, ki-higgidah ester mah hu-lah
And Mordecai came before the king; for Esther had told what he was unto her.

וַיָּסַר הַמֶּלֶךְ אֶת-טַבַּעְתּוֹ, אֲשֶׁר הֶעֱבִיר מֵהָמָן, וַיִּתְּנָהּ, לְמָרְדֳּכָי
vayasar hammelech et-tabba'to, asher he'evir mehaman, vayittenah lemordechai
And the king took off his ring, which he had taken from Haman, and gave it unto Mordecai.

וַתָּשֶׂם אֶסְתֵּר אֶת-מָרְדֳּכַי, עַל-בֵּית הָמָן
vattasem ester et-mordechai al-beit haman
And Esther set Mordecai over the house of Haman.

וַתּוֹסֶף אֶסְתֵּר, וַתְּדַבֵּר לִפְנֵי הַמֶּלֶךְ, וַתִּפֹּל, לִפְנֵי רַגְלָיו; וַתֵּבְךְּ וַתִּתְחַנֶּן-לוֹ
vattosef ester, vattedabber lifnei hammelech, vattippol lifnei raglav; vattevk vattitchannen-lo
And Esther spoke yet again before the king, and fell down at his feet, and besought him with tears

לְהַעֲבִיר אֶת-רָעַת הָמָן הָאֲגָגִי, וְאֵת מַחֲשַׁבְתּוֹ, אֲשֶׁר חָשַׁב עַל-הַיְּהוּדִים
leha'avir et-ra'at haman ha'agagi, ve'et machashavto, asher chashav al-hayehudim
to put away the mischief of Haman the Agagite, and his device that he had devised against the Jews.

וַיּוֹשֶׁט הַמֶּלֶךְ לְאֶסְתֵּר, אֵת שַׁרְבִט הַזָּהָב; וַתָּקָם אֶסְתֵּר, וַתַּעֲמֹד לִפְנֵי הַמֶּלֶךְ
vayoshet hammelech le'ester, et sharvit hazzahav; vattakom ester, vatta'amod lifnei hammelech
Then the king held out to Esther the golden sceptre. So Esther arose, and stood before the king.

וַתֹּאמֶר אִם-עַל-הַמֶּלֶךְ טוֹב וְאִם-מָצָאתִי חֵן לְפָנָיו, וְכָשֵׁר הַדָּבָר לִפְנֵי הַמֶּלֶךְ
vattomer im-'al-hammelech tov ve'im-matzati chen lefanav, vechasher haddavar lifnei hammelech
And she said: 'If it please the king, and if I have found favour in his sight, and the thing seem right before the king,

וְטוֹבָה אֲנִי, בְּעֵינָיו--יִכָּתֵב לְהָשִׁיב אֶת-הַסְּפָרִים, מַחֲשֶׁבֶת הָמָן בֶּן-הַמְּדָתָא הָאֲגָגִי
vetovah ani be'einav; yikkatev lehashiv et-hassefarim, machashevet haman ben-hammedata ha'agagi
and I be pleasing in his eyes, let it be written to reverse the letters devised by Haman the son of Hammedatha the Agagite,

אֲשֶׁר כָּתַב לְאַבֵּד אֶת-הַיְּהוּדִים, אֲשֶׁר בְּכָל-מְדִינוֹת הַמֶּלֶךְ
asher katav, le'abbed et-hayehudim, asher bechol-medinot hammelech
which he wrote to destroy the Jews that are in all the king's provinces;

אֶסְתֵּר

וַתֹּאמֶר אֶסְתֵּר--אִישׁ צַר וְאוֹיֵב, הָמָן הָרָע הַזֶּה
vattomer-'ester, ish tzar ve'oyev, haman hara hazzeh
And Esther said: 'An adversary and an enemy, even this wicked Haman.'

וְהָמָן נִבְעַת, מִלִּפְנֵי הַמֶּלֶךְ וְהַמַּלְכָּה
vehaman niv'at, millifnei hammelech vehammalkah
Then Haman was terrified before the king and the queen.

וְהַמֶּלֶךְ קָם בַּחֲמָתוֹ, מִמִּשְׁתֵּה הַיַּיִן, אֶל-גִּנַּת, הַבִּיתָן
vehammelech kam bachamato mimmishteh hayayin, el-ginnat habbitan
And the king arose in his wrath from the banquet of wine and went into the palace garden;

וְהָמָן עָמַד, לְבַקֵּשׁ עַל-נַפְשׁוֹ מֵאֶסְתֵּר הַמַּלְכָּה
vehaman amad, levakkesh al-nafsho me'ester hammalkah
but Haman remained to make request for his life to Esther the queen;

כִּי רָאָה, כִּי-כָלְתָה אֵלָיו הָרָעָה מֵאֵת הַמֶּלֶךְ
ki ra'ah, ki-chaletah elav hara'ah me'et hammelech
for he saw that there was evil determined against him by the king.

וְהַמֶּלֶךְ שָׁב מִגִּנַּת הַבִּיתָן אֶל-בֵּית מִשְׁתֵּה הַיַּיִן
vehammelech shav migginnat habbitan el-beit mishteh hayayin
Then the king returned out of the palace garden into the place of the banquet of wine;

וְהָמָן נֹפֵל עַל-הַמִּטָּה אֲשֶׁר אֶסְתֵּר עָלֶיהָ, וַיֹּאמֶר הַמֶּלֶךְ
vehaman nofel, al-hammittah asher ester aleiha, vayomer hammelech
and Haman was fallen upon the couch whereon Esther was. Then said the king:

הֲגַם לִכְבּוֹשׁ אֶת-הַמַּלְכָּה עִמִּי בַּבָּיִת
hagam lichbosh et-hammalkah immi babbayit
'Will he even force the queen before me in the house?'

הַדָּבָר, יָצָא מִפִּי הַמֶּלֶךְ, וּפְנֵי הָמָן, חָפוּ
haddavar, yatza mippi hammelech, ufenei haman chafu
As the word went out of the king's mouth, they covered Haman's face.

וַיֹּאמֶר חַרְבוֹנָה אֶחָד מִן-הַסָּרִיסִים לִפְנֵי הַמֶּלֶךְ
vayomer charvonah echad min-hassarisim lifnei hammelech
Then said Harbonah, one of the chamberlains that were before the king:

גַּם הִנֵּה-הָעֵץ אֲשֶׁר-עָשָׂה הָמָן לְמָרְדֳּכַי אֲשֶׁר דִּבֶּר-טוֹב עַל-הַמֶּלֶךְ
gam hinneh-ha'etz asher-'asah haman lemordechai asher dibber-tov al-hammelech
'Behold also, the gallows fifty cubits high, which Haman hath made for Mordecai, who spoke good for the king,

עֹמֵד בְּבֵית הָמָן--גָּבֹהַּ, חֲמִשִּׁים אַמָּה; וַיֹּאמֶר הַמֶּלֶךְ, תְּלֻהוּ עָלָיו
omed beveit haman, gavoha chamishim ammah; vayomer hammelech teluhu alav
standeth in the house of Haman.' And the king said: 'Hang him thereon.'

אֶסְתֵּר

ז

וַיָּבֹא הַמֶּלֶךְ וְהָמָן, לִשְׁתּוֹת עִם-אֶסְתֵּר הַמַּלְכָּה
Vayavo hammelech vehaman, lishtot im-'ester hammalkah
So the king and Haman came to banquet with Esther the queen.

וַיֹּאמֶר הַמֶּלֶךְ לְאֶסְתֵּר גַּם בַּיּוֹם הַשֵּׁנִי, בְּמִשְׁתֵּה הַיַּיִן
vayomer hammelech le'ester gam bayom hasheni bemishteh hayayin
And the king said again unto Esther on the second day at the banquet of wine:

מַה-שְּׁאֵלָתֵךְ אֶסְתֵּר הַמַּלְכָּה, וְתִנָּתֵן לָךְ
mah-she'elatech ester hammalkah vetinnaten lach
'Whatever thy petition, queen Esther, it shall be granted thee;

וּמַה-בַּקָּשָׁתֵךְ עַד-חֲצִי הַמַּלְכוּת, וְתֵעָשׂ
umah-bakkashatech ad-chatzi hammalchut vete'as
and whatever thy request, even to the half of the kingdom, it shall be performed.'

וַתַּעַן אֶסְתֵּר הַמַּלְכָּה, וַתֹּאמַר--אִם-מָצָאתִי חֵן בְּעֵינֶיךָ הַמֶּלֶךְ, וְאִם-עַל-הַמֶּלֶךְ טוֹב
vatta'an ester hammalkah vattomar, im-matzati chen be'eineicha hammelech, ve'im-'al-hammelech tov
Then Esther the queen answered and said: 'If I have found favour in thy sight, O king, and if it please the king,

תִּנָּתֶן-לִי נַפְשִׁי בִּשְׁאֵלָתִי, וְעַמִּי בְּבַקָּשָׁתִי
tinnaten-li nafshi bish'elati, ve'ammi bevakkashati
let my life be given me at my petition, and my people at my request;

כִּי נִמְכַּרְנוּ אֲנִי וְעַמִּי, לְהַשְׁמִיד לַהֲרוֹג וּלְאַבֵּד
ki nimkarnu ani ve'ammi, lehashmid laharog ule'abbed
for we are sold, I and my people, to be destroyed, to be slain, and to perish.

וְאִלּוּ לַעֲבָדִים וְלִשְׁפָחוֹת נִמְכַּרְנוּ, הֶחֱרַשְׁתִּי
ve'illu la'avadim velishfachot nimkarnu hecherashti
But if we had been sold for bondmen and bondwomen, I had held my peace,

כִּי אֵין הַצָּר שֹׁוֶה, בְּנֵזֶק הַמֶּלֶךְ
ki ein hatzar shoh benezek hammelech
for the adversary is not worthy that the king be endamaged.'

וַיֹּאמֶר הַמֶּלֶךְ אֲחַשְׁוֵרוֹשׁ, וַיֹּאמֶר לְאֶסְתֵּר הַמַּלְכָּה
vayomer hammelech achashverosh, vayomer le'ester hammalkah
Then spoke the king Ahasuerus and said unto Esther the queen:

מִי הוּא זֶה וְאֵי-זֶה הוּא, אֲשֶׁר-מְלָאוֹ לִבּוֹ לַעֲשׂוֹת כֵּן
mi hu zeh ve'ei-zeh hu, asher-mela'o libbo la'asot ken
'Who is he, and where is he, that durst presume in his heart to do so?'

אֶסְתֵּר

וַעֲשֵׂה-כֵן לְמָרְדֳּכַי הַיְּהוּדִי, הַיּוֹשֵׁב בְּשַׁעַר הַמֶּלֶךְ: אַל-תַּפֵּל דָּבָר, מִכֹּל אֲשֶׁר דִּבַּרְתָּ
va'aseh-chen lemordechai hayehudi, hayoshev besha'ar hammelech; al-tappel davar, mikkol asher dibbarta
and do even so to Mordecai the Jew, that sitteth at the king's gate; let nothing fail of all that thou hast spoken.'

וַיִּקַּח הָמָן אֶת-הַלְּבוּשׁ וְאֶת-הַסּוּס, וַיַּלְבֵּשׁ אֶת-מָרְדֳּכָי
vayikkach haman et-hallevush ve'et-hassus, vayalbesh et-mordechai
Then took Haman the apparel and the horse, and arrayed Mordecai,

וַיַּרְכִּיבֵהוּ, בִּרְחוֹב הָעִיר, וַיִּקְרָא לְפָנָיו
vayarkivehu birchov ha'ir, vayikra lefanav
and caused him to ride through the street of the city, and proclaimed before him:

כָּכָה יֵעָשֶׂה לָאִישׁ, אֲשֶׁר הַמֶּלֶךְ חָפֵץ בִּיקָרוֹ
kachah ye'aseh la'ish, asher hammelech chafetz bikaro
'Thus shall it be done unto the man whom the king delighteth to honour.'

וַיָּשָׁב מָרְדֳּכַי, אֶל-שַׁעַר הַמֶּלֶךְ; וְהָמָן נִדְחַף אֶל-בֵּיתוֹ, אָבֵל וַחֲפוּי רֹאשׁ
vayashov mordechai el-sha'ar hammelech; vehaman nidchaf el-beito, avel vachafui rosh
And Mordecai returned to the king's gate. But Haman hasted to his house, mourning and having his head covered.

וַיְסַפֵּר הָמָן לְזֶרֶשׁ אִשְׁתּוֹ, וּלְכָל-אֹהֲבָיו, אֵת, כָּל-אֲשֶׁר קָרָהוּ
vaysapper haman lezeresh ishto ulechal-'ohavav, et kol-'asher karahu
And Haman recounted unto Zeresh his wife and all his friends every thing that had befallen him.

וַיֹּאמְרוּ לוֹ חֲכָמָיו וְזֶרֶשׁ אִשְׁתּוֹ
vayomeru lo chachamav vezeresh ishto
Then said his wise men and Zeresh his wife unto him:

אִם מִזֶּרַע הַיְּהוּדִים מָרְדֳּכַי אֲשֶׁר הַחִלּוֹתָ לִנְפֹּל לְפָנָיו לֹא-תוּכַל לוֹ
im mizzera hayehudim mordechai asher hachillota linpol lefanav lo-tuchal lo
'If Mordecai, before whom thou hast begun to fall, be of the seed of the Jews, thou shalt not prevail against him,

כִּי-נָפוֹל תִּפּוֹל, לְפָנָיו
ki-nafol tippol lefanav
but shalt surely fall before him.'

עוֹדָם מְדַבְּרִים עִמּוֹ, וְסָרִיסֵי הַמֶּלֶךְ הִגִּיעוּ
'odam medabberim immo, vesarisei hammelech higgi'u
While they were yet talking with him, came the king's chamberlains,

וַיַּבְהִלוּ לְהָבִיא אֶת-הָמָן, אֶל-הַמִּשְׁתֶּה אֲשֶׁר-עָשְׂתָה אֶסְתֵּר
vayavhilu lehavi et-haman, el-hammishteh asher-'asetah ester
and hastened to bring Haman unto the banquet that Esther had prepared.

אֶסְתֵּר

וַיֹּאמְרוּ נַעֲרֵי הַמֶּלֶךְ, אֵלָיו--הִנֵּה הָמָן, עֹמֵד בֶּחָצֵר; וַיֹּאמֶר הַמֶּלֶךְ, יָבוֹא
vayomeru na'arei hammelech elav, hinneh haman omed bechatzer; vayomer hammelech yavo
And the king's servants said unto him: 'Behold, Haman standeth in the court.' And the king said: 'Let him come in.'

וַיָּבוֹא, הָמָן, וַיֹּאמֶר לוֹ הַמֶּלֶךְ
vayavo haman vayomer lo hammelech
So Haman came in. And the king said unto him:

מַה-לַּעֲשׂוֹת בָּאִישׁ אֲשֶׁר הַמֶּלֶךְ חָפֵץ בִּיקָרוֹ
mah-la'asot ba'ish asher hammelech chafetz bikaro
'What shall be done unto the man whom the king delighteth to honour?'

וַיֹּאמֶר הָמָן, בְּלִבּוֹ, לְמִי יַחְפֹּץ הַמֶּלֶךְ לַעֲשׂוֹת יְקָר, יוֹתֵר מִמֶּנִּי
vayomer haman belibbo, lemi yachpotz hammelech la'asot yekar yoter mimmenni
--Now Haman said in his heart: 'Whom would the king delight to honour besides myself?'--

וַיֹּאמֶר הָמָן, אֶל-הַמֶּלֶךְ: אִישׁ, אֲשֶׁר הַמֶּלֶךְ חָפֵץ בִּיקָרוֹ
vayomer haman el-hammelech; ish asher hammelech chafetz bikaro
And Haman said unto the king: 'For the man whom the king delighteth to honour,

יָבִיאוּ לְבוּשׁ מַלְכוּת, אֲשֶׁר לָבַשׁ-בּוֹ הַמֶּלֶךְ
yavi'u levush malchut, asher lavash-bo hammelech
let royal apparel be brought which the king useth to wear,

וְסוּס, אֲשֶׁר רָכַב עָלָיו הַמֶּלֶךְ, וַאֲשֶׁר נִתַּן כֶּתֶר מַלְכוּת, בְּרֹאשׁוֹ
vesus, asher rachav alav hammelech, va'asher nittan keter malchut berosho
and the horse that the king rideth upon, and on whose head a crown royal is set;

וְנָתוֹן הַלְּבוּשׁ וְהַסּוּס, עַל-יַד-אִישׁ מִשָּׂרֵי הַמֶּלֶךְ הַפַּרְתְּמִים
venaton hallevush vehassus, al-yad-'ish missarei hammelech happartemim
and let the apparel and the horse be delivered to the hand of one of the king's most noble princes,

וְהִלְבִּישׁוּ אֶת-הָאִישׁ, אֲשֶׁר הַמֶּלֶךְ חָפֵץ בִּיקָרוֹ
vehilbishu et-ha'ish, asher hammelech chafetz bikaro
that they may array the man therewith whom the king delighteth to honour,

וְהִרְכִּיבֻהוּ עַל-הַסּוּס, בִּרְחוֹב הָעִיר, וְקָרְאוּ לְפָנָיו
vehirkivuhu al-hassus birchov ha'ir, vekare'u lefanav
and cause him to ride on horseback through the street of the city, and proclaim before him:

כָּכָה יֵעָשֶׂה לָאִישׁ אֲשֶׁר הַמֶּלֶךְ חָפֵץ בִּיקָרוֹ
kachah ye'aseh la'ish, asher hammelech chafetz bikaro
Thus shall it be done to the man whom the king delighteth to honour.'

וַיֹּאמֶר הַמֶּלֶךְ לְהָמָן, מַהֵר קַח אֶת-הַלְּבוּשׁ וְאֶת-הַסּוּס כַּאֲשֶׁר דִּבַּרְתָּ
vayomer hammelech lehaman, maher kach et-hallevush ve'et-hassus ka'asher dibbarta
Then the king said to Haman: 'Make haste, and take the apparel and the horse, as thou hast said,

אֶסְתֵּר

וַתֹּאמֶר לוֹ זֶרֶשׁ אִשְׁתּוֹ וְכָל-אֹהֲבָיו, יַעֲשׂוּ-עֵץ גָּבֹהַּ חֲמִשִּׁים אַמָּה, וּבַבֹּקֶר
vattomer lo zeresh ishto vechol-'ohavav, ya'asu-'etz gavoah chamishim ammah uvabboker
Then said Zeresh his wife and all his friends unto him: 'Let a gallows be made of fifty cubits high, and in the morning '

אֱמֹר לַמֶּלֶךְ וְיִתְלוּ אֶת-מָרְדֳּכַי עָלָיו, וּבֹא-עִם-הַמֶּלֶךְ אֶל-הַמִּשְׁתֶּה שָׂמֵחַ
emor lammelech, veyitlu et-mordechai alav, uvo-'im-hammelech el-hammishteh sameach
speak thou unto the king that Mordecai may be hanged thereon; then go thou in merrily with the king unto the banquet.

וַיִּיטַב הַדָּבָר לִפְנֵי הָמָן, וַיַּעַשׂ הָעֵץ
vayitav haddavar lifnei haman vaya'as ha'etz
And the thing pleased Haman; and he caused the gallows to be made.

I

בַּלַּיְלָה הַהוּא, נָדְדָה שְׁנַת הַמֶּלֶךְ
Ballaylah hahu, nadedah shenat hammelech
On that night could not the king sleep;

וַיֹּאמֶר, לְהָבִיא אֶת-סֵפֶר הַזִּכְרֹנוֹת דִּבְרֵי הַיָּמִים, וַיִּהְיוּ נִקְרָאִים, לִפְנֵי הַמֶּלֶךְ
vayomer, lehavi et-sefer hazzichronot divrei hayamim, vayihyu nikra'im lifnei hammelech
and he commanded to bring the book of records of the chronicles, and they were read before the king.

וַיִּמָּצֵא כָתוּב, אֲשֶׁר הִגִּיד מָרְדֳּכַי עַל-בִּגְתָנָא וָתֶרֶשׁ שְׁנֵי סָרִיסֵי הַמֶּלֶךְ
vayimmatzei chatuv, asher higgid mordechai al-bigtana vateresh, shenei sarisei hammelech
And it was found written, that Mordecai had told of Bigthana and Teresh, two of the king's chamberlains,

מִשֹּׁמְרֵי, הַסַּף: אֲשֶׁר בִּקְשׁוּ לִשְׁלֹחַ יָד, בַּמֶּלֶךְ אֲחַשְׁוֵרוֹשׁ
mishomerei hassaf; asher bikshu lishloach yad, bammelech achashverosh
of those that kept the door, who had sought to lay hands on the king Ahasuerus.

וַיֹּאמֶר הַמֶּלֶךְ--מַה-נַּעֲשָׂה יְקָר וּגְדוּלָּה לְמָרְדֳּכַי, עַל-זֶה
vayomer hammelech, mah-na'asah yekar ugedullah lemordechai al-zeh
And the king said: 'What honour and dignity hath been done to Mordecai for this?'

וַיֹּאמְרוּ נַעֲרֵי הַמֶּלֶךְ, מְשָׁרְתָיו, לֹא-נַעֲשָׂה עִמּוֹ, דָּבָר
vayomeru na'arei hammelech mesharetav, lo-na'asah immo davar
Then said the king's servants that ministered unto him: 'There is nothing done for him.'

וַיֹּאמֶר הַמֶּלֶךְ, מִי בֶחָצֵר; וְהָמָן בָּא, לַחֲצַר בֵּית-הַמֶּלֶךְ הַחִיצוֹנָה
vayomer hammelech mi vechatzer; vehaman ba, lachatzar beit-hammelech hachitzonah
And the king said: 'Who is in the court?'--Now Haman was come into the outer court of the king's house,

לֵאמֹר לַמֶּלֶךְ, לִתְלוֹת אֶת-מָרְדֳּכַי עַל-הָעֵץ אֲשֶׁר-הֵכִין לוֹ
lemor lammelech, litlot et-mordechai, al-ha'etz asher-hechin lo
to speak unto the king to hang Mordecai on the gallows that he had prepared for him.--

אֶסְתֵּר

וַתַּעַן אֶסְתֵּר, וַתֹּאמַר: שְׁאֵלָתִי, וּבַקָּשָׁתִי
vatta'an ester vattomar; she'elati uvakkashati
Then answered Esther, and said: 'My petition and my request is--

אִם-מָצָאתִי חֵן בְּעֵינֵי הַמֶּלֶךְ, וְאִם-עַל-הַמֶּלֶךְ טוֹב, לָתֵת אֶת-שְׁאֵלָתִי, וְלַעֲשׂוֹת אֶת-בַּקָּשָׁתִי
'im-matzati chen be'einei hammelech, ve'im-'al-hammelech tov, latet et-she'elati, vela'asot et-bakkashati
if I have found favour in the sight of the king, and if it please the king to grant my petition, and to perform my request--

יָבוֹא הַמֶּלֶךְ וְהָמָן, אֶל-הַמִּשְׁתֶּה אֲשֶׁר אֶעֱשֶׂה לָהֶם, וּמָחָר אֶעֱשֶׂה, כִּדְבַר הַמֶּלֶךְ
yavo hammelech vehaman, el-hammishteh asher e'eseh lahem, umachar e'eseh kidvar hammelech
let the king and Haman come to the banquet that I shall prepare for them, and I will do to-morrow as the king hath said.'

וַיֵּצֵא הָמָן בַּיּוֹם הַהוּא, שָׂמֵחַ וְטוֹב לֵב; וְכִרְאוֹת הָמָן אֶת-מָרְדֳּכַי בְּשַׁעַר הַמֶּלֶךְ
vayetzei haman bayom hahu, sameach vetov lev; vechir'ot haman et-mordechai besha'ar hammelech
Then went Haman forth that day joyful and glad of heart; but when Haman saw Mordecai in the king's gate,

וְלֹא-קָם וְלֹא-זָע מִמֶּנּוּ--וַיִּמָּלֵא הָמָן עַל-מָרְדֳּכַי, חֵמָה
velo-kam velo-za mimmennu, vayimmalei haman al-mordechai chemah
that he stood not up, nor moved for him, Haman was filled with wrath against Mordecai.

וַיִּתְאַפַּק הָמָן, וַיָּבוֹא אֶל-בֵּיתוֹ; וַיִּשְׁלַח וַיָּבֵא אֶת-אֹהֲבָיו, וְאֶת-זֶרֶשׁ אִשְׁתּוֹ
vayit'appak haman, vayavo el-beito; vayishlach vayavei et-'ohavav ve'et-zeresh ishto
Nevertheless Haman refrained himself, and went home; and he sent and fetched his friends and Zeresh his wife.

וַיְסַפֵּר לָהֶם הָמָן אֶת-כְּבוֹד עָשְׁרוֹ, וְרֹב בָּנָיו
vaysapper lahem haman et-kevod oshero verov banav
And Haman recounted unto them the glory of his riches, and the multitude of his children,

וְאֵת כָּל-אֲשֶׁר גִּדְּלוֹ הַמֶּלֶךְ
ve'et kol-'asher giddelo hammelech
and everything as to how the king had promoted him,

וְאֵת אֲשֶׁר נִשְּׂאוֹ, עַל-הַשָּׂרִים וְעַבְדֵי הַמֶּלֶךְ
ve'et asher nisse'o, al-hassarim ve'avdei hammelech
and how he had advanced him above the princes and servants of the king.

וַיֹּאמֶר, הָמָן--אַף לֹא-הֵבִיאָה אֶסְתֵּר הַמַּלְכָּה עִם-הַמֶּלֶךְ
vayomer haman af lo-hevi'ah ester hammalkah im-hammelech
Haman said moreover: 'Yea, Esther the queen did let no man come in with the king

אֶל-הַמִּשְׁתֶּה אֲשֶׁר-עָשָׂתָה, כִּי אִם-אוֹתִי; וְגַם-לְמָחָר אֲנִי קָרוּא-לָהּ, עִם-הַמֶּלֶךְ
el-hammishteh asher-'asatah ki im-'oti; vegam-lemachar ani karu-lah im-hammelech
unto the banquet that she had prepared but myself; and to-morrow also am I invited by her together with the king.

וְכָל-זֶה, אֵינֶנּוּ שֹׁוֶה לִי: בְּכָל-עֵת, אֲשֶׁר אֲנִי רֹאֶה אֶת-מָרְדֳּכַי הַיְּהוּדִי--יוֹשֵׁב, בְּשַׁעַר הַמֶּלֶךְ
vechol-zeh einennu shoveh li; bechol-'et, asher ani ro'eh et-mordechai hayehudi, yoshev besha'ar hammelech
Yet all this availeth me nothing, so long as I see Mordecai the Jew sitting at the king's gate.'

אֶסְתֵּר

וְהַמֶּלֶךְ יוֹשֵׁב עַל-כִּסֵּא מַלְכוּתוֹ, בְּבֵית הַמַּלְכוּת, נֹכַח, פֶּתַח הַבָּיִת
vehammelech yoshev al-kissei malchuto beveit hammalchut, nochach petach habbayit
and the king sat upon his royal throne in the royal house, over against the entrance of the house.

וַיְהִי כִרְאוֹת הַמֶּלֶךְ אֶת-אֶסְתֵּר הַמַּלְכָּה, עֹמֶדֶת בֶּחָצֵר--נָשְׂאָה חֵן, בְּעֵינָיו
vayhi chir'ot hammelech et-'ester hammalkah, omedet bechatzer, nase'ah chen be'einav
And it was so, when the king saw Esther the queen standing in the court, that she obtained favour in his sight;

וַיּוֹשֶׁט הַמֶּלֶךְ לְאֶסְתֵּר, אֶת-שַׁרְבִיט הַזָּהָב אֲשֶׁר בְּיָדוֹ
vayoshet hammelech le'ester, et-sharvit hazzahav asher beyado
and the king held out to Esther the golden sceptre that was in his hand.

וַתִּקְרַב אֶסְתֵּר, וַתִּגַּע בְּרֹאשׁ הַשַּׁרְבִיט
vattikrav ester, vattigga berosh hasharvit
So Esther drew near, and touched the top of the sceptre.

וַיֹּאמֶר לָהּ הַמֶּלֶךְ, מַה-לָּךְ אֶסְתֵּר הַמַּלְכָּה
vayomer lah hammelech, mah-lach ester hammalkah
Then said the king unto her: 'What wilt thou, queen Esther?

וּמַה-בַּקָּשָׁתֵךְ עַד-חֲצִי הַמַּלְכוּת, וְיִנָּתֵן לָךְ
umah-bakkashatech ad-chatzi hammalchut veyinnaten lach
for whatever thy request, even to the half of the kingdom, it shall be given thee.'

וַתֹּאמֶר אֶסְתֵּר, אִם-עַל-הַמֶּלֶךְ טוֹב
vattomer ester, im-'al-hammelech tov
And Esther said: 'If it seem good unto the king,

יָבוֹא הַמֶּלֶךְ וְהָמָן הַיּוֹם, אֶל-הַמִּשְׁתֶּה אֲשֶׁר-עָשִׂיתִי לוֹ
yavo hammelech vehaman hayom, el-hammishteh asher-'asiti lo
let the king and Haman come this day unto the banquet that I have prepared for him.'

וַיֹּאמֶר הַמֶּלֶךְ--מַהֲרוּ אֶת-הָמָן, לַעֲשׂוֹת אֶת-דְּבַר אֶסְתֵּר
vayomer hammelech, maharu et-haman, la'asot et-devar ester
Then the king said: 'Cause Haman to make haste, that it may be done as Esther hath said.'

וַיָּבֹא הַמֶּלֶךְ וְהָמָן, אֶל-הַמִּשְׁתֶּה אֲשֶׁר-עָשְׂתָה אֶסְתֵּר
vayavo hammelech vehaman, el-hammishteh asher-'asetah ester
So the king and Haman came to the banquet that Esther had prepared.

וַיֹּאמֶר הַמֶּלֶךְ לְאֶסְתֵּר בְּמִשְׁתֵּה הַיַּיִן, מַה-שְּׁאֵלָתֵךְ וְיִנָּתֵן לָךְ
vayomer hammelech le'ester bemishteh hayayin, mah-she'elatech veyinnaten lach
And the king said unto Esther at the banquet of wine: 'Whatever thy petition, it shall be granted thee;

וּמַה-בַּקָּשָׁתֵךְ עַד-חֲצִי הַמַּלְכוּת, וְתֵעָשׂ
umah-bakkashatech ad-chatzi hammalchut vete'as
and whatever thy request, even to the half of the kingdom, it shall be performed.'

אֶסְתֵּר

אַל-תְּדַמִּי בְנַפְשֵׁךְ, לְהִמָּלֵט בֵּית-הַמֶּלֶךְ מִכָּל-הַיְּהוּדִים
al-tedammi venafshech, lehimmalet beit-hammelech mikkol-hayehudim
'Think not with thyself that thou shalt escape in the king's house, more than all the Jews.

כִּי אִם-הַחֲרֵשׁ תַּחֲרִישִׁי, בָּעֵת הַזֹּאת--רֶוַח וְהַצָּלָה יַעֲמוֹד לַיְּהוּדִים
ki im-hacharesh tacharishi ba'et hazzot revach vehatzalah ya'amod layehudim
For if thou altogether holdest thy peace at this time, then will relief and deliverance arise to the Jews

מִמָּקוֹם אַחֵר, וְאַתְּ וּבֵית-אָבִיךְ תֹּאבֵדוּ
mimmakom acher, ve'at uveit-'avich tovedu
from another place, but thou and thy father's house will perish;

וּמִי יוֹדֵעַ--אִם-לְעֵת כָּזֹאת, הִגַּעַתְּ לַמַּלְכוּת
umi yodea', im-le'et kazot, higga'at lammalchut
and who knoweth whether thou art not come to royal estate for such a time as this?'

וַתֹּאמֶר אֶסְתֵּר, לְהָשִׁיב אֶל-מָרְדֳּכָי
vattomer ester lehashiv el-mordechai
Then Esther bade them return answer unto Mordecai:

לֵךְ כְּנוֹס אֶת-כָּל-הַיְּהוּדִים הַנִּמְצְאִים בְּשׁוּשָׁן, וְצוּמוּ עָלַי וְאַל-תֹּאכְלוּ וְאַל-תִּשְׁתּוּ
lech kenos et-kol-hayehudim hannimtze'im beshushan, vetzumu alai ve'al-tochelu ve'al-tishtu
'Go, gather together all the Jews that are present in Shushan, and fast ye for me, and neither eat nor drink

שְׁלֹשֶׁת יָמִים לַיְלָה וָיוֹם--גַּם-אֲנִי וְנַעֲרֹתַי, אָצוּם כֵּן
sheloshet yamim laylah vayom, gam-'ani vena'arotai atzum ken
three days, night or day; I also and my maidens will fast in like manner;

וּבְכֵן אָבוֹא אֶל-הַמֶּלֶךְ, אֲשֶׁר לֹא-כַדָּת, וְכַאֲשֶׁר אָבַדְתִּי, אָבָדְתִּי
uvechen avo el-hammelech asher lo-chaddat, vecha'asher avadti avadeti
and so will I go in unto the king, which is not according to the law; and if I perish, I perish.'

וַיַּעֲבֹר, מָרְדֳּכָי; וַיַּעַשׂ, כְּכֹל אֲשֶׁר-צִוְּתָה עָלָיו אֶסְתֵּר
vaya'avor mordechai; vaya'as kechol asher-tzivvetah alav ester
So Mordecai went his way, and did according to all that Esther had commanded him.

ה

וַיְהִי בַּיּוֹם הַשְּׁלִישִׁי, וַתִּלְבַּשׁ אֶסְתֵּר מַלְכוּת
Vayhi bayom hashelishi, vattilbash ester malchut
Now it came to pass on the third day, that Esther put on her royal apparel,

וַתַּעֲמֹד בַּחֲצַר בֵּית-הַמֶּלֶךְ הַפְּנִימִית, נֹכַח בֵּית הַמֶּלֶךְ
vatta'amod bachatzar beit-hammelech happenimit, nochach beit hammelech
and stood in the inner court of the king's house, over against the king's house;

אֶסְתֵּר

וְאֵת פָּרָשַׁת הַכֶּסֶף, אֲשֶׁר אָמַר הָמָן לִשְׁקוֹל עַל-גִּנְזֵי הַמֶּלֶךְ בַּיְּהוּדִיִּים--לְאַבְּדָם
ve'et parashat hakkesef, asher amar haman lishkol al-ginzei hammelech bayehudiyim bayehudim le'abbedam
and the exact sum of the money that Haman had promised to pay to the king's treasuries for the Jews, to destroy them.

וְאֶת-פַּתְשֶׁגֶן כְּתָב-הַדָּת אֲשֶׁר-נִתַּן בְּשׁוּשָׁן לְהַשְׁמִידָם, נָתַן לוֹ
ve'et-patshegen ketav-haddot asher-nittan beshushan lehashmidam natan lo
Also he gave him the copy of the writing of the decree that was given out in Shushan to destroy them,

לְהַרְאוֹת אֶת-אֶסְתֵּר, וּלְהַגִּיד לָהּ; וּלְצַוּוֹת עָלֶיהָ, לָבוֹא אֶל-הַמֶּלֶךְ
lehar'ot et-'ester ulehaggid lah; uletzavvot aleiha, lavo el-hammelech
to show it unto Esther, and to declare it unto her; and to charge her that she should go in unto the king,

לְהִתְחַנֶּן-לוֹ וּלְבַקֵּשׁ מִלְּפָנָיו--עַל-עַמָּהּ
lehitchannen-lo ulevakkesh millefanav al-'ammah
to make supplication unto him, and to make request before him, for her people.

וַיָּבוֹא, הֲתָךְ; וַיַּגֵּד לְאֶסְתֵּר, אֵת דִּבְרֵי מָרְדֳּכָי
vayavo hatach; vayagged le'ester, et divrei mordechai
And Hathach came and told Esther the words of Mordecai.

וַתֹּאמֶר אֶסְתֵּר לַהֲתָךְ, וַתְּצַוֵּהוּ אֶל-מָרְדֳּכָי
vattomer ester lahatach, vattetzavvehu el-mordechai
Then Esther spoke unto Hathach, and gave him a message unto Mordecai:

כָּל-עַבְדֵי הַמֶּלֶךְ וְעַם-מְדִינוֹת הַמֶּלֶךְ יֹדְעִים, אֲשֶׁר כָּל-אִישׁ וְאִשָּׁה
kol-'avdei hammelech ve'am-medinot hammelech yode'im, asher kol-'ish ve'ishah
'All the king's servants, and the people of the king's provinces, do know, that whosoever, whether man or woman,

אֲשֶׁר יָבוֹא-אֶל-הַמֶּלֶךְ אֶל-הֶחָצֵר הַפְּנִימִית אֲשֶׁר לֹא-יִקָּרֵא אַחַת דָּתוֹ לְהָמִית
asher yavo-'el-hammelech el-hechatzer happenimit asher lo-yikkare, achat dato lehamit
shall come unto the king into the inner court, who is not called, there is one law for him, that he be put to death,

לְבַד מֵאֲשֶׁר יוֹשִׁיט-לוֹ הַמֶּלֶךְ אֶת-שַׁרְבִיט הַזָּהָב, וְחָיָה
levad me'asher yoshit-lo hammelech et-sharvit hazzahav vechayah
except such to whom the king shall hold out the golden sceptre, that he may live;

וַאֲנִי, לֹא נִקְרֵאתִי לָבוֹא אֶל-הַמֶּלֶךְ--זֶה, שְׁלוֹשִׁים יוֹם
va'ani, lo nikreti lavo el-hammelech, zeh sheloshim yom
but I have not been called to come in unto the king these thirty days.'

וַיַּגִּידוּ לְמָרְדֳּכָי, אֵת דִּבְרֵי אֶסְתֵּר
vayaggidu lemordechai, et divrei ester
And they told to Mordecai Esther's words.

וַיֹּאמֶר מָרְדֳּכַי, לְהָשִׁיב אֶל-אֶסְתֵּר
vayomer mordechai lehashiv el-'ester
Then Mordecai bade them to return answer unto Esther:

אֶסְתֵּר

ד

וּמָרְדֳּכַי, יָדַע אֶת-כָּל-אֲשֶׁר נַעֲשָׂה, וַיִּקְרַע מָרְדֳּכַי אֶת-בְּגָדָיו, וַיִּלְבַּשׁ שַׂק וָאֵפֶר
Umordechai, yada et-kol-'asher na'asah, vayikra mordechai et-begadav, vayilbash sak va'efer
Now when Mordecai knew all that was done, Mordecai rent his clothes, and put on sackcloth with ashes,

וַיֵּצֵא בְּתוֹךְ הָעִיר, וַיִּזְעַק זְעָקָה גְדוֹלָה וּמָרָה
vayetzei betoch ha'ir, vayiz'ak ze'akah gedolah umarah
and went out into the midst of the city, and cried with a loud and a bitter cry;

וַיָּבוֹא, עַד לִפְנֵי שַׁעַר-הַמֶּלֶךְ: כִּי אֵין לָבוֹא אֶל-שַׁעַר הַמֶּלֶךְ, בִּלְבוּשׁ שָׂק
vayavo ad lifnei sha'ar-hammelech; ki ein lavo el-sha'ar hammelech bilvush sak
and he came even before the king's gate; for none might enter within the king's gate clothed with sackcloth.

וּבְכָל-מְדִינָה וּמְדִינָה, מְקוֹם אֲשֶׁר דְּבַר-הַמֶּלֶךְ וְדָתוֹ מַגִּיעַ
uvechol-medinah umedinah, mekom asher devar-hammelech vedato maggia'
And in every province, whithersoever the king's commandment and his decree came,

אֵבֶל גָּדוֹל לַיְּהוּדִים, וְצוֹם וּבְכִי וּמִסְפֵּד; שַׂק וָאֵפֶר, יֻצַּע לָרַבִּים
evel gadol layehudim, vetzom uvechi umisped; sak va'efer, yutza larabbim
there was great mourning among the Jews, and fasting, and weeping, and wailing; and many lay in sackcloth and ashes.

וַתָּבוֹאנָה נַעֲרוֹת אֶסְתֵּר וְסָרִיסֶיהָ, וַיַּגִּידוּ לָהּ, וַתִּתְחַלְחַל הַמַּלְכָּה, מְאֹד
vattavonah na'arot ester vesariseiha vayaggidu lah, vattitchalchal hammalkah me'od
And Esther's maidens and her chamberlains came and told it her; and the queen was exceedingly pained;

וַתִּשְׁלַח בְּגָדִים לְהַלְבִּישׁ אֶת-מָרְדֳּכַי, וּלְהָסִיר שַׂקּוֹ מֵעָלָיו--וְלֹא קִבֵּל
vattishlach begadim lehalbish et-mordechai, ulehasir sakko me'alav velo kibbel
and she sent raiment to clothe Mordecai; and to take his sackcloth from off him; but he accepted it not.

וַתִּקְרָא אֶסְתֵּר לַהֲתָךְ מִסָּרִיסֵי הַמֶּלֶךְ, אֲשֶׁר הֶעֱמִיד לְפָנֶיהָ
vattikra ester lahatach missarisei hammelech asher he'emid lefaneiha
Then called Esther for Hathach, one of the king's chamberlains, whom he had appointed to attend upon her,

וַתְּצַוֵּהוּ, עַל-מָרְדֳּכָי--לָדַעַת מַה-זֶּה, וְעַל-מַה-זֶּה
vattetzavvehu al-mordechai; lada'at mah-zeh ve'al-mah-zeh
and charged him to go to Mordecai, to know what this was, and why it was.

וַיֵּצֵא הֲתָךְ, אֶל-מָרְדֳּכָי--אֶל-רְחוֹב הָעִיר, אֲשֶׁר לִפְנֵי שַׁעַר-הַמֶּלֶךְ
vayetzei hatach el-mordechai; el-rechov ha'ir, asher lifnei sha'ar-hammelech
So Hathach went forth to Mordecai unto the broad place of the city, which was before the king's gate.

וַיַּגֶּד-לוֹ מָרְדֳּכַי, אֵת כָּל-אֲשֶׁר קָרָהוּ
vayagged-lo mordechai, et kol-'asher karahu
And Mordecai told him of all that had happened unto him,

אֶסְתֵּר

וַיִּקָּרְאוּ סֹפְרֵי הַמֶּלֶךְ בַּחֹדֶשׁ הָרִאשׁוֹן, בִּשְׁלוֹשָׁה עָשָׂר יוֹם בּוֹ
vayikkare'u soferei hammelech bachodesh harishon, bishloshah asar yom bo
Then were the king's scribes called in the first month, on the thirteenth day thereof,

וַיִּכָּתֵב כְּכָל-אֲשֶׁר-צִוָּה הָמָן אֶל אֲחַשְׁדַּרְפְּנֵי-הַמֶּלֶךְ
vayikkatev kechol-'asher-tzivvah haman el achashdarpenei-hammelech
and there was written, according to all that Haman commanded, unto the king's satraps,

וְאֶל-הַפַּחוֹת אֲשֶׁר עַל-מְדִינָה וּמְדִינָה
ve'el-happachot asher al-medinah umedinah
and to the governors that were over every province, and to the princes of every people;

וְאֶל-שָׂרֵי עַם וָעָם, מְדִינָה וּמְדִינָה כִּכְתָבָהּ וְעַם וָעָם כִּלְשׁוֹנוֹ
ve'el-sarei am va'am, medinah umedinah kichtavah, ve'am va'am kilshono
to every province according to the writing thereof, and to every people after their language;

בְּשֵׁם הַמֶּלֶךְ אֲחַשְׁוֵרֹשׁ נִכְתָּב, וְנֶחְתָּם בְּטַבַּעַת הַמֶּלֶךְ
beshem hammelech achashverosh nichtav, venechtam betabba'at hammelech
in the name of king Ahasuerus was it written, and it was sealed with the king's ring.

וְנִשְׁלוֹחַ סְפָרִים בְּיַד הָרָצִים, אֶל-כָּל-מְדִינוֹת הַמֶּלֶךְ--לְהַשְׁמִיד לַהֲרֹג וּלְאַבֵּד
venishloach sefarim beyad haratzim el-kol-medinot hammelech lehashmid laharog ule'abbed
And letters were sent by posts into all the king's provinces, to destroy, to slay, and to cause to perish,

אֶת-כָּל-הַיְּהוּדִים מִנַּעַר וְעַד-זָקֵן טַף וְנָשִׁים בְּיוֹם אֶחָד
et-kol-hayehudim minna'ar ve'ad-zaken taf venashim beyom echad
all Jews, both young and old, little children and women, in one day,

בִּשְׁלוֹשָׁה עָשָׂר לְחֹדֶשׁ שְׁנֵים-עָשָׂר הוּא-חֹדֶשׁ אֲדָר; וּשְׁלָלָם, לָבוֹז
bishloshah asar lechodesh sheneim-'asar hu-chodesh adar; ushelalam lavoz
even upon the thirteenth day of the twelfth month, which is the month Adar, and to take the spoil of them for a prey.

פַּתְשֶׁגֶן הַכְּתָב, לְהִנָּתֵן דָּת בְּכָל-מְדִינָה וּמְדִינָה, גָּלוּי, לְכָל-הָעַמִּים
patshegen hakketav, lehinnaten dat bechol-medinah umedinah, galui lechol-ha'ammim
The copy of the writing, to be given out for a decree in every province, was to be published unto all peoples,

לִהְיוֹת עֲתִדִים, לַיּוֹם הַזֶּה
lihyot atidim layom hazzeh
that they should be ready against that day.

הָרָצִים יָצְאוּ דְחוּפִים, בִּדְבַר הַמֶּלֶךְ, וְהַדָּת נִתְּנָה, בְּשׁוּשַׁן הַבִּירָה
haratzim yatze'u dechufim bidvar hammelech, vehaddat nittenah beshushan habbirah
The posts went forth in haste by the king's commandment, and the decree was given out in Shushan the castle;

וְהַמֶּלֶךְ וְהָמָן יָשְׁבוּ לִשְׁתּוֹת, וְהָעִיר שׁוּשָׁן נָבוֹכָה
vehammelech vehaman yashevu lishtot, veha'ir shushan navochah
and the king and Haman sat down to drink; but the city of Shushan was perplexed.

אֶסְתֵּר

וַיִּבֶז בְּעֵינָיו, לִשְׁלֹחַ יָד בְּמָרְדֳּכַי לְבַדּוֹ
vayivez be'einav, lishloch yad bemordechai levaddo
But it seemed contemptible in his eyes to lay hands on Mordecai alone;

כִּי-הִגִּידוּ לוֹ, אֶת-עַם מָרְדֳּכָי; וַיְבַקֵּשׁ הָמָן, לְהַשְׁמִיד אֶת-כָּל-הַיְּהוּדִים
ki-higgidu lo et-'am mordechai; vayvakkesh haman, lehashmid et-kol-hayehudim
for they had made known to him the people of Mordecai; wherefore Haman sought to destroy all the Jews

אֲשֶׁר בְּכָל-מַלְכוּת אֲחַשְׁוֵרוֹשׁ--עַם מָרְדֳּכָי
asher bechol-malchut achashverosh am mordechai
that were throughout the whole kingdom of Ahasuerus, even the people of Mordecai.

בַּחֹדֶשׁ הָרִאשׁוֹן, הוּא-חֹדֶשׁ נִיסָן, בִּשְׁנַת שְׁתֵּים עֶשְׂרֵה, לַמֶּלֶךְ אֲחַשְׁוֵרוֹשׁ: הִפִּיל פּוּר הוּא הַגּוֹרָל
bachodesh harishon hu-chodesh nisan, bishnat sheteim esreh, lammelech achashverosh; hippil pur hu haggoral
In the first month, which is the month Nisan, in the twelfth year of king Ahasuerus, they cast pur, that is, the lot,

לִפְנֵי הָמָן, מִיּוֹם לְיוֹם וּמֵחֹדֶשׁ לְחֹדֶשׁ שְׁנֵים-עָשָׂר--הוּא-חֹדֶשׁ אֲדָר
lifnei haman, miyom leyom umechodesh lechodesh sheneim-'asar hu-chodesh adar
before Haman from day to day, and from month to month, to the twelfth month, which is the month Adar.

וַיֹּאמֶר הָמָן, לַמֶּלֶךְ אֲחַשְׁוֵרוֹשׁ--יֶשְׁנוֹ עַם-אֶחָד מְפֻזָּר וּמְפֹרָד
vayomer haman lammelech achashverosh, yeshno am-'echad, mefuzzar umeforad
And Haman said unto king Ahasuerus: 'There is a certain people scattered abroad and dispersed

בֵּין הָעַמִּים, בְּכֹל מְדִינוֹת מַלְכוּתֶךָ; וְדָתֵיהֶם שֹׁנוֹת מִכָּל-עָם
bein ha'ammim, bechol medinot malchutecha; vedateihem shonot mikkol-'am
among the peoples in all the provinces of thy kingdom; and their laws are diverse from those of every people;

וְאֶת-דָּתֵי הַמֶּלֶךְ אֵינָם עֹשִׂים, וְלַמֶּלֶךְ אֵין-שֹׁוֶה, לְהַנִּיחָם
ve'et-datei hammelech einam osim, velammelech ein-shoh lehannicham
neither keep they the king's laws; therefore it profiteth not the king to suffer them.

אִם-עַל-הַמֶּלֶךְ טוֹב, יִכָּתֵב לְאַבְּדָם; וַעֲשֶׂרֶת אֲלָפִים כִּכַּר-כֶּסֶף, אֶשְׁקוֹל
'im-'al-hammelech tov, yikkatev le'abbedam; va'aseret alafim kikkar-kesef, eshkol
If it please the king, let it be written that they be destroyed; and I will pay ten thousand talents of silver

עַל-יְדֵי עֹשֵׂי הַמְּלָאכָה, לְהָבִיא, אֶל-גִּנְזֵי הַמֶּלֶךְ
al-yedei osei hammelachah, lehavi el-ginzei hammelech
into the hands of those that have the charge of the king's business, to bring it into the king's treasuries.'

וַיָּסַר הַמֶּלֶךְ אֶת-טַבַּעְתּוֹ, מֵעַל יָדוֹ; וַיִּתְּנָהּ, לְהָמָן בֶּן-הַמְּדָתָא הָאֲגָגִי--צֹרֵר הַיְּהוּדִים
vayasar hammelech et-tabba'to me'al yado; vayittenah, lehaman ben-hammedata ha'agagi tzorer hayehudim
And the king took his ring from his hand, and gave it unto Haman the son of Hammedatha the Agagite, the Jews' enemy.

וַיֹּאמֶר הַמֶּלֶךְ לְהָמָן, הַכֶּסֶף נָתוּן לָךְ; וְהָעָם, לַעֲשׂוֹת בּוֹ כַּטּוֹב בְּעֵינֶיךָ
vayomer hammelech lehaman, hakkesef natun lach; veha'am la'asot bo kattov be'eineicha
And the king said unto Haman: 'The silver is given to thee, the people also, to do with them as it seemeth good to thee.'

אֶסְתֵּר

ג

אַחַר הַדְּבָרִים הָאֵלֶּה, גִּדַּל הַמֶּלֶךְ אֲחַשְׁוֵרוֹשׁ אֶת-הָמָן בֶּן-הַמְּדָתָא הָאֲגָגִי
Achar haddevarim ha'elleh, giddal hammelech achashverosh et-haman ben-hammedata ha'agagi
After these things did king Ahasuerus promote Haman the son of Hammedatha the Agagite,

וַיְנַשְּׂאֵהוּ; וַיָּשֶׂם, אֶת-כִּסְאוֹ, מֵעַל, כָּל-הַשָּׂרִים אֲשֶׁר אִתּוֹ
vaynasse'ehu; vayasem et-kis'o, me'al kol-hassarim asher itto
and advanced him, and set his seat above all the princes that were with him.

וְכָל-עַבְדֵי הַמֶּלֶךְ אֲשֶׁר-בְּשַׁעַר הַמֶּלֶךְ, כֹּרְעִים
vechol-'avdei hammelech asher-besha'ar hammelech, kore'im
And all the king's servants, that were in the king's gate, bowed down,

וּמִשְׁתַּחֲוִים לְהָמָן--כִּי-כֵן, צִוָּה-לוֹ הַמֶּלֶךְ
umishtachavim lehaman, ki-chen tzivvah-lo hammelech
and prostrated themselves before Haman; for the king had so commanded concerning him.

וּמָרְדֳּכַי--לֹא יִכְרַע, וְלֹא יִשְׁתַּחֲוֶה
umordechai, lo yichra velo yishtachaveh
But Mordecai bowed not down, nor prostrated himself before him.

וַיֹּאמְרוּ עַבְדֵי הַמֶּלֶךְ, אֲשֶׁר-בְּשַׁעַר הַמֶּלֶךְ--לְמָרְדֳּכָי
vayomeru avdei hammelech asher-besha'ar hammelech lemordechai
Then the king's servants, that were in the king's gate, said unto Mordecai:

מַדּוּעַ אַתָּה עוֹבֵר, אֵת מִצְוַת הַמֶּלֶךְ
maddua attah over, et mitzvat hammelech
'Why transgressest thou the king's commandment?'

וַיְהִי, כְּאָמְרָם אֵלָיו יוֹם וָיוֹם, וְלֹא שָׁמַע, אֲלֵיהֶם; וַיַּגִּידוּ לְהָמָן
vayehi, ke'ameram elav yom vayom, velo shama aleihem; vayaggidu lehaman
Now it came to pass, when they spoke daily unto him, and he hearkened not unto them, that they told Haman,

לִרְאוֹת הֲיַעַמְדוּ דִּבְרֵי מָרְדֳּכַי--כִּי-הִגִּיד לָהֶם, אֲשֶׁר-הוּא יְהוּדִי
lir'ot haya'amdu divrei mordechai, ki-higgid lahem asher-hu yehudi
to see whether Mordecai's words would stand; for he had told them that he was a Jew.

וַיַּרְא הָמָן--כִּי-אֵין מָרְדֳּכַי, כֹּרֵעַ
vayar haman, ki-'ein mordechai, korea
And when Haman saw that Mordecai bowed not down,

וּמִשְׁתַּחֲוֶה לוֹ; וַיִּמָּלֵא הָמָן, חֵמָה
umishtachaveh lo; vayimmalei haman chemah
nor prostrated himself before him, then was Haman full of wrath.

אֶסְתֵּר

וַיָּשֶׂם כֶּתֶר-מַלְכוּת בְּרֹאשָׁהּ, וַיַּמְלִיכֶהָ תַּחַת וַשְׁתִּי
vayasem keter-malchut beroshah, vayamlicheha tachat vashti
so that he set the royal crown upon her head, and made her queen instead of Vashti.

וַיַּעַשׂ הַמֶּלֶךְ מִשְׁתֶּה גָדוֹל, לְכָל-שָׂרָיו וַעֲבָדָיו--אֵת, מִשְׁתֵּה אֶסְתֵּר
vaya'as hammelech mishteh gadol, lechol-sarav va'avadav, et mishteh ester
Then the king made a great feast unto all his princes and his servants, even Esther's feast;

וַהֲנָחָה לַמְּדִינוֹת עָשָׂה, וַיִּתֵּן מַשְׂאֵת כְּיַד הַמֶּלֶךְ
vahanachah lammedinot asah, vayitten mas'et keyad hammelech
and he made a release to the provinces, and gave gifts, according to the bounty of the king.

וּבְהִקָּבֵץ בְּתוּלוֹת, שֵׁנִית; וּמָרְדֳּכַי, יֹשֵׁב בְּשַׁעַר-הַמֶּלֶךְ
uvehikkavetz betulot shenit; umordechai yoshev besha'ar-hammelech
And when the virgins were gathered together the second time, and Mordecai sat in the king's gate--

אֵין אֶסְתֵּר, מַגֶּדֶת מוֹלַדְתָּהּ וְאֶת-עַמָּהּ, כַּאֲשֶׁר צִוָּה עָלֶיהָ, מָרְדֳּכָי
'ein ester, maggedet moladtah ve'et-'ammah, ka'asher tzivvah aleiha mordechai
Esther had not yet made known her kindred nor her people; as Mordecai had charged her;

וְאֶת-מַאֲמַר מָרְדֳּכַי אֶסְתֵּר עֹשָׂה, כַּאֲשֶׁר הָיְתָה בְאָמְנָה אִתּוֹ
ve'et-ma'amar mordechai ester osah, ka'asher hayetah ve'amenah itto
for Esther did the commandment of Mordecai, like as when she was brought up with him--

בַּיָּמִים הָהֵם, וּמָרְדֳּכַי יוֹשֵׁב בְּשַׁעַר-הַמֶּלֶךְ; קָצַף
bayamim hahem, umordechai yoshev besha'ar-hammelech; katzaf
in those days, while Mordecai sat in the king's gate, two of the king's chamberlains,

בִּגְתָן וָתֶרֶשׁ שְׁנֵי-סָרִיסֵי הַמֶּלֶךְ, מִשֹּׁמְרֵי הַסַּף, וַיְבַקְשׁוּ לִשְׁלֹחַ יָד, בַּמֶּלֶךְ אֲחַשְׁוֵרוֹשׁ
bigtan vateresh shenei-sarisei hammelech mishomerei hassaf, vayvakshu lishloach yad, bammelech achashverosh
Bigthan and Teresh, of those that kept the door, were wroth, and sought to lay hands on the king Ahasuerus.

וַיִּוָּדַע הַדָּבָר לְמָרְדֳּכַי, וַיַּגֵּד לְאֶסְתֵּר הַמַּלְכָּה
vayivvada haddavar lemordechai, vayagged le'ester hammalkah
And the thing became known to Mordecai, who told it unto Esther the queen;

וַתֹּאמֶר אֶסְתֵּר לַמֶּלֶךְ, בְּשֵׁם מָרְדֳּכָי
vattomer ester lammelech beshem mordechai
and Esther told the king thereof in Mordecai's name.

וַיְבֻקַּשׁ הַדָּבָר וַיִּמָּצֵא, וַיִּתָּלוּ שְׁנֵיהֶם עַל-עֵץ
vayvukkash haddavar vayimmatze, vayittalu sheneihem al-'etz
And when inquisition was made of the matter, and it was found to be so, they were both hanged on a tree;

וַיִּכָּתֵב, בְּסֵפֶר דִּבְרֵי הַיָּמִים--לִפְנֵי הַמֶּלֶךְ
vayikkatev, besefer divrei hayamim lifnei hammelech
and it was written in the book of the chronicles before the king.

אֶסְתֵּר

שִׁשָּׁה חֳדָשִׁים, בְּשֶׁמֶן הַמֹּר, וְשִׁשָּׁה חֳדָשִׁים בַּבְּשָׂמִים, וּבְתַמְרוּקֵי הַנָּשִׁים
shishah chodashim beshemen hammor, veshishah chodashim babbesamim, uvetamrukei hannashim
six months with oil of myrrh, and six month with sweet odours, and with other ointments of the women--

וּבָזֶה, הַנַּעֲרָה בָּאָה אֶל-הַמֶּלֶךְ--אֵת כָּל-אֲשֶׁר תֹּאמַר יִנָּתֵן לָהּ
uvazeh hanna'arah ba'ah el-hammelech; et kol-'asher tomar yinnaten lah
when then the maiden came unto the king, whatsoever she desired was given her

לָבוֹא עִמָּהּ, מִבֵּית הַנָּשִׁים, עַד-בֵּית הַמֶּלֶךְ
lavo immah, mibbeit hannashim ad-beit hammelech
to go with her out of the house of the women unto the king's house.

בָּעֶרֶב הִיא בָאָה, וּבַבֹּקֶר הִיא שָׁבָה אֶל-בֵּית הַנָּשִׁים שֵׁנִי
ba'erev hi va'ah, uvabboker hi shavah el-beit hannashim sheni
In the evening she went, and on the morrow she returned into the second house of the women,

אֶל-יַד שַׁעֲשְׁגַז סְרִיס הַמֶּלֶךְ, שֹׁמֵר הַפִּילַגְשִׁים
el-yad sha'ashgaz seris hammelech shomer happilagshim
to the custody of Shaashgaz, the king's chamberlain, who kept the concubines;

לֹא-תָבוֹא עוֹד אֶל-הַמֶּלֶךְ, כִּי אִם-חָפֵץ בָּהּ הַמֶּלֶךְ וְנִקְרְאָה בְשֵׁם
lo-tavo od el-hammelech, ki im-chafetz bah hammelech venikre'ah veshem
she came in unto the king no more, except the king delighted in her, and she were called by name.

וּבְהַגִּיעַ תֹּר-אֶסְתֵּר בַּת-אֲבִיחַיִל דֹּד מָרְדֳּכַי אֲשֶׁר לָקַח-לוֹ לְבַת
uvehaggia tor-'ester bat-'avichayil dod mordechai asher lakach-lo levat
Now when the turn of Esther, the daughter of Abihail the uncle of Mordecai, who had taken her for his daughter,

לָבוֹא אֶל-הַמֶּלֶךְ, לֹא בִקְשָׁה דָּבָר--כִּי אִם אֶת-אֲשֶׁר יֹאמַר הֵגַי סְרִיס-הַמֶּלֶךְ
lavo el-hammelech, lo vikshah davar, ki im et-'asher yomar hegai seris-hammelech
was come to go in unto the king, she required nothing but what Hegai the king's chamberlain,

שֹׁמֵר הַנָּשִׁים; וַתְּהִי אֶסְתֵּר נֹשֵׂאת חֵן, בְּעֵינֵי כָּל-רֹאֶיהָ
shomer hannashim; vattehi ester noset chen, be'einei kol-ro'eiha
the keeper of the women, appointed. And Esther obtained favour in the sight of all them that looked upon her.

וַתִּלָּקַח אֶסְתֵּר אֶל-הַמֶּלֶךְ אֲחַשְׁוֵרוֹשׁ, אֶל-בֵּית מַלְכוּתוֹ, בַּחֹדֶשׁ הָעֲשִׂירִי
vattillakach ester el-hammelech achashverosh el-beit malchuto, bachodesh ha'asiri
So Esther was taken unto king Ahasuerus into his house royal in the tenth month,

הוּא-חֹדֶשׁ טֵבֵת--בִּשְׁנַת-שֶׁבַע, לְמַלְכוּתוֹ
hu-chodesh tevet; bishnat-sheva lemalchuto
which is the month Tebeth, in the seventh year of his reign.

וַיֶּאֱהַב הַמֶּלֶךְ אֶת-אֶסְתֵּר מִכָּל-הַנָּשִׁים, וַתִּשָּׂא-חֵן וָחֶסֶד לְפָנָיו מִכָּל-הַבְּתוּלֹת
vaye'ehav hammelech et-'ester mikkol-hannashim, vattissa-chen vachesed lefanav mikkol-habbetulot
And the king loved Esther above all the women, and she obtained grace and favour in his sight more than all the virgins;

אֶסְתֵּר

לְקָחָהּ מָרְדֳּכַי לוֹ לְבַת
lekachah mordechai lo levat
Mordecai took her for his own daughter.

וַיְהִי, בְּהִשָּׁמַע דְּבַר-הַמֶּלֶךְ וְדָתוֹ
vayhi, behishama devar-hammelech vedato
So it came to pass, when the king's commandment and his decree was published,

וּבְהִקָּבֵץ נְעָרוֹת רַבּוֹת אֶל-שׁוּשַׁן הַבִּירָה, אֶל-יַד הֵגָי
uvehikkavetz ne'arot rabbot el-shushan habbirah el-yad hegai
and when many maidens were gathered together unto Shushan the castle, to the custody of Hegai,

וַתִּלָּקַח אֶסְתֵּר אֶל-בֵּית הַמֶּלֶךְ, אֶל-יַד הֵגַי שֹׁמֵר הַנָּשִׁים
vattillakach ester el-beit hammelech, el-yad hegai shomer hannashim
that Esther was taken into the king's house, to the custody of Hegai, keeper of the women.

וַתִּיטַב הַנַּעֲרָה בְעֵינָיו, וַתִּשָּׂא חֶסֶד לְפָנָיו, וַיְבַהֵל אֶת-תַּמְרוּקֶיהָ
vattitav hanna'arah ve'einav vattissa chesed lefanav vayvahel et-tamrukeiha
And the maiden pleased him, and she obtained kindness of him; and he speedily gave her her ointments,

וְאֶת-מָנוֹתֶהָ לָתֵת לָהּ, וְאֵת שֶׁבַע הַנְּעָרוֹת הָרְאֻיוֹת לָתֶת-לָהּ מִבֵּית הַמֶּלֶךְ
ve'et-manoteha latet lah, ve'et sheva hanne'arot, hare'uyot latet-lah mibbeit hammelech
with her portions, and the seven maidens, who were meet to be given her out of the king's house;

וַיְשַׁנֶּהָ וְאֶת-נַעֲרוֹתֶיהָ לְטוֹב, בֵּית הַנָּשִׁים
vayshanneha ve'et-na'aroteiha letov beit hannashim
and he advanced her and her maidens to the best place in the house of the women.

לֹא-הִגִּידָה אֶסְתֵּר, אֶת-עַמָּהּ וְאֶת-מוֹלַדְתָּהּ: כִּי מָרְדֳּכַי צִוָּה עָלֶיהָ, אֲשֶׁר לֹא-תַגִּיד
lo-higgidah ester, et-'ammah ve'et-moladetah; ki mordechai tzivvah aleiha asher lo-taggid
Esther had not made known her people nor her kindred; for Mordecai had charged her that she should not tell it.

וּבְכָל-יוֹם וָיוֹם--מָרְדֳּכַי מִתְהַלֵּךְ, לִפְנֵי חֲצַר בֵּית-הַנָּשִׁים
uvechol-yom vayom, mordechai mit'hallech, lifnei chatzar beit-hannashim
And Mordecai walked every day before the court of the women's house,

לָדַעַת אֶת-שְׁלוֹם אֶסְתֵּר, וּמַה-יֵּעָשֶׂה בָּהּ
lada'at et-shelom ester, umah-ye'aseh bah
to know how Esther did, and what would become of her.

וּבְהַגִּיעַ תֹּר נַעֲרָה וְנַעֲרָה לָבוֹא אֶל-הַמֶּלֶךְ אֲחַשְׁוֵרוֹשׁ, מִקֵּץ הֱיוֹת לָהּ
uvehaggia tor na'arah vena'arah lavo el-hammelech achashverosh, mikketz heyot lah
Now when the turn of every maiden was come to go in to king Ahasuerus, after that it had been done to her

כְּדָת הַנָּשִׁים שְׁנֵים עָשָׂר חֹדֶשׁ--כִּי כֵּן יִמְלְאוּ, יְמֵי מְרוּקֵיהֶן
kedat hannashim sheneim asar chodesh, ki ken yimle'u yemei merukeihen
according to the law for the women, twelve months--for so were the days of their anointing accomplished, to wit,

אֶסְתֵּר

זָכַר אֶת-וַשְׁתִּי וְאֵת אֲשֶׁר-עָשָׂתָה, וְאֵת אֲשֶׁר-נִגְזַר עָלֶיהָ
zachar et-vashti ve'et asher-'asatah, ve'et asher-nigzar aleiha
he remembered Vashti, and what she had done, and what was decreed against her.

וַיֹּאמְרוּ נַעֲרֵי-הַמֶּלֶךְ, מְשָׁרְתָיו: יְבַקְשׁוּ לַמֶּלֶךְ נְעָרוֹת בְּתוּלוֹת, טוֹבוֹת מַרְאֶה
vayomeru na'arei-hammelech mesharetav; yevakshu lammelech ne'arot betulot tovot mar'eh
Then said the king's servants that ministered unto him: 'Let there be sought for the king young virgins fair to look on;

וְיַפְקֵד הַמֶּלֶךְ פְּקִידִים, בְּכָל-מְדִינוֹת מַלְכוּתוֹ
veyafked hammelech pekidim bechol-medinot malchuto
and let the king appoint officers in all the provinces of his kingdom,

וְיִקְבְּצוּ אֶת-כָּל-נַעֲרָה-בְתוּלָה טוֹבַת מַרְאֶה אֶל-שׁוּשַׁן הַבִּירָה אֶל-בֵּית הַנָּשִׁים
veyikbetzu et-kol-na'arah-vetulah tovat mar'eh el-shushan habbirah el-beit hannashim
that they may gather together all the fair young virgins unto Shushan the castle, to the house of the women,

אֶל-יַד הֵגֶא סְרִיס הַמֶּלֶךְ שֹׁמֵר הַנָּשִׁים; וְנָתוֹן, תַּמְרוּקֵיהֶן
el-yad hegei seris hammelech shomer hannashim; venaton tamrukeihen
unto the custody of Hegai the king's chamberlain, keeper of the women; and let their ointments be given them;

וְהַנַּעֲרָה, אֲשֶׁר תִּיטַב בְּעֵינֵי הַמֶּלֶךְ--תִּמְלֹךְ, תַּחַת וַשְׁתִּי; וַיִּיטַב הַדָּבָר בְּעֵינֵי הַמֶּלֶךְ, וַיַּעַשׂ כֵּן
vehanna'arah, asher titav be'einei hammelech, timloch tachat vashti; vayitav haddavar be'einei hammelech vaya'as ken
and let the maiden that pleaseth the king be queen instead of Vashti.' And the thing pleased the king; and he did so.

אִישׁ יְהוּדִי, הָיָה בְּשׁוּשַׁן הַבִּירָה
'ish yehudi, hayah beshushan habbirah
There was a certain Jew in Shushan the castle,

וּשְׁמוֹ מָרְדֳּכַי, בֶּן יָאִיר בֶּן-שִׁמְעִי בֶּן-קִישׁ--אִישׁ יְמִינִי
ushemo mordechai, ben ya'ir ben-shim'i ben-kish ish yemini
whose name was Mordecai the son of Jair the son of Shimei the son of Kish, a Benjamite,

אֲשֶׁר הָגְלָה, מִירוּשָׁלַיִם, עִם-הַגֹּלָה אֲשֶׁר הָגְלְתָה, עִם יְכָנְיָה מֶלֶךְ-יְהוּדָה
'asher hagelah miyerushalayim, im-haggolah asher hageletah, im yechaneyah melech-yehudah
who had been carried away from Jerusalem with the captives that had been carried away with Jeconiah king of Judah,

אֲשֶׁר הֶגְלָה, נְבוּכַדְנֶצַּר מֶלֶךְ בָּבֶל
asher heglah, nevuchadnetzar melech bavel
whom Nebuchadnezzar the king of Babylon had carried away.

וַיְהִי אֹמֵן אֶת-הֲדַסָּה, הִיא אֶסְתֵּר בַּת-דֹּדוֹ--כִּי אֵין לָהּ, אָב וָאֵם
vayhi omen et-hadassah, hi ester bat-dodo, ki ein lah av va'em
And he brought up Hadassah, that is, Esther, his uncle's daughter; for she had neither father nor mother,

וְהַנַּעֲרָה יְפַת-תֹּאַר, וְטוֹבַת מַרְאֶה, וּבְמוֹת אָבִיהָ וְאִמָּהּ
vehanna'arah yefat-to'ar vetovat mar'eh, uvemot aviha ve'immah
and the maiden was of beautiful form and fair to look on; and when her father and mother were dead,

אֶסְתֵּר

וּכְדַי, בִּזָּיוֹן וָקָצֶף
uchedai bizzayon vakatzef
So will there arise enough contempt and wrath.

אִם-עַל-הַמֶּלֶךְ טוֹב, יֵצֵא דְבַר-מַלְכוּת מִלְּפָנָיו, וְיִכָּתֵב בְּדָתֵי
'im-'al-hammelech tov, yetzei devar-malchut millefanav, veyikkatev bedatei
If it please the king, let there go forth a royal commandment from him, and let it be written among the laws

פָּרַס-וּמָדַי, וְלֹא יַעֲבוֹר: אֲשֶׁר לֹא-תָבוֹא וַשְׁתִּי, לִפְנֵי הַמֶּלֶךְ אֲחַשְׁוֵרוֹשׁ
faras-umadai velo ya'avor; asher lo-tavo vashti, lifnei hammelech achashverosh
of the Persians and the Medes, that it be not altered, that Vashti come no more before king Ahasuerus,

וּמַלְכוּתָהּ יִתֵּן הַמֶּלֶךְ, לִרְעוּתָהּ הַטּוֹבָה מִמֶּנָּה
umalchutah yitten hammelech, lir'utah hattovah mimmennah
and that the king give her royal estate unto another that is better than she.

וְנִשְׁמַע פִּתְגָם הַמֶּלֶךְ אֲשֶׁר-יַעֲשֶׂה בְּכָל-מַלְכוּתוֹ
venishma pitgam hammelech asher-ya'aseh bechol-malchuto
And when the king's decree which he shall make shall be published throughout all his kingdom,

כִּי רַבָּה הִיא; וְכָל-הַנָּשִׁים, יִתְּנוּ יְקָר לְבַעְלֵיהֶן--לְמִגָּדוֹל, וְעַד-קָטָן
ki rabbah hi; vechol-hannashim, yittenu yekar leva'leihen, lemiggadol ve'ad-katan
great though it be, all the wives will give to their husbands honour, both to great and small.'

וַיִּיטַב, הַדָּבָר, בְּעֵינֵי הַמֶּלֶךְ, וְהַשָּׂרִים; וַיַּעַשׂ הַמֶּלֶךְ, כִּדְבַר מְמוּכָן
vayitav haddavar, be'einei hammelech vehassarim; vaya'as hammelech kidvar memuchan
And the word pleased the king and the princes; and the king did according to the word of Memucan;

וַיִּשְׁלַח סְפָרִים, אֶל-כָּל-מְדִינוֹת הַמֶּלֶךְ--אֶל-מְדִינָה וּמְדִינָה כִּכְתָבָהּ
vayishlach sefarim el-kol-medinot hammelech, el-medinah umedinah kichtavah
for he sent letters into all the king's provinces, into every province according to the writing thereof,

וְאֶל-עַם וָעָם כִּלְשׁוֹנוֹ: לִהְיוֹת כָּל-אִישׁ שֹׂרֵר בְּבֵיתוֹ
ve'el-'am va'am kilshono; lihyot kol-'ish sorer beveito
and to every people after their language, that every man should bear rule in his own house,

וּמְדַבֵּר כִּלְשׁוֹן עַמּוֹ
umedabber kilshon ammo
and speak according to the language of his people.

ב

אַחַר, הַדְּבָרִים הָאֵלֶּה, כְּשֹׁךְ, חֲמַת הַמֶּלֶךְ אֲחַשְׁוֵרוֹשׁ
Achar haddevarim ha'elleh, keshoch chamat hammelech achashverosh
After these things, when the wrath of king Ahasuerus was assuaged,

אֶסְתֵּר

וַיֹּאמֶר הַמֶּלֶךְ, לַחֲכָמִים יֹדְעֵי הָעִתִּים
vayomer hammelech, lachachamim yode'ei ha'ittim
Then the king said to the wise men, who knew the times—

כִּי-כֵן, דְּבַר הַמֶּלֶךְ, לִפְנֵי, כָּל-יֹדְעֵי דָּת וָדִין
ki-chen devar hammelech, lifnei kol-yode'ei dat vadin
for so was the king's manner toward all that knew law and judgment;

וְהַקָּרֹב אֵלָיו, כַּרְשְׁנָא שֵׁתָר אַדְמָתָא תַרְשִׁישׁ, מֶרֶס מַרְסְנָא, מְמוּכָן
vehakkarov elav, karshena shetar admata tarshish, meres marsena memuchan
and the next unto him was Carshena, Shethar, Admatha, Tarshish, Meres, Marsena, and Memucan,

שִׁבְעַת שָׂרֵי פָּרַס וּמָדַי, רֹאֵי פְּנֵי הַמֶּלֶךְ, הַיֹּשְׁבִים רִאשֹׁנָה, בַּמַּלְכוּת
shiv'at sarei paras umadai, ro'ei penei hammelech, hayoshevim rishonah bammalchut
the seven princes of Persia and Media, who saw the king's face, and sat the first in the kingdom:

כְּדָת, מַה-לַּעֲשׂוֹת, בַּמַּלְכָּה, וַשְׁתִּי
kedat mah-la'asot, bammalkah vashti
'What shall we do unto the queen Vashti according to law,

עַל אֲשֶׁר לֹא-עָשְׂתָה, אֶת-מַאֲמַר הַמֶּלֶךְ אֲחַשְׁוֵרוֹשׁ, בְּיַד, הַסָּרִיסִים
al asher lo-'asetah, et-ma'amar hammelech achashverosh, beyad hassarisim
forasmuch as she hath not done the bidding of the king Ahasuerus by the chamberlains?'

וַיֹּאמֶר מְמוּכָן, לִפְנֵי הַמֶּלֶךְ וְהַשָּׂרִים, לֹא עַל-הַמֶּלֶךְ לְבַדּוֹ, עָוְתָה וַשְׁתִּי הַמַּלְכָּה
vayomer memuchan, lifnei hammelech vehassarim, lo al-hammelech levaddo, avetah vashti hammalkah
And Memucan answered before the king and the princes: 'Vashti the queen hath not done wrong to the king only,

כִּי עַל-כָּל-הַשָּׂרִים, וְעַל-כָּל-הָעַמִּים, אֲשֶׁר, בְּכָל-מְדִינוֹת הַמֶּלֶךְ אֲחַשְׁוֵרוֹשׁ
ki al-kol-hassarim ve'al-kol-ha'ammim, asher bechol-medinot hammelech achashverosh
but also to all the princes, and to all the peoples, that are in all the provinces of the king Ahasuerus.

כִּי-יֵצֵא דְבַר-הַמַּלְכָּה עַל-כָּל-הַנָּשִׁים, לְהַבְזוֹת בַּעְלֵיהֶן בְּעֵינֵיהֶן
ki-yetzei devar-hammalkah al-kol-hannashim, lehavzot ba'leihen be'eineihen
For this deed of the queen will come abroad unto all women, to make their husbands contemptible in their eyes,

בְּאָמְרָם, הַמֶּלֶךְ אֲחַשְׁוֵרוֹשׁ אָמַר לְהָבִיא אֶת-וַשְׁתִּי הַמַּלְכָּה לְפָנָיו--וְלֹא-בָאָה
be'omeram, hammelech achashverosh amar lehavi et-vashti hammalkah lefanav velo-va'ah
when it will be said: The king Ahasuerus commanded Vashti the queen to be brought in before him, but she came not.

וְהַיּוֹם הַזֶּה תֹּאמַרְנָה שָׂרוֹת פָּרַס-וּמָדַי
vehayom hazzeh tomarnah sarot paras-umadai
And this day will the princesses of Persia and Media

אֲשֶׁר שָׁמְעוּ אֶת-דְּבַר הַמַּלְכָּה, לְכֹל, שָׂרֵי הַמֶּלֶךְ
asher shame'u et-devar hammalkah, lechol sarei hammelech
who have heard of the deed of the queen say the like unto all the king's princes.

אֶסְתֵּר

עַל רִצְפַת בַּהַט-וָשֵׁשׁ--וְדַר וְסֹחָרֶת
al ritzfat bahat-vashesh vedar vesocharet
upon a pavement of green, and white, and shell, and onyx marble.

וְהַשְׁקוֹת בִּכְלֵי זָהָב, וְכֵלִים מִכֵּלִים שׁוֹנִים
vehashkot bichlei zahav, vechelim mikkelim shonim
And they gave them drink in vessels of gold--the vessels being diverse one from another--

וְיֵין מַלְכוּת רָב, כְּיַד הַמֶּלֶךְ
veyein malchut rav keyad hammelech
and royal wine in abundance, according to the bounty of the king.

וְהַשְּׁתִיָּה כַדָּת, אֵין אֹנֵס: כִּי-כֵן יִסַּד הַמֶּלֶךְ, עַל כָּל-רַב בֵּיתוֹ
vehashetiyah chaddat ein ones; ki-chen yissad hammelech, al kol-rav beito
And the drinking was according to the law; none did compel; for so the king had appointed to all the officers of his house,

לַעֲשׂוֹת, כִּרְצוֹן אִישׁ-וָאִישׁ
la'asot kirtzon ish-va'ish
that they should do according to every man's pleasure.

גַּם וַשְׁתִּי הַמַּלְכָּה, עָשְׂתָה מִשְׁתֵּה נָשִׁים--בֵּית, הַמַּלְכוּת, אֲשֶׁר, לַמֶּלֶךְ אֲחַשְׁוֵרוֹשׁ
gam vashti hammalkah, asetah mishteh nashim; beit hammalchut, asher lammelech achashverosh
Also Vashti the queen made a feast for the women in the royal house which belonged to king Ahasuerus.

בַּיּוֹם, הַשְּׁבִיעִי, כְּטוֹב לֵב-הַמֶּלֶךְ, בַּיָּיִן--אָמַר לִמְהוּמָן בִּזְּתָא חַרְבוֹנָא בִּגְתָא
bayom hashevi'i, ketov lev-hammelech bayayin; amar limhumon bizzeta charvona bigta
On the seventh day, when the heart of the king was merry with wine, he commanded Mehuman, Bizzetha, Harbona, Bigtha,

וַאֲבַגְתָא, זֵתַר וְכַרְכַּס, שִׁבְעַת הַסָּרִיסִים, הַמְשָׁרְתִים, אֶת-פְּנֵי הַמֶּלֶךְ אֲחַשְׁוֵרוֹשׁ
va'avagta zetar vecharkas, shiv'at hassarisim, hamsharetim, et-penei hammelech achashverosh
and Abagtha, Zethar, and Carcas, the seven chamberlains that ministered in the presence of Ahasuerus the king,

לְהָבִיא אֶת-וַשְׁתִּי הַמַּלְכָּה, לִפְנֵי הַמֶּלֶךְ--בְּכֶתֶר מַלְכוּת
lehavi et-vashti hammalkah lifnei hammelech becheter malchut
to bring Vashti the queen before the king with the crown royal,

לְהַרְאוֹת הָעַמִּים וְהַשָּׂרִים אֶת-יָפְיָהּ, כִּי-טוֹבַת מַרְאֶה הִיא
lehar'ot ha'ammim vehassarim et-yofiyah, ki-tovat mar'eh hi
to show the peoples and the princes her beauty; for she was fair to look on.

וַתְּמָאֵן הַמַּלְכָּה וַשְׁתִּי, לָבוֹא בִּדְבַר הַמֶּלֶךְ, אֲשֶׁר, בְּיַד הַסָּרִיסִים
vattema'en hammalkah vashti, lavo bidvar hammelech, asher beyad hassarisim
But the queen Vashti refused to come at the king's commandment by the chamberlains;

וַיִּקְצֹף הַמֶּלֶךְ מְאֹד, וַחֲמָתוֹ בָּעֲרָה בוֹ
vayiktzof hammelech me'od, vachamato ba'arah vo
therefore was the king very wroth, and his anger burned in him.

אֶסְתֵּר

אֶסְתֵּר א

וַיְהִי, בִּימֵי אֲחַשְׁוֵרוֹשׁ: הוּא אֲחַשְׁוֵרוֹשׁ, הַמֹּלֵךְ
Vayhi biymei achashverosh; hu achashverosh, hammolech
Now it came to pass in the days of Ahasuerus--this is Ahasuerus who reigned,

מֵהֹדּוּ וְעַד-כּוּשׁ--שֶׁבַע וְעֶשְׂרִים וּמֵאָה, מְדִינָה
mehoddu ve'ad-kush, sheva ve'esrim ume'ah medinah
from India even unto Ethiopia, over a hundred and seven and twenty provinces--

בַּיָּמִים, הָהֵם--כְּשֶׁבֶת הַמֶּלֶךְ אֲחַשְׁוֵרוֹשׁ, עַל כִּסֵּא מַלְכוּתוֹ, אֲשֶׁר, בְּשׁוּשַׁן הַבִּירָה
bayamim hahem; keshevet hammelech achashverosh, al kissei malchuto, asher beshushan habbirah
that in those days, when the king Ahasuerus sat on the throne of his kingdom, which was in Shushan the castle,

בִּשְׁנַת שָׁלוֹשׁ, לְמָלְכוֹ, עָשָׂה מִשְׁתֶּה, לְכָל-שָׂרָיו וַעֲבָדָיו
bishnat shalosh lemolecho, asah mishteh, lechol-sarav va'avadav
in the third year of his reign, he made a feast unto all his princes and his servants;

חֵיל פָּרַס וּמָדַי, הַפַּרְתְּמִים וְשָׂרֵי הַמְּדִינוֹת--לְפָנָיו
cheil paras umadai, happartemim vesarei hammedinot lefanav
the army of Persia and Media, the nobles and princes of the provinces, being before him;

בְּהַרְאֹתוֹ, אֶת-עֹשֶׁר כְּבוֹד מַלְכוּתוֹ, וְאֶת-יְקָר, תִּפְאֶרֶת גְּדוּלָּתוֹ
behar'oto, et-'osher kevod malchuto, ve'et-yekar, tif'eret gedullato
when he showed the riches of his glorious kingdom and the honour of his excellent majesty,

יָמִים רַבִּים, שְׁמוֹנִים וּמְאַת יוֹם
yamim rabbim, shemonim ume'at yom
many days, even a hundred and fourscore days.

וּבִמְלוֹאת הַיָּמִים הָאֵלֶּה, עָשָׂה הַמֶּלֶךְ לְכָל-הָעָם הַנִּמְצְאִים בְּשׁוּשַׁן הַבִּירָה
uvimlot hayamim ha'elleh, asah hammelech lechol-ha'am hannimtze'im beshushan habbirah
And when these days were fulfilled, the king made a feast unto all the people that were present in Shushan the castle,

לְמִגָּדוֹל וְעַד-קָטָן מִשְׁתֶּה--שִׁבְעַת יָמִים: בַּחֲצַר, גִּנַּת בִּיתַן הַמֶּלֶךְ
lemiggadol ve'ad-katan mishteh shiv'at yamim; bachatzar ginnat bitan hammelech
both great and small, seven days, in the court of the garden of the king's palace;

חוּר כַּרְפַּס וּתְכֵלֶת, אָחוּז בְּחַבְלֵי-בוּץ וְאַרְגָּמָן
chur karpas utechelet, achuz bechavlei-vutz ve'argaman
there were hangings of white, fine cotton, and blue, bordered with cords of fine linen and purple,

עַל-גְּלִילֵי כֶסֶף, וְעַמּוּדֵי שֵׁשׁ; מִטּוֹת זָהָב וָכֶסֶף
al-gelilei chesef ve'ammudei shesh; mittot zahav vachesef
upon silver rods and pillars of marble; the couches were of gold and silver,

קֹהֶלֶת

כִּי, אֶת-כָּל-מַעֲשֶׂה, הָאֱלֹהִים יָבִא בְמִשְׁפָּט, עַל כָּל-נֶעְלָם: אִם-טוֹב, וְאִם-רָע
ki et-kol-ma'aseh, ha'elohim yavi vemishpat al kol-ne'lam; im-tov ve'im-ra
For God shall bring every work into the judgment concerning every hidden thing, whether it be good or whether it be evil.

קֹהֶלֶת

וְתָפֵר הָאֲבִיּוֹנָה: כִּי-הֹלֵךְ הָאָדָם אֶל-בֵּית עוֹלָמוֹ, וְסָבְבוּ בַשּׁוּק הַסּוֹפְדִים
vetafer ha'aviyonah; ki-holech ha'adam el-beit olamo, vesavevu vashuk hassofedim
and the caperberry shall fail; because man goeth to his long home, and the mourners go about the streets;

עַד אֲשֶׁר לֹא-יֵרָתֵק חֶבֶל הַכֶּסֶף, וְתָרוּץ גֻּלַּת הַזָּהָב
'ad asher lo-yeratek chevel hakkesef, vetarutz gullat hazzahav
Before the silver cord is snapped asunder, and the golden bowl is shattered,

וְתִשָּׁבֶר כַּד עַל-הַמַּבּוּעַ, וְנָרֹץ הַגַּלְגַּל אֶל-הַבּוֹר
vetishaver kad al-hammabbua', venarotz haggalgal el-habbor
and the pitcher is broken at the fountain, and the wheel falleth shattered, into the pit;

וְיָשֹׁב הֶעָפָר עַל-הָאָרֶץ, כְּשֶׁהָיָה; וְהָרוּחַ תָּשׁוּב, אֶל-הָאֱלֹהִים אֲשֶׁר נְתָנָהּ.
veyashov he'afar al-ha'aretz keshehayah; veharuach tashuv, el-ha'elohim asher netanah
And the dust returneth to the earth as it was, and the spirit returneth unto God who gave it.

הֲבֵל הֲבָלִים אָמַר הַקּוֹהֶלֶת, הַכֹּל הָבֶל
havel havalim amar hakkohelet hakkol havel
Vanity of vanities, saith Koheleth; all is vanity.

וְיֹתֵר, שֶׁהָיָה קֹהֶלֶת חָכָם: עוֹד, לִמַּד-דַּעַת אֶת-הָעָם
veyoter shehayah kohelet chacham; od, limmad-da'at et-ha'am
And besides that Koheleth was wise, he also taught the people knowledge;

וְאִזֵּן וְחִקֵּר, תִּקֵּן מְשָׁלִים הַרְבֵּה
ve'izzen vechikker, tikken meshalim harbeh
yea, he pondered, and sought out, and set in order many proverbs.

בִּקֵּשׁ קֹהֶלֶת, לִמְצֹא דִּבְרֵי-חֵפֶץ; וְכָתוּב יֹשֶׁר, דִּבְרֵי אֱמֶת
bikkesh kohelet, limtzo divrei-chefetz; vechatuv yosher divrei emet
Koheleth sought to find out words of delight, and that which was written uprightly, even words of truth.

דִּבְרֵי חֲכָמִים כַּדָּרְבֹנוֹת, וּכְמַשְׂמְרוֹת נְטוּעִים
divrei chachamim kaddarevonot, uchemasmerot netu'im
The words of the wise are as goads, and as nails well fastened

בַּעֲלֵי אֲסֻפּוֹת; נִתְּנוּ, מֵרֹעֶה אֶחָד
ba'alei asuppot; nittenu mero'eh echad
are those that are composed in collections; they are given from one shepherd.

וְיֹתֵר מֵהֵמָּה, בְּנִי הִזָּהֵר: עֲשׂוֹת סְפָרִים הַרְבֵּה אֵין קֵץ, וְלַהַג הַרְבֵּה יְגִעַת בָּשָׂר
veyoter mehemmah beni hizzaher; asot sefarim harbeh ein ketz, velahag harbeh yegi'at basar
And furthermore, my son, be admonished: of making many books there is no end; and much study is a weariness of the flesh.

סוֹף דָּבָר, הַכֹּל נִשְׁמָע: אֶת-הָאֱלֹהִים יְרָא וְאֶת-מִצְוֹתָיו שְׁמוֹר, כִּי-זֶה כָּל-הָאָדָם
sof davar hakkol nishma'; et-ha'elohim yera ve'et-mitzvotav shemor, ki-zeh kol-ha'adam
The end of the matter, all having been heard: fear God, and keep His commandments; for this is the whole man.

קֹהֶלֶת

וּבְמַרְאֵי עֵינֶיךָ; וְדָע, כִּי עַל-כָּל-אֵלֶּה יְבִיאֲךָ הָאֱלֹהִים בַּמִּשְׁפָּט
uvemar'ei eineicha; veda ki al-kol-'elleh yevi'acha ha'elohim bammishpat
and in the sight of thine eyes; but know thou, that for all these things God will bring thee into judgment.

וְהָסֵר כַּעַס מִלִּבֶּךָ, וְהַעֲבֵר רָעָה מִבְּשָׂרֶךָ: כִּי-הַיַּלְדוּת וְהַשַּׁחֲרוּת, הָבֶל
vehaser ka'as millibbecha, veha'aver ra'ah mibbesarecha; ki-hayaldut vehashacharut havel
Therefore remove vexation from thy heart, and put away evil from thy flesh; for childhood and youth are vanity.

יב

וּזְכֹר, אֶת-בּוֹרְאֶיךָ, בִּימֵי, בְּחוּרֹתֶיךָ: עַד אֲשֶׁר לֹא-יָבֹאוּ, יְמֵי הָרָעָה
Uzechor et-bore'eicha, bimei bechuroteicha; ad asher lo-yavo'u yemei hara'ah
Remember then thy Creator in the days of thy youth, before the evil days come,

וְהִגִּיעוּ שָׁנִים, אֲשֶׁר תֹּאמַר אֵין-לִי בָהֶם חֵפֶץ
vehiggi'u shanim, asher tomar, ein-li vahem chefetz
and the years draw nigh, when thou shalt say: 'I have no pleasure in them';

עַד אֲשֶׁר לֹא-תֶחְשַׁךְ הַשֶּׁמֶשׁ, וְהָאוֹר, וְהַיָּרֵחַ, וְהַכּוֹכָבִים; וְשָׁבוּ הֶעָבִים, אַחַר הַגָּשֶׁם
'ad asher lo-techshach hashemesh veha'or, vehayareach vehakkochavim; veshavu he'avim achar haggashem
Before the sun, and the light, and the moon, and the stars, are darkened, and the clouds return after the rain;

בַּיּוֹם, שֶׁיָּזֻעוּ שֹׁמְרֵי הַבַּיִת, וְהִתְעַוְּתוּ, אַנְשֵׁי הֶחָיִל
bayom, sheyazu'u shomerei habbayit, vehit'avvetu anshei hechayil
In the day when the keepers of the house shall tremble, and the strong men shall bow themselves,

וּבָטְלוּ הַטֹּחֲנוֹת כִּי מִעֵטוּ, וְחָשְׁכוּ הָרֹאוֹת בָּאֲרֻבּוֹת
uvatelu hattochanot ki mi'etu, vechashechu haro'ot ba'arubbot
and the grinders cease because they are few, and those that look out shall be darkened in the windows,

וְסֻגְּרוּ דְלָתַיִם בַּשּׁוּק, בִּשְׁפַל קוֹל הַטַּחֲנָה
vesuggeru delatayim bashuk, bishfal kol hattachanah
And the doors shall be shut in the street, when the sound of the grinding is low;

וְיָקוּם לְקוֹל הַצִּפּוֹר, וְיִשַּׁחוּ כָּל-בְּנוֹת הַשִּׁיר
veyakum lekol hatzippor, veyishachu kol-benot hashir
and one shall start up at the voice of a bird, and all the daughters of music shall be brought low;

גַּם מִגָּבֹהַּ יִרָאוּ, וְחַתְחַתִּים בַּדֶּרֶךְ
gam miggavoha yira'u vechatchattim badderech
Also when they shall be afraid of that which is high, and terrors shall be in the way;

וְיָנֵאץ הַשָּׁקֵד וְיִסְתַּבֵּל הֶחָגָב
veyanetz hashaked veyistabbel hechagav
and the almond-tree shall blossom, and the grasshopper shall drag itself along,

קֹהֶלֶת

תֶּן-חֵלֶק לְשִׁבְעָה, וְגַם לִשְׁמוֹנָה: כִּי לֹא תֵדַע, מַה-יִּהְיֶה רָעָה עַל-הָאָרֶץ
ten-chelek leshiv'ah vegam lishmonah; ki lo teda', mah-yihyeh ra'ah al-ha'aretz
Divide a portion into seven, yea, even into eight; for thou knowest not what evil shall be upon the earth.

אִם-יִמָּלְאוּ הֶעָבִים גֶּשֶׁם עַל-הָאָרֶץ יָרִיקוּ, וְאִם-יִפּוֹל עֵץ בַּדָּרוֹם
'im-yimmale'u he'avim geshem al-ha'aretz yariku, ve'im-yippol etz baddarom
If the clouds be full of rain, they empty themselves upon the earth; and if a tree fall in the south,

וְאִם בַּצָּפוֹן--מְקוֹם שֶׁיִּפּוֹל הָעֵץ, שָׁם יְהוּא
ve'im batzafon; mekom sheyippol ha'etz sham yehu
or in the north, in the place where the tree falleth, there shall it be.

שֹׁמֵר רוּחַ, לֹא יִזְרָע; וְרֹאֶה בֶעָבִים, לֹא יִקְצוֹר
shomer ruach lo yizra'; vero'eh ve'avim lo yiktzor
He that observeth the wind shall not sow; and he that regardeth the clouds shall not reap.

כַּאֲשֶׁר אֵינְךָ יוֹדֵעַ מַה-דֶּרֶךְ הָרוּחַ, כַּעֲצָמִים בְּבֶטֶן הַמְּלֵאָה
ka'asher einecha yodea mah-derech haruach, ka'atzamim beveten hammele'ah
As thou knowest not what is the way of the wind, nor how the bones do grow in the womb of her that is with child;

כָּכָה, לֹא תֵדַע אֶת-מַעֲשֵׂה הָאֱלֹהִים, אֲשֶׁר יַעֲשֶׂה, אֶת-הַכֹּל
kachah, lo teda et-ma'aseh ha'elohim, asher ya'aseh et-hakkol
even so thou knowest not the work of God who doeth all things.

בַּבֹּקֶר זְרַע אֶת-זַרְעֶךָ, וְלָעֶרֶב אַל-תַּנַּח יָדֶךָ
babboker zera et-zar'echa, vela'erev al-tannach yadecha
In the morning sow thy seed, and in the evening withhold not thy hand;

כִּי אֵינְךָ יוֹדֵעַ אֵי זֶה יִכְשָׁר, הֲזֶה אוֹ-זֶה, וְאִם-שְׁנֵיהֶם כְּאֶחָד, טוֹבִים
ki einecha yodei ei zeh yichshar hazeh o-zeh, ve'im-sheneihem ke'echad tovim
for thou knowest not which shall prosper, whether this or that, or whether they both shall be alike good.

וּמָתוֹק, הָאוֹר; וְטוֹב לַעֵינַיִם, לִרְאוֹת אֶת-הַשָּׁמֶשׁ
umatok ha'or; vetov la'einayim lir'ot et-hashamesh
And the light is sweet, and a pleasant thing it is for the eyes to behold the sun.

כִּי אִם-שָׁנִים הַרְבֵּה יִחְיֶה הָאָדָם, בְּכֻלָּם יִשְׂמָח; וְיִזְכֹּר אֶת-יְמֵי הַחֹשֶׁךְ, כִּי-הַרְבֵּה יִהְיוּ
ki im-shanim harbeh yichyeh ha'adam bechullam yismach; veyizkor et-yemei hachoshech, ki-harbeh yihyu
For if a man live many years, let him rejoice in them all, and remember the days of darkness, for they shall be many.

כָּל-שֶׁבָּא הָבֶל
kol-shebba havel
All that cometh is vanity.

שְׂמַח בָּחוּר בְּיַלְדוּתֶיךָ, וִיטִיבְךָ לִבְּךָ בִּימֵי בְחוּרוֹתֶיךָ, וְהַלֵּךְ בְּדַרְכֵי לִבְּךָ
semach bachur beyalduteicha, vitivecha libbecha bimei vechurotecha, vehallech bedarchei libbecha
Rejoice, O young man, in thy youth; and let thy heart cheer thee in the days of thy youth, and walk in the ways of thy heart,

קֹהֶלֶת

דִּבְרֵי פִי-חָכָם, חֵן; וְשִׂפְתוֹת כְּסִיל, תְּבַלְּעֶנּוּ
divrei fi-chacham chen; vesiftot kesil tevalle'ennu
The words of a wise man's mouth are gracious; but the lips of a fool will swallow up himself.

תְּחִלַּת דִּבְרֵי-פִיהוּ, סִכְלוּת; וְאַחֲרִית פִּיהוּ, הוֹלֵלוּת רָעָה
techillat divrei-fihu sichlut; ve'acharit pihu, holelut ra'ah
The beginning of the words of his mouth is foolishness; and the end of his talk is grievous madness.

וְהַסָּכָל, יַרְבֶּה דְבָרִים; לֹא-יֵדַע הָאָדָם, מַה-שֶּׁיִּהְיֶה, וַאֲשֶׁר יִהְיֶה מֵאַחֲרָיו, מִי יַגִּיד לוֹ
vehassachal yarbeh devarim; lo-yeda ha'adam mah-sheyihyeh, va'asher yihyeh me'acharav, mi yaggid lo
A fool also multiplieth words; yet man knoweth not what shall be; and that which shall be after him, who can tell him?

עֲמַל הַכְּסִילִים, תְּיַגְּעֶנּוּ--אֲשֶׁר לֹא-יָדַע, לָלֶכֶת אֶל-עִיר
'amal hakkesilim teyagge'ennu; asher lo-yada lalechet el-'ir
The labour of fools wearieth every one of them, for he knoweth not how to go to the city.

אִי-לָךְ אֶרֶץ, שֶׁמַּלְכֵּךְ נָעַר; וְשָׂרַיִךְ, בַּבֹּקֶר יֹאכֵלוּ
'i-lach eretz, shemmalkech na'ar; vesarayich babboker yochelu
Woe to thee, O land, when thy king is a boy, and thy princes feast in the morning!

אַשְׁרֵיךְ אֶרֶץ, שֶׁמַּלְכֵּךְ בֶּן-חוֹרִים; וְשָׂרַיִךְ בָּעֵת יֹאכֵלוּ, בִּגְבוּרָה וְלֹא בַשְּׁתִי
'ashreich eretz, shemmalkech ben-chorim; vesarayich ba'et yochelu, bigvurah velo vasheti
Happy art thou, O land, when thy king is a free man, and thy princes eat in due season, in strength, and not in drunkenness!

בַּעֲצַלְתַּיִם, יִמַּךְ הַמְּקָרֶה; וּבְשִׁפְלוּת יָדַיִם, יִדְלֹף הַבָּיִת
ba'atzaltayim yimmach hammekareh; uveshiflut yadayim yidlof habbayit
By slothfulness the rafters sink in; and through idleness of the hands the house leaketh.

לִשְׂחוֹק עֹשִׂים לֶחֶם, וְיַיִן יְשַׂמַּח חַיִּים; וְהַכֶּסֶף, יַעֲנֶה אֶת-הַכֹּל
lischok osim lechem, veyayin yesammach chayim; vehakkesef ya'aneh et-hakkol
A feast is made for laughter, and wine maketh glad the life; and money answereth all things.

גַּם בְּמַדָּעֲךָ, מֶלֶךְ אַל-תְּקַלֵּל, וּבְחַדְרֵי מִשְׁכָּבְךָ, אַל-תְּקַלֵּל עָשִׁיר
gam bemadda'acha, melech al-tekallel, uvechadrei mishkavcha, al-tekallel ashir
Curse not the king, no, not in thy thought, and curse not the rich in thy bedchamber;

כִּי עוֹף הַשָּׁמַיִם יוֹלִיךְ אֶת-הַקּוֹל, וּבַעַל כְּנָפַיִם יַגֵּיד דָּבָר
ki of hashamayim yolich et-hakkol, uva'al kenafayim yaggeid davar
for a bird of the air shall carry the voice, and that which hath wings shall tell the matter.

יא

שַׁלַּח לַחְמְךָ, עַל-פְּנֵי הַמָּיִם: כִּי-בְרֹב הַיָּמִים, תִּמְצָאֶנּוּ
Shallach lachmecha al-penei hammayim; ki-verov hayamim timtza'ennu
Cast thy bread upon the waters, for thou shalt find it after many days.

קֹהֶלֶת

I

זְבוּבֵי מָוֶת, יַבְאִישׁ יַבִּיעַ שֶׁמֶן רוֹקֵחַ; יָקָר מֵחָכְמָה מִכָּבוֹד, סִכְלוּת מְעָט
Zevuvei mavet, yav'ish yabbia shemen rokeach; yakar mechachemah mikkavod sichlut me'at
Dead flies make the ointment of the perfumer fetid and putrid; so doth a little folly outweigh wisdom and honour.

לֵב חָכָם לִימִינוֹ, וְלֵב כְּסִיל לִשְׂמֹאלוֹ
lev chacham limino, velev kesil lismolo
A wise man's understanding is at his right hand; but a fool's understanding at his left.

וְגַם-בַּדֶּרֶךְ כְּשֶׁסָּכָל הֹלֵךְ, לִבּוֹ חָסֵר; וְאָמַר לַכֹּל, סָכָל הוּא
vegam-badderech keshessachal holech libbo chaser; ve'amar lakkol sachal hu
Yea also, when a fool walketh by the way, his understanding faileth him, and he saith to every one that he is a fool.

אִם-רוּחַ הַמּוֹשֵׁל תַּעֲלֶה עָלֶיךָ, מְקוֹמְךָ אַל-תַּנַּח: כִּי מַרְפֵּא, יַנִּיחַ חֲטָאִים גְּדוֹלִים
'im-ruach hammoshel ta'aleh aleicha, mekomecha al-tannach; ki marpe, yanniach chata'im gedolim
If the spirit of the ruler rise up against thee, leave not thy place; for gentleness allayeth great offences.

יֵשׁ רָעָה, רָאִיתִי תַּחַת הַשָּׁמֶשׁ--כִּשְׁגָגָה, שֶׁיֹּצָא מִלִּפְנֵי הַשַּׁלִּיט
yesh ra'ah, ra'iti tachat hashamesh; kishgagah sheyotza millifnei hashallit
There is an evil which I have seen under the sun, like an error which proceedeth from a ruler:

נִתַּן הַסֶּכֶל, בַּמְּרוֹמִים רַבִּים; וַעֲשִׁירִים, בַּשֵּׁפֶל יֵשֵׁבוּ
nittan hassechel, bammeromim rabbim; va'ashirim bashefel yeshevu
Folly is set on great heights, and the rich sit in low place.

רָאִיתִי עֲבָדִים, עַל-סוּסִים; וְשָׂרִים הֹלְכִים כַּעֲבָדִים, עַל-הָאָרֶץ
ra'iti avadim al-susim; vesarim holechim ka'avadim al-ha'aretz
I have seen servants upon horses, and princes walking as servants upon the earth.

חֹפֵר גּוּמָּץ, בּוֹ יִפּוֹל; וּפֹרֵץ גָּדֵר, יִשְּׁכֶנּוּ נָחָשׁ
chofer gummatz bo yippol; uforetz gader yishechennu nachash
He that diggeth a pit shall fall into it; and whoso breaketh through a fence, a serpent shall bite him.

מַסִּיעַ אֲבָנִים, יֵעָצֵב בָּהֶם; בּוֹקֵעַ עֵצִים, יִסָּכֶן בָּם
massia avanim, ye'atzev bahem; bokea etzim yissachen bam
Whoso quarrieth stones shall be hurt therewith; and he that cleaveth wood is endangered thereby.

אִם-קֵהָה הַבַּרְזֶל, וְהוּא לֹא-פָנִים קִלְקַל, וַחֲיָלִים, יְגַבֵּר; וְיִתְרוֹן הַכְשֵׁיר, חָכְמָה
'im-kehah habbarzel, vehu lo-fanim kilkal, vachayalim yegabber; veyitron hachsheir chochmah
If the iron be blunt, and one do not whet the edge, then must he put to more strength; but wisdom is profitable to direct.

אִם-יִשֹּׁךְ הַנָּחָשׁ, בְּלוֹא-לָחַשׁ; וְאֵין יִתְרוֹן, לְבַעַל הַלָּשׁוֹן
'im-yishoch hannachash belo-lachash; ve'ein yitron, leva'al hallashon
If the serpent bite before it is charmed, then the charmer hath no advantage.

קֹהֶלֶת

וְגַם לֹא לַנְּבֹנִים עֹשֶׁר, וְגַם לֹא לַיֹּדְעִים, חֵן: כִּי-עֵת וָפֶגַע, יִקְרֶה אֶת-כֻּלָּם
vegam lo lannevonim osher, vegam lo layode'im chen; ki-'et vafega yikreh et-kullam
nor yet riches to men of understanding, nor yet favour to men of skill; but time and chance happeneth to them all.

כִּי גַם לֹא-יֵדַע הָאָדָם אֶת-עִתּוֹ, כַּדָּגִים שֶׁנֶּאֱחָזִים בִּמְצוֹדָה רָעָה, וְכַצִּפֳּרִים, הָאֲחֻזוֹת בַּפָּח
ki gam lo-yeda ha'adam et-'itto, kaddagim shenne'echazim bimtzodah ra'ah, vechatzipporim, ha'achuzot bappach
For man also knoweth not his time; as the fishes that are taken in an evil net, and as the birds that are caught in the snare,

כָּהֵם, יוּקָשִׁים בְּנֵי הָאָדָם, לְעֵת רָעָה, כְּשֶׁתִּפּוֹל עֲלֵיהֶם פִּתְאֹם
kahem, yukashim benei ha'adam, le'et ra'ah, keshettippol aleihem pit'om
even so are the sons of men snared in an evil time, when it falleth suddenly upon them.

גַּם-זֹה רָאִיתִי חָכְמָה, תַּחַת הַשָּׁמֶשׁ; וּגְדוֹלָה הִיא, אֵלָי
gam-zoh ra'iti chochmah tachat hashamesh; ugedolah hi elai
This also have I seen as wisdom under the sun, and it seemed great unto me:

עִיר קְטַנָּה, וַאֲנָשִׁים בָּהּ מְעָט; וּבָא-אֵלֶיהָ מֶלֶךְ גָּדוֹל
'ir ketannah, va'anashim bah me'at; uva-'eleiha melech gadol
there was a little city, and few men within it; and there came a great king against it,

וְסָבַב אֹתָהּ, וּבָנָה עָלֶיהָ, מְצוֹדִים גְּדֹלִים
vesavav otah, uvanah aleiha metzodim gedolim
and besieged it, and built great bulwarks against it;

וּמָצָא בָהּ, אִישׁ מִסְכֵּן חָכָם, וּמִלַּט-הוּא אֶת-הָעִיר, בְּחָכְמָתוֹ
umatza vah, ish misken chacham, umillat-hu et-ha'ir bechochmato
now there was found in it a man poor and wise, and he by his wisdom delivered the city;

וְאָדָם לֹא זָכַר, אֶת-הָאִישׁ הַמִּסְכֵּן הַהוּא
ve'adam lo zachar, et-ha'ish hammisken hahu
yet no man remembered that same poor man.

וְאָמַרְתִּי אָנִי, טוֹבָה חָכְמָה מִגְּבוּרָה
ve'amarti ani, tovah chochmah miggevurah
Then said I: 'Wisdom is better than strength;

וְחָכְמַת הַמִּסְכֵּן בְּזוּיָה, וּדְבָרָיו אֵינָם נִשְׁמָעִים
vechachemat hammisken bezuyah, udevarav einam nishma'im
nevertheless the poor man's wisdom is despised, and his words are not heard.'

דִּבְרֵי חֲכָמִים, בְּנַחַת נִשְׁמָעִים--מִזַּעֲקַת מוֹשֵׁל, בַּכְּסִילִים
divrei chachamim, benachat nishma'im; mizza'akat moshel bakkesilim
The words of the wise spoken in quiet are more acceptable than the cry of a ruler among fools.

טוֹבָה חָכְמָה, מִכְּלֵי קְרָב; וְחוֹטֶא אֶחָד, יְאַבֵּד טוֹבָה הַרְבֵּה
tovah chochmah mikkelei kerav; vechotei echad, ye'abbed tovah harbeh
Wisdom is better than weapons of war; but one sinner destroyeth much good.

קֹהֶלֶת

כִּי-מִי אֲשֶׁר יְחֻבַּר, אֶל כָּל-הַחַיִּים יֵשׁ בִּטָּחוֹן: כִּי-לְכֶלֶב חַי הוּא טוֹב, מִן-הָאַרְיֵה הַמֵּת
ki-mi asher yechubbar, el kol-hachayim yesh bittachon; ki-lechelev chai hu tov, min-ha'aryeh hammet
For to him that is joined to all the living there is hope; for a living dog is better than a dead lion.

כִּי הַחַיִּים יוֹדְעִים, שֶׁיָּמֻתוּ; וְהַמֵּתִים אֵינָם יוֹדְעִים מְאוּמָה
ki hachayim yode'im sheyamutu; vehammetim einam yode'im me'umah
For the living know that they shall die; but the dead know not any thing,

וְאֵין-עוֹד לָהֶם שָׂכָר--כִּי נִשְׁכַּח, זִכְרָם
ve'ein-'od lahem sachar, ki nishkach zichram
neither have they any more a reward; for the memory of them is forgotten.

גַּם אַהֲבָתָם גַּם-שִׂנְאָתָם גַּם-קִנְאָתָם, כְּבָר אָבָדָה
gam ahavatam gam-sin'atam gam-kin'atam kevar avadah
As well their love, as their hatred and their envy, is long ago perished;

וְחֵלֶק אֵין-לָהֶם עוֹד לְעוֹלָם, בְּכֹל אֲשֶׁר-נַעֲשָׂה תַּחַת הַשָּׁמֶשׁ
vechelek ein-lahem od le'olam, bechol asher-na'asah tachat hashamesh
neither have they any more a portion for ever in any thing that is done under the sun.

לֵךְ אֱכֹל בְּשִׂמְחָה לַחְמֶךָ, וּשְׁתֵה בְלֶב-טוֹב יֵינֶךָ: כִּי כְבָר, רָצָה הָאֱלֹהִים אֶת-מַעֲשֶׂיךָ.
lech echol besimchah lachmecha, ushateh velev-tov yeinecha; ki chevar, ratzah ha'elohim et-ma'aseicha
Go thy way, eat thy bread with joy, and drink thy wine with a merry heart; for God hath already accepted thy works.

בְּכָל-עֵת, יִהְיוּ בְגָדֶיךָ לְבָנִים; וְשֶׁמֶן, עַל-רֹאשְׁךָ אַל-יֶחְסָר
bechol-'et yihyu vegadeicha levanim; veshemen al-roshecha al-yechsar
Let thy garments be always white; and let thy head lack no oil.

רְאֵה חַיִּים עִם-אִשָּׁה אֲשֶׁר-אָהַבְתָּ, כָּל-יְמֵי חַיֵּי הֶבְלֶךָ, אֲשֶׁר נָתַן-לְךָ תַּחַת הַשֶּׁמֶשׁ
re'eh chayim im-'ishah asher-'ahavta, kol-yemei chayei hevlecha, asher natan-lecha tachat hashemesh
Enjoy life with the wife whom thou lovest all the days of the life of thy vanity, which He hath given thee under the sun,

כֹּל יְמֵי הֶבְלֶךָ: כִּי הוּא חֶלְקְךָ, בַּחַיִּים, וּבַעֲמָלְךָ, אֲשֶׁר-אַתָּה עָמֵל תַּחַת הַשָּׁמֶשׁ
kol yemei hevlecha; ki hu chelkecha bachayim, uva'amalecha, asher-'attah amel tachat hashamesh
all the days of thy vanity; for that is thy portion in life, and in thy labour wherein thou labourest under the sun.

כֹּל אֲשֶׁר תִּמְצָא יָדְךָ, לַעֲשׂוֹת בְּכֹחֲךָ--עֲשֵׂה
kol asher timtza yadecha la'asot bechochacha aseh
Whatsoever thy hand attaineth to do by thy strength, that do;

כִּי אֵין מַעֲשֶׂה וְחֶשְׁבּוֹן, וְדַעַת וְחָכְמָה, בִּשְׁאוֹל, אֲשֶׁר אַתָּה הֹלֵךְ שָׁמָּה
ki ein ma'aseh vecheshbon veda'at vechochemah, bish'ol asher attah holech shammah
for there is no work, nor device, nor knowledge, nor wisdom, in the grave, whither thou goest.

שַׁבְתִּי וְרָאֹה תַחַת-הַשֶּׁמֶשׁ, כִּי לֹא לַקַּלִּים הַמֵּרוֹץ וְלֹא לַגִּבּוֹרִים הַמִּלְחָמָה וְגַם לֹא לַחֲכָמִים לֶחֶם
shavti vera'oh tachat-hashemesh, ki lo lakkallim hammerotz velo laggibborim hammilchamah, vegam lo lachachamim lechem
I returned, and saw under the sun, that the race is not to the swift, nor the battle to the strong, neither yet bread to the wise,

קֹהֶלֶת

וְרָאִיתִי, אֶת-כָּל-מַעֲשֵׂה הָאֱלֹהִים, כִּי לֹא יוּכַל הָאָדָם לִמְצוֹא אֶת-הַמַּעֲשֶׂה אֲשֶׁר נַעֲשָׂה תַחַת-הַשֶּׁמֶשׁ
vera'iti et-kol-ma'aseh ha'elohim ki lo yuchal ha'adam, limtzo et-hamma'aseh asher na'asah tachat-hashemesh
then I beheld all the work of God, that man cannot find out the work that is done under the sun;

בְּשֶׁל אֲשֶׁר יַעֲמֹל הָאָדָם לְבַקֵּשׁ וְלֹא יִמְצָא
beshel asher ya'amol ha'adam levakkesh velo yimtza
because though a man labour to seek it out, yet he shall not find it; yea further,

וְגַם אִם-יֹאמַר הֶחָכָם לָדַעַת, לֹא יוּכַל לִמְצֹא
vegam im-yomar hechacham lada'at, lo yuchal limtzo
though a wise man think to know it, yet shall he not be able to find it.

ט

כִּי אֶת-כָּל-זֶה נָתַתִּי אֶל-לִבִּי, וְלָבוּר אֶת-כָּל-זֶה, אֲשֶׁר הַצַּדִּיקִים וְהַחֲכָמִים וַעֲבָדֵיהֶם
Ki et-kol-zeh natatti el-libbi velavur et-kol-zeh, asher hatzaddikim vehachachamim va'avadeihem
For all this I laid to my heart, even to make clear all this: that the righteous, and the wise, and their works,

בְּיַד הָאֱלֹהִים; גַּם-אַהֲבָה גַם-שִׂנְאָה, אֵין יוֹדֵעַ הָאָדָם--הַכֹּל, לִפְנֵיהֶם
beyad ha'elohim; gam-'ahavah gam-sin'ah, ein yodea ha'adam, hakkol lifneihem
are in the hand of God; whether it be love or hatred, man knoweth it not; all is before them.

הַכֹּל כַּאֲשֶׁר לַכֹּל, מִקְרֶה אֶחָד לַצַּדִּיק וְלָרָשָׁע לַטּוֹב
hakkol ka'asher lakkol, mikreh echad latzaddik velarasha lattov
All things come alike to all; there is one event to the righteous and to the wicked; to the good

וְלַטָּהוֹר וְלַטָּמֵא, וְלַזֹּבֵחַ, וְלַאֲשֶׁר אֵינֶנּוּ זֹבֵחַ
velattahor velattame, velazzoveach, vela'asher einennu zoveach
and to the clean and to the unclean; to him that sacrificeth and to him that sacrificeth not;

כַּטּוֹב, כַּחֹטֶא--הַנִּשְׁבָּע, כַּאֲשֶׁר שְׁבוּעָה יָרֵא
kattov kachote, hannishba ka'asher shevu'ah yare
as is the good, so is the sinner, and he that sweareth, as he that feareth an oath.

זֶה רָע, בְּכֹל אֲשֶׁר-נַעֲשָׂה תַּחַת הַשֶּׁמֶשׁ--כִּי-מִקְרֶה אֶחָד, לַכֹּל
zeh ra', bechol asher-na'asah tachat hashemesh, ki-mikreh echad lakkol
This is an evil in all that is done under the sun, that there is one event unto all;

וְגַם לֵב בְּנֵי-הָאָדָם מָלֵא-רָע
vegam lev benei-ha'adom male-ra
yea also, the heart of the sons of men is full of evil,

וְהוֹלֵלוֹת בִּלְבָבָם, בְּחַיֵּיהֶם, וְאַחֲרָיו, אֶל-הַמֵּתִים
veholelot bilvavam bechayeihem, ve'acharav el-hammetim
and madness is in their heart while they live, and after that they go to the dead.

קֹהֶלֶת

עַל-כֵּן מָלֵא לֵב בְּנֵי-הָאָדָם, בָּהֶם--לַעֲשׂוֹת רָע
al-ken malei lev benei-ha'adam bahem la'asot ra
therefore the heart of the sons of men is fully set in them to do evil;

אֲשֶׁר חֹטֶא, עֹשֶׂה רָע מְאַת--וּמַאֲרִיךְ לוֹ
'asher chote, oseh ra me'at uma'arich lo
because a sinner doeth evil a hundred times, and prolongeth his days--

כִּי, גַּם-יוֹדֵעַ אָנִי, אֲשֶׁר יִהְיֶה-טּוֹב לְיִרְאֵי הָאֱלֹהִים, אֲשֶׁר יִירְאוּ מִלְּפָנָיו
ki gam-yodea ani, asher yihyeh-tov leyir'ei ha'elohim, asher yire'u millefanav
though yet I know that it shall be well with them that fear God, that fear before Him;

וְטוֹב לֹא-יִהְיֶה לָרָשָׁע, וְלֹא-יַאֲרִיךְ יָמִים כַּצֵּל
vetov lo-yihyeh larasha', velo-ya'arich yamim katzel
but it shall not be well with the wicked, neither shall he prolong his days, which are as a shadow,

אֲשֶׁר אֵינֶנּוּ יָרֵא, מִלִּפְנֵי אֱלֹהִים
asher einennu yarei millifnei elohim
because he feareth not before God.

יֶשׁ-הֶבֶל, אֲשֶׁר נַעֲשָׂה עַל-הָאָרֶץ, אֲשֶׁר יֵשׁ צַדִּיקִים
yesh-hevel asher na'asah al-ha'aretz asher yesh tzaddikim
There is a vanity which is done upon the earth: that there are righteous men,

אֲשֶׁר מַגִּיעַ אֲלֵהֶם כְּמַעֲשֵׂה הָרְשָׁעִים, וְיֵשׁ רְשָׁעִים
asher maggia alehem kema'aseh haresha'im, veyesh resha'im
unto whom it happeneth according to the work of the wicked; again, there are wicked men,

שֶׁמַּגִּיעַ אֲלֵהֶם כְּמַעֲשֵׂה הַצַּדִּיקִים: אָמַרְתִּי, שֶׁגַּם-זֶה הָבֶל
shemmaggia alehem kema'aseh hatzaddikim; amarti sheggam-zeh havel
to whom it happeneth according to the work of the righteous--I said that this also is vanity.

וְשִׁבַּחְתִּי אֲנִי, אֶת-הַשִּׂמְחָה, אֲשֶׁר אֵין-טוֹב לָאָדָם תַּחַת הַשֶּׁמֶשׁ, כִּי אִם-לֶאֱכֹל וְלִשְׁתּוֹת וְלִשְׂמוֹחַ
veshibbachti ani et-hassimchah, asher ein-tov la'adam tachat hashemesh, ki im-le'echol velishtot velismoach
So I commended mirth, that a man hath no better thing under the sun, than to eat, and to drink, and to be merry,

וְהוּא יִלְוֶנּוּ בַעֲמָלוֹ, יְמֵי חַיָּיו אֲשֶׁר-נָתַן-לוֹ הָאֱלֹהִים--תַּחַת הַשָּׁמֶשׁ
vehu yilvennu va'amalo, yemei chayav asher-natan-lo ha'elohim tachat hashamesh
and that this should accompany him in his labour all the days of his life which God hath given him under the sun.

כַּאֲשֶׁר נָתַתִּי אֶת-לִבִּי, לָדַעַת חָכְמָה, וְלִרְאוֹת אֶת-הָעִנְיָן, אֲשֶׁר נַעֲשָׂה עַל-הָאָרֶץ
ka'asher natatti et-libbi lada'at chochmah velir'ot et-ha'inyan, asher na'asah al-ha'aretz
When I applied my heart to know wisdom, and to see the business that is done upon the earth--

כִּי גַם בַּיּוֹם, וּבַלַּיְלָה--שֵׁנָה, בְּעֵינָיו אֵינֶנּוּ רֹאֶה
ki gam bayom uvallaylah, shenah be'einav einennu ro'eh
for neither day nor night do men see sleep with their eyes—

קֹהֶלֶת

אַל-תִּבָּהֵל מִפָּנָיו תֵּלֵךְ, אַל-תַּעֲמֹד בְּדָבָר רָע: כִּי כָּל-אֲשֶׁר יַחְפֹּץ, יַעֲשֶׂה
'al-tibbahel mippanav telech, al-ta'amod bedavar ra'; ki kol-'asher yachpotz ya'aseh
Be not hasty to go out of his presence; stand not in an evil thing; for he doeth whatsoever pleaseth him.

בַּאֲשֶׁר דְּבַר-מֶלֶךְ, שִׁלְטוֹן; וּמִי יֹאמַר-לוֹ, מַה-תַּעֲשֶׂה
ba'asher devar-melech shilton; umi yomar-lo mah-ta'aseh
Forasmuch as the king's word hath power; and who may say unto him: 'What doest thou?'

שׁוֹמֵר מִצְוָה, לֹא יֵדַע דָּבָר רָע; וְעֵת וּמִשְׁפָּט, יֵדַע לֵב חָכָם
shomer mitzvah, lo yeda davar ra'; ve'et umishpat, yeda lev chacham
Whoso keepeth the commandment shall know no evil thing; and a wise man's heart discerneth time and judgment.

כִּי לְכָל-חֵפֶץ, יֵשׁ עֵת וּמִשְׁפָּט: כִּי-רָעַת הָאָדָם, רַבָּה עָלָיו
ki lechol-chefetz, yesh et umishpat; ki-ra'at ha'adam rabbah alav
For to every matter there is a time and judgment; for the evil of man is great upon him.

כִּי-אֵינֶנּוּ יֹדֵעַ, מַה-שֶּׁיִּהְיֶה: כִּי כַּאֲשֶׁר יִהְיֶה, מִי יַגִּיד לוֹ
ki-'einennu yodea mah-sheyihyeh; ki ka'asher yihyeh, mi yaggid lo
For he knoweth not that which shall be; for even when it cometh to pass, who shall declare it unto him?

אֵין אָדָם שַׁלִּיט בָּרוּחַ, לִכְלוֹא אֶת-הָרוּחַ, וְאֵין שִׁלְטוֹן בְּיוֹם הַמָּוֶת
'ein adam shallit baruach lichlo et-haruach, ve'ein shilton beyom hammavet
There is no man that hath power over the wind to retain the wind; neither hath he power over the day of death;

וְאֵין מִשְׁלַחַת בַּמִּלְחָמָה; וְלֹא-יְמַלֵּט רֶשַׁע, אֶת-בְּעָלָיו
ve'ein mishlachat bammilchamah; velo-yemallet resha et-be'alav
and there is no discharge in war; neither shall wickedness deliver him that is given to it.

אֶת-כָּל-זֶה רָאִיתִי, וְנָתוֹן אֶת-לִבִּי, לְכָל-מַעֲשֶׂה, אֲשֶׁר נַעֲשָׂה תַּחַת הַשָּׁמֶשׁ
'et-kol-zeh ra'iti venaton et-libbi, lechol-ma'aseh, asher na'asah tachat hashamesh
All this have I seen, even applied my heart thereto, whatever the work that is done under the sun;

עֵת, אֲשֶׁר שָׁלַט הָאָדָם בְּאָדָם--לְרַע לוֹ
et, asher shalat ha'adam be'adam lera lo
what time one man had power over another to his hurt.

וּבְכֵן רָאִיתִי רְשָׁעִים קְבֻרִים וָבָאוּ
uvechen ra'iti resha'im kevurim vava'u
And so I saw the wicked buried, and they entered into their rest;

וּמִמְּקוֹם קָדוֹשׁ יְהַלֵּכוּ, וְיִשְׁתַּכְּחוּ בָעִיר אֲשֶׁר כֵּן-עָשׂוּ; גַּם-זֶה, הָבֶל
umimmekom kadosh yehallechu, veyishtakkechu va'ir asher ken-'asu; gam-zeh havel
but they that had done right went away from the holy place, and were forgotten in the city; this also is vanity.

אֲשֶׁר אֵין-נַעֲשָׂה פִתְגָם, מַעֲשֵׂה הָרָעָה מְהֵרָה
'asher ein-na'asah fitgam, ma'aseh hara'ah meherah
Because sentence against an evil work is not executed speedily,

קֹהֶלֶת

סַבּוֹתִי אֲנִי וְלִבִּי לָדַעַת וְלָתוּר, וּבַקֵּשׁ חָכְמָה וְחֶשְׁבּוֹן
sabboti ani velibbi lada'at velatur, uvakkesh chochmah vecheshbon
I turned about, and applied my heart to know and to search out, and to seek wisdom and the reason of things,

וְלָדַעַת רֶשַׁע כֶּסֶל, וְהַסִּכְלוּת הוֹלֵלוֹת
velada'at resha kesel, vehassichlut holelot
and to know wickedness to be folly, and foolishness to be madness;

וּמוֹצֶא אֲנִי מַר מִמָּוֶת, אֶת-הָאִשָּׁה אֲשֶׁר-הִיא מְצוֹדִים וַחֲרָמִים לִבָּהּ--אֲסוּרִים יָדֶיהָ
umotzei ani mar mimmavet, et-ha'ishah asher-hi metzodim vacharamim libbah asurim yadeiha
and I find more bitter than death the woman, whose heart is snares and nets, and her hands as bands;

טוֹב לִפְנֵי הָאֱלֹהִים, יִמָּלֵט מִמֶּנָּה, וְחוֹטֵא, יִלָּכֶד בָּהּ
tov lifnei ha'elohim yimmalet mimmennah, vechotei yillached bah
whoso pleaseth God shall escape from her; but the sinner shall be taken by her.

רְאֵה זֶה מָצָאתִי, אָמְרָה קֹהֶלֶת; אַחַת לְאַחַת, לִמְצֹא חֶשְׁבּוֹן
re'eh zeh matzati, amerah kohelet; achat le'achat limtzo cheshbon
Behold, this have I found, saith Koheleth, adding one thing to another, to find out the account;

אֲשֶׁר עוֹד-בִּקְשָׁה נַפְשִׁי, וְלֹא מָצָאתִי: אָדָם אֶחָד מֵאֶלֶף, מָצָאתִי
'asher od-bikshah nafshi velo matzati; adam echad me'elef matzati
which yet my soul sought, but I found not; one man among a thousand have I found;

וְאִשָּׁה בְכָל-אֵלֶּה, לֹא מָצָאתִי
ve'ishah vechol-'elleh lo matzati
but a woman among all those have I not found.

לְבַד רְאֵה-זֶה מָצָאתִי, אֲשֶׁר עָשָׂה הָאֱלֹהִים אֶת-הָאָדָם יָשָׁר; וְהֵמָּה בִקְשׁוּ, חִשְּׁבֹנוֹת רַבִּים
levad re'eh-zeh matzati, asher asah ha'elohim et-ha'adam yashar; vehemmah vikshu chishevonot rabbim
Behold, this only have I found, that God made man upright; but they have sought out many inventions.

ח

מִי, כְּהֶחָכָם, וּמִי יוֹדֵעַ, פֵּשֶׁר דָּבָר
Mi kehechacham, umi yodea pesher davar
Who is as the wise man? and who knoweth the interpretation of a thing?

חָכְמַת אָדָם תָּאִיר פָּנָיו, וְעֹז פָּנָיו יְשֻׁנֶּא
chochemat adam ta'ir panav, ve'oz panav yeshunne
A man's wisdom maketh his face to shine, and the boldness of his face is changed.

אֲנִי, פִּי-מֶלֶךְ שְׁמֹר, וְעַל, דִּבְרַת שְׁבוּעַת אֱלֹהִים
'ani pi-melech shemor, ve'al divrat shevu'at elohim
I [counsel thee]: keep the king's command, and that in regard of the oath of God.

קֹהֶלֶת

אֶת-הַכֹּל רָאִיתִי, בִּימֵי הֶבְלִי; יֵשׁ צַדִּיק, אֹבֵד בְּצִדְקוֹ
'et-hakkol ra'iti biymei hevli; yesh tzaddik oved betzidko
All things have I seen in the days of my vanity; there is a righteous man that perisheth in his righteousness,

וְיֵשׁ רָשָׁע, מַאֲרִיךְ בְּרָעָתוֹ
veyesh rasha', ma'arich bera'ato
and there is a wicked man that prolongeth his life in his evil-doing.

אַל-תְּהִי צַדִּיק הַרְבֵּה, וְאַל-תִּתְחַכַּם יוֹתֵר: לָמָּה, תִּשּׁוֹמֵם
'al-tehi tzaddik harbeh, ve'al-titchakkam yoter; lammah tishomem
Be not righteous overmuch; neither make thyself overwise; why shouldest thou destroy thyself?

אַל-תִּרְשַׁע הַרְבֵּה, וְאַל-תְּהִי סָכָל: לָמָּה תָמוּת, בְּלֹא עִתֶּךָ
'al-tirsha harbeh ve'al-tehi sachal; lammah tamut belo ittecha
Be not overmuch wicked, neither be thou foolish; why shouldest thou die before thy time?

טוֹב אֲשֶׁר תֶּאֱחֹז בָּזֶה, וְגַם-מִזֶּה אַל-תַּנַּח אֶת-יָדֶךָ
tov asher te'echoz bazeh, vegam-mizzeh al-tannach et-yadecha
It is good that thou shouldest take hold of the one; yea, also from the other withdraw not thy hand;

כִּי-יְרֵא אֱלֹהִים, יֵצֵא אֶת-כֻּלָּם
ki-yerei elohim yetzei et-kullam
for he that feareth God shall discharge himself of them all.

הַחָכְמָה, תָּעֹז לֶחָכָם--מֵעֲשָׂרָה, שַׁלִּיטִים, אֲשֶׁר הָיוּ, בָּעִיר
hachochemah ta'oz lechacham; me'asarah shallitim, asher hayu ba'ir
Wisdom is a stronghold to the wise man more than ten rulers that are in a city.

כִּי אָדָם, אֵין צַדִּיק בָּאָרֶץ--אֲשֶׁר יַעֲשֶׂה-טּוֹב, וְלֹא יֶחֱטָא
ki adam, ein tzaddik ba'aretz; asher ya'aseh-tov velo yecheta
For there is not a righteous man upon earth, that doeth good, and sinneth not.

גַּם לְכָל-הַדְּבָרִים אֲשֶׁר יְדַבֵּרוּ, אַל-תִּתֵּן לִבֶּךָ: אֲשֶׁר לֹא-תִשְׁמַע אֶת-עַבְדְּךָ, מְקַלְלֶךָ
gam lechol-haddevarim asher yedabberu, al-titten libbecha; asher lo-tishma et-'avdecha mekalelecha
Also take not heed unto all words that are spoken, lest thou hear thy servant curse thee;

כִּי גַּם-פְּעָמִים רַבּוֹת, יָדַע לִבֶּךָ: אֲשֶׁר גַּם-אַתָּה, קִלַּלְתָּ אֲחֵרִים
ki gam-pe'amim rabbot yada libbecha; asher gam-'attah killalta acherim
for oftentimes also thine own heart knoweth that thou thyself likewise hast cursed others.

כָּל-זֹה, נִסִּיתִי בַחָכְמָה; אָמַרְתִּי אֶחְכָּמָה, וְהִיא רְחוֹקָה מִמֶּנִּי
kol-zoh nissiti vachochemah; amarti echkamah, vehi rechokah mimmenni
All this have I tried by wisdom; I said: 'I will get wisdom'; but it was far from me.

רָחוֹק, מַה-שֶּׁהָיָה; וְעָמֹק עָמֹק, מִי יִמְצָאֶנּוּ
rachok mah-shehayah; ve'amok amok mi yimtza'ennu
That which is is far off, and exceeding deep; who can find it out?

קֹהֶלֶת

כִּי כְקוֹל הַסִּירִים תַּחַת הַסִּיר, כֵּן שְׂחֹק הַכְּסִיל; וְגַם-זֶה, הָבֶל
ki chekol hassirim tachat hassir, ken sechok hakkesil; vegam-zeh havel
For as the crackling of thorns under a pot, so is the laughter of the fool; this also is vanity.

כִּי הָעֹשֶׁק, יְהוֹלֵל חָכָם; וִיאַבֵּד אֶת-לֵב, מַתָּנָה
ki ha'oshek yeholel chacham; vi'abbed et-lev mattanah
Surely oppression turneth a wise man into a fool; and a gift destroyeth the understanding.

טוֹב אַחֲרִית דָּבָר, מֵרֵאשִׁיתוֹ; טוֹב אֶרֶךְ-רוּחַ, מִגְּבַהּ-רוּחַ
tov acharit davar mereshito; tov erech-ruach miggevah-ruach
Better is the end of a thing than the beginning thereof; and the patient in spirit is better than the proud in spirit.

אַל-תְּבַהֵל בְּרוּחֲךָ, לִכְעוֹס: כִּי כַעַס, בְּחֵיק כְּסִילִים יָנוּחַ
'al-tevahel beruchacha lich'os; ki cha'as, becheik kesilim yanuach
Be not hasty in thy spirit to be angry; for anger resteth in the bosom of fools.

אַל-תֹּאמַר, מֶה הָיָה--שֶׁהַיָּמִים הָרִאשֹׁנִים, הָיוּ טוֹבִים מֵאֵלֶּה
'al-tomar meh hayah, shehayamim harishonim, hayu tovim me'elleh
Say not thou: 'How was it that the former days were better than these?'

כִּי לֹא מֵחָכְמָה, שָׁאַלְתָּ עַל-זֶה
ki lo mechochmah sha'alta al-zeh
for it is not out of wisdom that thou inquirest concerning this.

טוֹבָה חָכְמָה, עִם-נַחֲלָה; וְיֹתֵר, לְרֹאֵי הַשָּׁמֶשׁ
tovah chochmah im-nachalah; veyoter lero'ei hashamesh
Wisdom is good with an inheritance, yea, a profit to them that see the sun.

כִּי בְּצֵל הַחָכְמָה, בְּצֵל הַכָּסֶף; וְיִתְרוֹן דַּעַת
ki betzel hachochemah betzel hakkasef; veyitron da'at
For wisdom is a defence, even as money is a defence; but the excellency of knowledge is,

הַחָכְמָה תְּחַיֶּה בְעָלֶיהָ
hachochemah techayeh ve'aleiha
that wisdom preserveth the life of him that hath it.

רְאֵה, אֶת-מַעֲשֵׂה הָאֱלֹהִים: כִּי מִי יוּכַל לְתַקֵּן, אֵת אֲשֶׁר עִוְּתוֹ
re'eh et-ma'aseh ha'elohim; ki mi yuchal letakken, et asher ivveto
Consider the work of God; for who can make that straight, which He hath made crooked?

בְּיוֹם טוֹבָה הֱיֵה בְטוֹב, וּבְיוֹם רָעָה רְאֵה
beyom tovah heyeh vetov, uveyom ra'ah re'eh
In the day of prosperity be joyful, and in the day of adversity consider;

גַּם אֶת-זֶה לְעֻמַּת-זֶה, עָשָׂה הָאֱלֹהִים, עַל-דִּבְרַת שֶׁלֹּא יִמְצָא הָאָדָם אַחֲרָיו, מְאוּמָה
gam et-zeh le'ummat-zeh asah ha'elohim, al-divrat, shello yimtza ha'adam acharav me'umah
God hath made even the one as well as the other, to the end that man should find nothing after him.

קֹהֶלֶת

מַה-שֶּׁהָיָה, כְּבָר נִקְרָא שְׁמוֹ, וְנוֹדָע, אֲשֶׁר-הוּא אָדָם

mah-shehayah, kevar nikra shemo, venoda asher-hu adam
Whatsoever cometh into being, the name thereof was given long ago, and it is foreknown what man is;

וְלֹא-יוּכַל לָדִין, עִם שֶׁתַּקִּיף מִמֶּנּוּ

velo-yuchal ladin, im shehatkif shettakkif mimmennu
neither can he contend with Him that is mightier than he.

כִּי יֵשׁ-דְּבָרִים הַרְבֵּה, מַרְבִּים הָבֶל; מַה-יֹּתֵר, לָאָדָם

ki yesh-devarim harbeh marbim havel; mah-yoter la'adam
Seeing there are many words that increase vanity, what is man the better?

כִּי מִי-יוֹדֵעַ מַה-טּוֹב לָאָדָם בַּחַיִּים, מִסְפַּר יְמֵי-חַיֵּי הֶבְלוֹ--וְיַעֲשֵׂם כַּצֵּל

ki mi-yodea mah-tov la'adam bachayim, mispar yemei-chayei hevlo veya'asem katzel
For who knoweth what is good for man in his life, all the days of his vain life which he spendeth as a shadow?

אֲשֶׁר מִי-יַגִּיד לָאָדָם, מַה-יִּהְיֶה אַחֲרָיו תַּחַת הַשָּׁמֶשׁ

asher mi-yaggid la'adam, mah-yihyeh acharav tachat hashamesh
for who can tell a man what shall be after him under the sun?

ז

טוֹב שֵׁם, מִשֶּׁמֶן טוֹב; וְיוֹם הַמָּוֶת, מִיּוֹם הִוָּלְדוֹ

Tov shem mishemen tov; veyom hammavet, miyom hivvaledo
A good name is better than precious oil; and the day of death than the day of one's birth.

טוֹב לָלֶכֶת אֶל-בֵּית-אֵבֶל, מִלֶּכֶת אֶל-בֵּית מִשְׁתֶּה

tov lalechet el-beit-'evel, millechet el-beit mishteh
It is better to go to the house of mourning, than to go to the house of feasting;

בַּאֲשֶׁר, הוּא סוֹף כָּל-הָאָדָם; וְהַחַי, יִתֵּן אֶל-לִבּוֹ

ba'asher hu sof kol-ha'adam; vehachai yitten el-libbo
for that is the end of all men, and the living will lay it to his heart.

טוֹב כַּעַס, מִשְּׂחוֹק: כִּי-בְרֹעַ פָּנִים, יִיטַב לֵב

tov ka'as missechok; ki-veroa panim yitav lev
Vexation is better than laughter; for by the sadness of the countenance the heart may be gladdened.

לֵב חֲכָמִים בְּבֵית אֵבֶל, וְלֵב כְּסִילִים בְּבֵית שִׂמְחָה

lev chachamim beveit evel, velev kesilim beveit simchah
The heart of the wise is in the house of mourning; but the heart of fools is in the house of mirth.

טוֹב, לִשְׁמֹעַ גַּעֲרַת חָכָם--מֵאִישׁ, שֹׁמֵעַ שִׁיר כְּסִילִים

tov lishmoa ga'arat chacham; me'ish shomea shir kesilim
It is better to hear the rebuke of the wise, than for a man to hear the song of fools.

קֹהֶלֶת

I

יֵשׁ רָעָה, אֲשֶׁר רָאִיתִי תַּחַת הַשָּׁמֶשׁ; וְרַבָּה הִיא, עַל-הָאָדָם
Yesh ra'ah, asher ra'iti tachat hashamesh; verabbah hi al-ha'adam
There is an evil which I have seen under the sun, and it is heavy upon men:

אִישׁ אֲשֶׁר יִתֶּן-לוֹ הָאֱלֹהִים עֹשֶׁר וּנְכָסִים וְכָבוֹד וְאֵינֶנּוּ חָסֵר לְנַפְשׁוֹ מִכֹּל אֲשֶׁר-יִתְאַוֶּה
'ish asher yitten-lo ha'elohim osher unechasim vechavod ve'einennu chaser lenafsho mikkol asher-yit'avveh
a man to whom God giveth riches, wealth, and honour, so that he wanteth nothing for his soul of all that he desireth,

וְלֹא-יַשְׁלִיטֶנּוּ הָאֱלֹהִים לֶאֱכֹל מִמֶּנּוּ--כִּי אִישׁ נָכְרִי, יֹאכְלֶנּוּ: זֶה הֶבֶל וָחֳלִי רָע, הוּא
velo-yashlitennu ha'elohim le'echol mimmennu, ki ish nochri yochalennu; zeh hevel vocholi ra hu
yet God giveth him not power to eat thereof, but a stranger eateth it; this is vanity, and it is an evil disease.

אִם-יוֹלִיד אִישׁ מֵאָה וְשָׁנִים רַבּוֹת יִחְיֶה וְרַב שֶׁיִּהְיוּ יְמֵי-שָׁנָיו
'im-yolid ish me'ah veshanim rabbot yichyeh verav sheyihyu yemei-shanav
If a man beget a hundred children, and live many years, so that the days of his years are many,

וְנַפְשׁוֹ לֹא-תִשְׂבַּע מִן-הַטּוֹבָה, וְגַם-קְבוּרָה, לֹא-הָיְתָה לּוֹ--אָמַרְתִּי, טוֹב מִמֶּנּוּ הַנָּפֶל
venafsho lo-tisba min-hattovah, vegam-kevurah lo-hayetah lo; amarti tov mimmennu hannafel
but his soul have not enough of good, and moreover he have no burial; I say, that an untimely birth is better than he;

כִּי-בַהֶבֶל בָּא, וּבַחֹשֶׁךְ יֵלֵךְ; וּבַחֹשֶׁךְ, שְׁמוֹ יְכֻסֶּה
ki-vahevel ba uvachoshech yelech; uvachoshech shemo yechusseh
for it cometh in vanity, and departeth in darkness, and the name thereof is covered with darkness;

גַּם-שֶׁמֶשׁ לֹא-רָאָה, וְלֹא יָדָע; נַחַת לָזֶה, מִזֶּה
gam-shemesh lo-ra'ah velo yada'; nachat lazeh mizzeh
moreover it hath not seen the sun nor known it; this hath gratification rather than the other;

וְאִלּוּ חָיָה, אֶלֶף שָׁנִים פַּעֲמַיִם, וְטוֹבָה, לֹא רָאָה--הֲלֹא אֶל-מָקוֹם אֶחָד, הַכֹּל הוֹלֵךְ
ve'illu chayah, elef shanim pa'amayim, vetovah lo ra'ah; halo el-makom echad hakkol holech
yea, though he live a thousand years twice told, and enjoy no good; do not all go to one place?

כָּל-עֲמַל הָאָדָם, לְפִיהוּ; וְגַם-הַנֶּפֶשׁ, לֹא תִמָּלֵא
kol-'amal ha'adam lefihu; vegam-hannefesh lo timmale
All the labour of man is for his mouth, and yet the appetite is not filled.

כִּי מַה-יּוֹתֵר לֶחָכָם, מִן-הַכְּסִיל; מַה-לֶּעָנִי יוֹדֵעַ, לַהֲלֹךְ נֶגֶד הַחַיִּים
ki mah-yoter lechacham min-hakkesil; mah-le'ani yodea', lahaloch neged hachayim
For what advantage hath the wise more than the fool? or the poor man that hath understanding, in walking before the living?

טוֹב מַרְאֵה עֵינַיִם, מֵהֲלָךְ-נָפֶשׁ; גַּם-זֶה הֶבֶל, וּרְעוּת רוּחַ
tov mar'eh einayim mehalach-nafesh; gam-zeh hevel ure'ut ruach
Better is the seeing of the eyes than the wandering of the desire; this also is vanity and a striving after wind.

קֹהֶלֶת

יֵשׁ רָעָה חוֹלָה, רָאִיתִי תַּחַת הַשָּׁמֶשׁ: עֹשֶׁר שָׁמוּר לִבְעָלָיו, לְרָעָתוֹ
yesh ra'ah cholah, ra'iti tachat hashamesh; osher shamur liv'alav lera'ato
There is a grievous evil which I have seen under the sun, namely, riches kept by the owner thereof to his hurt;

וְאָבַד הָעֹשֶׁר הַהוּא, בְּעִנְיַן רָע; וְהוֹלִיד בֵּן, וְאֵין בְּיָדוֹ מְאוּמָה
ve'avad ha'osher hahu be'inyan ra'; veholid ben, ve'ein beyado me'umah
and those riches perish by evil adventure; and if he hath begotten a son, there is nothing in his hand.

כַּאֲשֶׁר יָצָא מִבֶּטֶן אִמּוֹ, עָרוֹם יָשׁוּב לָלֶכֶת כְּשֶׁבָּא
ka'asher yatza mibbeten immo, arom yashuv lalechet keshebba
As he came forth of his mother's womb, naked shall he go back as he came,

וּמְאוּמָה לֹא-יִשָּׂא בַעֲמָלוֹ, שֶׁיֹּלֵךְ בְּיָדוֹ
ume'umah lo-yissa va'amalo, sheyolech beyado
and shall take nothing for his labour, which he may carry away in his hand.

וְגַם-זֹה רָעָה חוֹלָה, כָּל-עֻמַּת שֶׁבָּא כֵּן יֵלֵךְ
vegam-zoh ra'ah cholah, kol-'ummat shebba ken yelech
And this also is a grievous evil, that in all points as he came, so shall he go;

וּמַה-יִּתְרוֹן לוֹ, שֶׁיַּעֲמֹל לָרוּחַ
umah-yitron lo, sheya'amol laruach
and what profit hath he that he laboureth for the wind?

גַּם כָּל-יָמָיו, בַּחֹשֶׁךְ יֹאכֵל; וְכָעַס הַרְבֵּה, וְחָלְיוֹ וָקָצֶף
gam kol-yamav bachoshech yochel; vecha'as harbeh vecholyo vakatzef
All his days also he eateth in darkness, and he hath much vexation and sickness and wrath.

הִנֵּה אֲשֶׁר-רָאִיתִי אָנִי, טוֹב אֲשֶׁר-יָפֶה לֶאֱכוֹל-וְלִשְׁתּוֹת וְלִרְאוֹת טוֹבָה בְּכָל-עֲמָלוֹ
hinneh asher-ra'iti ani, tov asher-yafeh le'echol-velishtot velir'ot tovah bechol-'amalo
Behold that which I have seen: it is good, yea, it is comely for one to eat and to drink, and to enjoy pleasure for all his labour,

שֶׁיַּעֲמֹל תַּחַת-הַשֶּׁמֶשׁ מִסְפַּר יְמֵי-חַיָּיו אֲשֶׁר-נָתַן-לוֹ הָאֱלֹהִים--כִּי-הוּא חֶלְקוֹ
sheya'amol tachat-hashemesh, mispar yemei-chayav yemei-chayav asher-natan-lo ha'elohim ki-hu chelko
wherein he laboureth under the sun, all the days of his life which God hath given him; for this is his portion.

גַּם כָּל-הָאָדָם אֲשֶׁר נָתַן-לוֹ הָאֱלֹהִים עֹשֶׁר וּנְכָסִים וְהִשְׁלִיטוֹ לֶאֱכֹל מִמֶּנּוּ
gam kol-ha'adam asher natan-lo ha'elohim osher unechasim vehishlito le'echol mimmennu
Every man also to whom God hath given riches and wealth, and hath given him power to eat thereof,

וְלָשֵׂאת אֶת-חֶלְקוֹ, וְלִשְׂמֹחַ בַּעֲמָלוֹ--זֹה, מַתַּת אֱלֹהִים הִיא
velaset et-chelko, velismoach ba'amalo; zoh mattat elohim hi
and to take his portion, and to rejoice in his labour--this is the gift of God.

כִּי לֹא הַרְבֵּה, יִזְכֹּר אֶת-יְמֵי חַיָּיו: כִּי הָאֱלֹהִים מַעֲנֶה, בְּשִׂמְחַת לִבּוֹ
ki lo harbeh, yizkor et-yemei chayav; ki ha'elohim ma'aneh besimchat libbo
For let him remember the days of his life that they are not many; for God answereth him in the joy of his heart.

קֹהֶלֶת

כַּאֲשֶׁר תִּדֹּר נֶדֶר לֵאלֹהִים, אַל-תְּאַחֵר לְשַׁלְּמוֹ--כִּי אֵין חֵפֶץ, בַּכְּסִילִים: אֵת אֲשֶׁר-תִּדֹּר, שַׁלֵּם
ka'asher tiddor neder le'elohim, al-te'acher leshallemo, ki ein chefetz bakkesilim; et asher-tiddor shallem
When thou vowest a vow unto God, defer not to pay it; for He hath no pleasure in fools; pay that which thou vowest.

טוֹב, אֲשֶׁר לֹא-תִדֹּר--מִשֶּׁתִּדּוֹר, וְלֹא תְשַׁלֵּם
tov asher lo-tiddor; mishettiddor velo teshallem
Better is it that thou shouldest not vow, than that thou shouldest vow and not pay.

אַל-תִּתֵּן אֶת-פִּיךָ, לַחֲטִיא אֶת-בְּשָׂרֶךָ, וְאַל-תֹּאמַר לִפְנֵי הַמַּלְאָךְ, כִּי שְׁגָגָה הִיא
'al-titten et-picha lachati et-besarecha, ve'al-tomar lifnei hammal'ach, ki shegagah hi
Suffer not thy mouth to bring thy flesh into guilt, neither say thou before the messenger, that it was an error;

לָמָּה יִקְצֹף הָאֱלֹהִים עַל-קוֹלֶךָ, וְחִבֵּל אֶת-מַעֲשֵׂה יָדֶיךָ
lammah yiktzof ha'elohim al-kolecha, vechibbel et-ma'aseh yadeicha
wherefore should God be angry at thy voice, and destroy the work of thy hands?

כִּי בְרֹב חֲלֹמוֹת וַהֲבָלִים, וּדְבָרִים הַרְבֵּה: כִּי אֶת-הָאֱלֹהִים, יְרָא
ki verov chalomot vahavalim, udevarim harbeh; ki et-ha'elohim yera
For through the multitude of dreams and vanities there are also many words; but fear thou God.

אִם-עֹשֶׁק רָשׁ וְגֵזֶל מִשְׁפָּט וָצֶדֶק, תִּרְאֶה בַמְּדִינָה
'im-'oshek rash vegezel mishpat vatzedek tir'eh vammedinah
If thou seest the oppression of the poor, and the violent perverting of justice and righteousness in the state,

אַל-תִּתְמַהּ, עַל-הַחֵפֶץ: כִּי גָבֹהַּ מֵעַל גָּבֹהַּ, שֹׁמֵר, וּגְבֹהִים, עֲלֵיהֶם
al-titmah al-hachefetz; ki gavoha me'al gavoha shomer, ugevohim aleihem
marvel not at the matter; for one higher than the high watcheth, and there are higher than they.

וְיִתְרוֹן אֶרֶץ, בַּכֹּל הוּא--מֶלֶךְ לְשָׂדֶה, נֶעֱבָד
veyitron eretz bakkol hu; melech lesadeh ne'evad
But the profit of a land every way is a king that maketh himself servant to the field.

אֹהֵב כֶּסֶף לֹא-יִשְׂבַּע כֶּסֶף, וּמִי-אֹהֵב בֶּהָמוֹן לֹא תְבוּאָה; גַּם-זֶה, הָבֶל
'ohev kesef lo-yisba kesef, umi-'ohev behamon lo tevu'ah; gam-zeh havel
He that loveth silver shall not be satisfied with silver; nor he that loveth abundance, with increase; this also is vanity.

בִּרְבוֹת, הַטּוֹבָה, רַבּוּ, אוֹכְלֶיהָ
birvot hattovah, rabbu ocheleiha
When goods increase, they are increased that eat them;

וּמַה-כִּשְׁרוֹן, לִבְעָלֶיהָ, כִּי, אִם-רְאוּת עֵינָיו
umah-kishron liv'aleiha, ki im-re'ut einav
and what advantage is there to the owner thereof, saving the beholding of them with his eyes?

מְתוּקָה שְׁנַת הָעֹבֵד, אִם-מְעַט וְאִם-הַרְבֵּה יֹאכֵל; וְהַשָּׂבָע, לֶעָשִׁיר--אֵינֶנּוּ מַנִּיחַ לוֹ, לִישׁוֹן
metukah shenat ha'oved, im-me'at ve'im-harbeh yochel; vehassava le'ashir, einennu manniach lo lishon
Sweet is the sleep of a labouring man, whether he eat little or much; but the satiety of the rich will not suffer him to sleep.

קֹהֶלֶת

טוֹב יֶלֶד מִסְכֵּן, וְחָכָם--מִמֶּלֶךְ זָקֵן וּכְסִיל
tov yeled misken vechacham; mimmelech zaken uchesil
Better is a poor and wise child than an old and foolish king,

אֲשֶׁר לֹא-יָדַע לְהִזָּהֵר עוֹד
asher lo-yada lehizzaher od
who knoweth not how to receive admonition any more.

כִּי-מִבֵּית הָסוּרִים, יָצָא לִמְלֹךְ: כִּי גַּם בְּמַלְכוּתוֹ, נוֹלַד רָשׁ
ki-mibbeit hasurim yatza limloch; ki gam bemalchuto nolad rash
For out of prison he came forth to be king; although in his kingdom he was born poor.

רָאִיתִי, אֶת-כָּל-הַחַיִּים, הַמְהַלְּכִים, תַּחַת הַשָּׁמֶשׁ--עִם הַיֶּלֶד הַשֵּׁנִי, אֲשֶׁר יַעֲמֹד תַּחְתָּיו
ra'iti et-kol-hachayim, hamhallechim tachat hashamesh; im hayeled hasheni, asher ya'amod tachtav
I saw all the living that walk under the sun, that they were with the child, the second, that was to stand up in his stead.

אֵין-קֵץ לְכָל-הָעָם, לְכֹל אֲשֶׁר-הָיָה לִפְנֵיהֶם
'ein-ketz lechol-ha'am, lechol asher-hayah lifneihem
There was no end of all the people, even of all them whom he did lead;

גַּם הָאַחֲרוֹנִים, לֹא יִשְׂמְחוּ-בוֹ: כִּי-גַם-זֶה הֶבֶל, וְרַעְיוֹן רוּחַ
gam ha'acharonim lo yismechu-vo; ki-gam-zeh hevel vera'yon ruach
yet they that come after shall not rejoice in him. Surely this also is vanity and a striving after wind.

שְׁמֹר רַגְלְךָ, כַּאֲשֶׁר תֵּלֵךְ אֶל-בֵּית הָאֱלֹהִים, וְקָרוֹב לִשְׁמֹעַ
shemor raglecha, ka'asher telech el-beit ha'elohim, vekarov lishmoa'
Guard thy foot when thou goest to the house of God, and be ready to hearken:

מִתֵּת הַכְּסִילִים זָבַח: כִּי-אֵינָם יוֹדְעִים, לַעֲשׂוֹת רָע
mittet hakkesilim zavach; ki-'einam yode'im la'asot ra
it is better than when fools give sacrifices; for they know not that they do evil.

ה

אַל-תְּבַהֵל עַל-פִּיךָ וְלִבְּךָ אַל-יְמַהֵר, לְהוֹצִיא דָבָר--לִפְנֵי הָאֱלֹהִים
Al-tevahel al-picha velibbecha al-yemaher lehotzi davar lifnei ha'elohim
Be not rash with thy mouth, and let not thy heart be hasty to utter a word before God;

כִּי הָאֱלֹהִים בַּשָּׁמַיִם וְאַתָּה עַל-הָאָרֶץ, עַל-כֵּן יִהְיוּ דְבָרֶיךָ מְעַטִּים
ki ha'elohim bashamayim ve'attah al-ha'aretz, al-ken yihyu devareicha me'attim
for God is in heaven, and thou upon earth; therefore let thy words be few.

כִּי בָּא הַחֲלוֹם, בְּרֹב עִנְיָן; וְקוֹל כְּסִיל, בְּרֹב דְּבָרִים
ki ba hachalom berov inyan; vekol kesil berov devarim
For a dream cometh through a multitude of business; and a fool's voice through a multitude of words.

קֹהֶלֶת

גַּם-זֶה הֶבֶל, וּרְעוּת רוּחַ
gam-zeh hevel ure'ut ruach
This also is vanity and a striving after wind.

הַכְּסִיל חֹבֵק אֶת-יָדָיו, וְאֹכֵל אֶת-בְּשָׂרוֹ
hakkesil chovek et-yadav, ve'ochel et-besaro
The fool foldeth his hands together, and eateth his own flesh.

טוֹב, מְלֹא כַף נָחַת--מִמְּלֹא חָפְנַיִם עָמָל, וּרְעוּת רוּחַ
tov melo chaf nachat; mimmelo chafenayim amal ure'ut ruach
Better is a handful of quietness, than both the hands full of labour and striving after wind.

וְשַׁבְתִּי אֲנִי וָאֶרְאֶה הֶבֶל, תַּחַת הַשָּׁמֶשׁ
veshavti ani va'er'eh hevel tachat hashamesh
Then I returned and saw vanity under the sun.

יֵשׁ אֶחָד וְאֵין שֵׁנִי גַּם בֵּן וָאָח אֵין-לוֹ
yesh echad ve'ein sheni gam ben va'ach ein-lo
There is one that is alone, and he hath not a second; yea, he hath neither son nor brother;

וְאֵין קֵץ לְכָל-עֲמָלוֹ--גַּם-עֵינוֹ, לֹא-תִשְׂבַּע עֹשֶׁר
ve'ein ketz lechol-'amalo, gam-'eino lo-tisba osher
yet is there no end of all his labour, neither is his eye satisfied with riches:

וּלְמִי אֲנִי עָמֵל, וּמְחַסֵּר אֶת-נַפְשִׁי מִטּוֹבָה--גַּם-זֶה הֶבֶל וְעִנְיַן רָע, הוּא
ulemi ani amel, umechasser et-nafshi mittovah, gam-zeh hevel ve'inyan ra hu
'for whom then do I labour, and bereave my soul of pleasure?' This also is vanity, yea, it is a grievous business.

טוֹבִים הַשְּׁנַיִם, מִן-הָאֶחָד: אֲשֶׁר יֵשׁ-לָהֶם שָׂכָר טוֹב, בַּעֲמָלָם
tovim hashenayim min-ha'echad; asher yesh-lahem sachar tov ba'amalam
Two are better than one; because they have a good reward for their labour.

כִּי אִם-יִפֹּלוּ, הָאֶחָד יָקִים אֶת-חֲבֵרוֹ
ki im-yippolu, ha'echad yakim et-chavero
For if they fall, the one will lift up his fellow;

וְאִילוֹ, הָאֶחָד שֶׁיִּפּוֹל, וְאֵין שֵׁנִי, לַהֲקִימוֹ
ve'ilo, ha'echad sheyippol, ve'ein sheni lahakimo
but woe to him that is alone when he falleth, and hath not another to lift him up.

גַּם אִם-יִשְׁכְּבוּ שְׁנַיִם, וְחַם לָהֶם; וּלְאֶחָד, אֵיךְ יֵחָם
gam im-yishkevu shenayim vecham lahem; ule'echad eich yecham
Again, if two lie together, then they have warmth; but how can one be warm alone?

וְאִם-יִתְקְפוֹ, הָאֶחָד--הַשְּׁנַיִם, יַעַמְדוּ נֶגְדּוֹ; וְהַחוּט, הַמְשֻׁלָּשׁ, לֹא בִמְהֵרָה, יִנָּתֵק
ve'im-yitkefo ha'echad, hashenayim ya'amdu negdo; vehachut hamshullash, lo vimherah yinnatek
And if a man prevail against him that is alone, two shall withstand him; and a threefold cord is not quickly broken.

קֹהֶלֶת

הַכֹּל הוֹלֵךְ, אֶל-מָקוֹם אֶחָד; הַכֹּל הָיָה מִן-הֶעָפָר, וְהַכֹּל שָׁב אֶל-הֶעָפָר
hakkol holech el-makom echad; hakkol hayah min-he'afar, vehakkol shav el-he'afar
All go unto one place; all are of the dust, and all return to dust.

מִי יוֹדֵעַ, רוּחַ בְּנֵי הָאָדָם--הָעֹלָה הִיא, לְמָעְלָה
mi yodea', ruach benei ha'adam, ha'olah hi lema'elah
Who knoweth the spirit of man whether it goeth upward,

וְרוּחַ, הַבְּהֵמָה--הַיֹּרֶדֶת הִיא, לְמַטָּה לָאָרֶץ
veruach habbehemah, hayoredet hi lemattah la'aretz
and the spirit of the beast whether it goeth downward to the earth?

וְרָאִיתִי, כִּי אֵין טוֹב מֵאֲשֶׁר יִשְׂמַח הָאָדָם בְּמַעֲשָׂיו
vera'iti, ki ein tov me'asher yismach ha'adam bema'asav
Wherefore I perceived that there is nothing better, than that a man should rejoice in his works;

כִּי-הוּא, חֶלְקוֹ: כִּי מִי יְבִיאֶנּוּ לִרְאוֹת, בְּמֶה שֶׁיִּהְיֶה אַחֲרָיו
ki-hu chelko; ki mi yevi'ennu lir'ot, bemeh sheyihyeh acharav
for that is his portion; for who shall bring him to see what shall be after him?

ד

וְשַׁבְתִּי אֲנִי, וָאֶרְאֶה אֶת-כָּל-הָעֲשֻׁקִים, אֲשֶׁר נַעֲשִׂים, תַּחַת הַשָּׁמֶשׁ
Veshavti ani, va'er'eh et-kol-ha'ashukim, asher na'asim tachat hashamesh
But I returned and considered all the oppressions that are done under the sun;

וְהִנֵּה דִּמְעַת הָעֲשֻׁקִים
vehinneh dim'at ha'ashukim
and behold the tears of such as were oppressed,

וְאֵין לָהֶם מְנַחֵם, וּמִיַּד עֹשְׁקֵיהֶם כֹּחַ, וְאֵין לָהֶם מְנַחֵם
ve'ein lahem menachem, umiyad oshekeihem koach, ve'ein lahem menachem
and they had no comforter; and on the side of their oppressors there was power, but they had no comforter.

וְשַׁבֵּחַ אֲנִי אֶת-הַמֵּתִים, שֶׁכְּבָר מֵתוּ--מִן-הַחַיִּים, אֲשֶׁר הֵמָּה חַיִּים עֲדֶנָה
veshabbeach ani et-hammetim shekkevar metu; min-hachayim, asher hemmah chayim adenah
Wherefore I praised the dead that are already dead more than the living that are yet alive;

וְטוֹב, מִשְּׁנֵיהֶם--אֵת אֲשֶׁר-עֲדֶן, לֹא הָיָה: אֲשֶׁר לֹא-רָאָה אֶת-הַמַּעֲשֶׂה הָרָע, אֲשֶׁר נַעֲשָׂה תַּחַת הַשָּׁמֶשׁ
vetov misheneihem, et asher-'aden lo hayah; asher lo-ra'ah et-hamma'aseh hara', asher na'asah tachat hashamesh
but better than they both is he that hath not yet been, who hath not seen the evil work that is done under the sun.

וְרָאִיתִי אֲנִי אֶת-כָּל-עָמָל, וְאֵת כָּל-כִּשְׁרוֹן הַמַּעֲשֶׂה--כִּי הִיא קִנְאַת-אִישׁ, מֵרֵעֵהוּ
vera'iti ani et-kol-'amal, ve'et kol-kishron hamma'aseh, ki hi kin'at-'ish mere'ehu
Again, I considered all labour and all excelling in work, that it is a man's rivalry with his neighbour.

קֹהֶלֶת

וְגַם כָּל-הָאָדָם שֶׁיֹּאכַל וְשָׁתָה, וְרָאָה טוֹב בְּכָל-עֲמָלוֹ--מַתַּת אֱלֹהִים, הִיא
vegam kol-ha'adam sheyochal veshatah, vera'ah tov bechol-'amalo; mattat elohim hi
But also that every man should eat and drink, and enjoy pleasure for all his labour, is the gift of God.

יָדַעְתִּי, כִּי כָּל-אֲשֶׁר יַעֲשֶׂה הָאֱלֹהִים הוּא יִהְיֶה לְעוֹלָם--עָלָיו אֵין לְהוֹסִיף
yada'ti, ki kol-'asher ya'aseh ha'elohim hu yihyeh le'olam, alav ein lehosif
I know that, whatsoever God doeth, it shall be for ever; nothing can be added to it,

וּמִמֶּנּוּ אֵין לִגְרֹעַ; וְהָאֱלֹהִים עָשָׂה, שֶׁיִּרְאוּ מִלְּפָנָיו
umimmennu ein ligroa'; veha'elohim asah, sheyir'u millefanav
nor any thing taken from it; and God hath so made it, that men should fear before Him.

מַה-שֶּׁהָיָה כְּבָר הוּא, וַאֲשֶׁר לִהְיוֹת כְּבָר הָיָה; וְהָאֱלֹהִים, יְבַקֵּשׁ אֶת-נִרְדָּף
mah-shehayah kevar hu, va'asher lihyot kevar hayah; veha'elohim yevakkesh et-nirdaf
That which is hath been long ago, and that which is to be hath already been; and God seeketh that which is pursued.

וְעוֹד רָאִיתִי, תַּחַת הַשָּׁמֶשׁ: מְקוֹם הַמִּשְׁפָּט שָׁמָּה הָרֶשַׁע
ve'od ra'iti tachat hashamesh; mekom hammishpat shammah haresha'
And moreover I saw under the sun, in the place of justice, that wickedness was there;

וּמְקוֹם הַצֶּדֶק שָׁמָּה הָרָשַׁע
umekom hatzedek shammah harasha
and in the place of righteousness, that wickedness was there.

אָמַרְתִּי אֲנִי, בְּלִבִּי--אֶת-הַצַּדִּיק וְאֶת-הָרָשָׁע, יִשְׁפֹּט הָאֱלֹהִים
'amarti ani belibbi, et-hatzaddik ve'et-harasha', yishpot ha'elohim
I said in my heart: 'The righteous and the wicked God will judge;

כִּי-עֵת לְכָל-חֵפֶץ, וְעַל כָּל-הַמַּעֲשֶׂה שָׁם
ki-'et lechol-chefetz, ve'al kol-hamma'aseh sham
for there is a time there for every purpose and for every work.'

אָמַרְתִּי אֲנִי, בְּלִבִּי--עַל-דִּבְרַת בְּנֵי הָאָדָם, לְבָרָם הָאֱלֹהִים
'amarti ani belibbi, al-divrat benei ha'adam, levaram ha'elohim
I said in my heart: 'It is because of the sons of men, that God may sift them,

וְלִרְאוֹת, שְׁהֶם-בְּהֵמָה הֵמָּה לָהֶם
velir'ot shehem-behemah hemmah lahem
and that they may see that they themselves are but as beasts.'

כִּי מִקְרֶה בְנֵי-הָאָדָם וּמִקְרֶה הַבְּהֵמָה, וּמִקְרֶה אֶחָד לָהֶם--כְּמוֹת זֶה
ki mikreh venei-ha'adam umikreh habbehemah, umikreh echad lahem, kemot zeh
For that which befalleth the sons of men befalleth beasts; even one thing befalleth them; as the one dieth,

כֵּן מוֹת זֶה, וְרוּחַ אֶחָד לַכֹּל; וּמוֹתַר הָאָדָם מִן-הַבְּהֵמָה אָיִן, כִּי הַכֹּל הָבֶל
ken mot zeh, veruach echad lakkol; umotar ha'adam min-habbehemah ayin, ki hakkol havel
so dieth the other; yea, they have all one breath; so that man hath no pre-eminence above a beast; for all is vanity.

קֹהֶלֶת

עֵת לַהֲרוֹג וְעֵת לִרְפּוֹא, עֵת לִפְרוֹץ וְעֵת לִבְנוֹת
'et laharog ve'et lirpo, et lifrotz ve'et livnot
A time to kill, and a time to heal; a time to break down, and a time to build up;

עֵת לִבְכּוֹת וְעֵת לִשְׂחוֹק, עֵת סְפוֹד וְעֵת רְקוֹד
'et livkot ve'et lischok, et sefod ve'et rekod
A time to weep, and a time to laugh; a time to mourn, and a time to dance;

עֵת לְהַשְׁלִיךְ אֲבָנִים, וְעֵת כְּנוֹס אֲבָנִים
'et lehashlich avanim, ve'et kenos avanim
A time to cast away stones, and a time to gather stones together;

עֵת לַחֲבוֹק, וְעֵת לִרְחֹק מֵחַבֵּק
et lachavok, ve'et lirchok mechabbek
a time to embrace, and a time to refrain from embracing;

עֵת לְבַקֵּשׁ וְעֵת לְאַבֵּד, עֵת לִשְׁמוֹר וְעֵת לְהַשְׁלִיךְ
'et levakkesh ve'et le'abbed, et lishmor ve'et lehashlich
A time to seek, and a time to lose; a time to keep, and a time to cast away;

עֵת לִקְרוֹעַ וְעֵת לִתְפּוֹר, עֵת לַחֲשׁוֹת וְעֵת לְדַבֵּר
'et likroa ve'et litpor, et lachashot ve'et ledabber
A time to rend, and a time to sew; a time to keep silence, and a time to speak;

עֵת לֶאֱהֹב וְעֵת לִשְׂנֹא, עֵת מִלְחָמָה וְעֵת שָׁלוֹם
'et le'ehov ve'et lisno, et milchamah ve'et shalom
A time to love, and a time to hate; a time for war, and a time for peace.

מַה-יִּתְרוֹן, הָעוֹשֶׂה, בַּאֲשֶׁר, הוּא עָמֵל
mah-yitron ha'oseh, ba'asher hu amel
What profit hath he that worketh in that he laboureth?

רָאִיתִי אֶת-הָעִנְיָן, אֲשֶׁר נָתַן אֱלֹהִים לִבְנֵי הָאָדָם--לַעֲנוֹת בּוֹ
ra'iti et-ha'inyan, asher natan elohim livnei ha'adam la'anot bo
I have seen the task which God hath given to the sons of men to be exercised therewith.

אֶת-הַכֹּל עָשָׂה, יָפֶה בְעִתּוֹ; גַּם אֶת-הָעֹלָם, נָתַן בְּלִבָּם
'et-hakkol asah yafeh ve'itto; gam et-ha'olam natan belibbam
He hath made every thing beautiful in its time; also He hath set the world in their heart,

מִבְּלִי אֲשֶׁר לֹא-יִמְצָא הָאָדָם אֶת-הַמַּעֲשֶׂה אֲשֶׁר-עָשָׂה הָאֱלֹהִים, מֵרֹאשׁ וְעַד-סוֹף
mibbeli asher lo-yimtza ha'adam, et-hamma'aseh asher-'asah ha'elohim merosh ve'ad-sof
yet so that man cannot find out the work that God hath done from the beginning even to the end.

יָדַעְתִּי, כִּי אֵין טוֹב בָּם--כִּי אִם-לִשְׂמוֹחַ, וְלַעֲשׂוֹת טוֹב בְּחַיָּיו
yada'ti ki ein tov bam; ki im-lismoach, vela'asot tov bechayav
I know that there is nothing better for them, than to rejoice, and to get pleasure so long as they live.

קֹהֶלֶת

כִּי מֶה-הֹוֶה לָאָדָם, בְּכָל-עֲמָלוֹ, וּבְרַעְיוֹן, לִבּוֹ--שֶׁהוּא עָמֵל, תַּחַת הַשָּׁמֶשׁ

ki meh-hoh la'adam bechol-'amalo, uvera'yon libbo; shehu amel tachat hashamesh
For what hath a man of all his labour, and of the striving of his heart, wherein he laboureth under the sun?

כִּי כָל-יָמָיו מַכְאֹבִים, וָכַעַס עִנְיָנוֹ

ki chol-yamav mach'ovim, vacha'as inyano
For all his days are pains, and his occupation vexation;

גַּם-בַּלַּיְלָה, לֹא-שָׁכַב לִבּוֹ; גַּם-זֶה, הֶבֶל הוּא

gam-ballaylah lo-shachav libbo; gam-zeh hevel hu
yea, even in the night his heart taketh not rest. This also is vanity.

אֵין-טוֹב בָּאָדָם שֶׁיֹּאכַל וְשָׁתָה, וְהֶרְאָה אֶת-נַפְשׁוֹ טוֹב בַּעֲמָלוֹ

'ein-tov ba'adam sheyochal veshatah, veher'ah et-nafsho tov ba'amalo
There is nothing better for a man than that he should eat and drink, and make his soul enjoy pleasure for his labour.

גַּם-זֹה רָאִיתִי אָנִי, כִּי מִיַּד הָאֱלֹהִים הִיא

gam-zoh ra'iti ani, ki miyad ha'elohim hi
This also I saw, that it is from the hand of God.

כִּי מִי יֹאכַל וּמִי יָחוּשׁ, חוּץ מִמֶּנִּי

ki mi yochal umi yachush chutz mimmenni
For who will eat, or who will enjoy, if not I?

כִּי לְאָדָם שֶׁטּוֹב לְפָנָיו, נָתַן חָכְמָה וְדַעַת וְשִׂמְחָה

ki le'adam shettov lefanav, natan chochmah veda'at vesimchah
For to the man that is good in His sight He giveth wisdom, and knowledge, and joy;

וְלַחוֹטֶא נָתַן עִנְיָן לֶאֱסוֹף וְלִכְנוֹס

velachotei natan inyan le'esof velichnos
but to the sinner He giveth the task, to gather and to heap up,

לָתֵת לְטוֹב לִפְנֵי הָאֱלֹהִים--גַּם-זֶה הֶבֶל, וּרְעוּת רוּחַ

latet letov lifnei ha'elohim, gam-zeh hevel ure'ut ruach
that he may leave to him that is good in the sight of God. This also is vanity and a striving after wind.

ג

לַכֹּל, זְמָן; וְעֵת לְכָל-חֵפֶץ, תַּחַת הַשָּׁמָיִם

Lakkol zeman; ve'et lechol-chefetz tachat hashamayim
To every thing there is a season, and a time to every purpose under the heaven:

עֵת לָלֶדֶת, וְעֵת לָמוּת; עֵת לָטַעַת, וְעֵת לַעֲקוֹר נָטוּעַ

'et laledet ve'et lamut; et lata'at, ve'et la'akor natua
A time to be born, and a time to die; a time to plant, and a time to pluck up that which is planted;

קֹהֶלֶת

וְאָמַרְתִּי אֲנִי בְּלִבִּי, כְּמִקְרֵה הַכְּסִיל גַּם-אֲנִי יִקְרֵנִי
ve'amarti ani belibbi, kemikreh hakkesil gam-'ani yikreni
Then said I in my heart: 'As it happeneth to the fool, so will it happen even to me;

וְלָמָּה חָכַמְתִּי אֲנִי, אָז יֹתֵר; וְדִבַּרְתִּי בְלִבִּי, שֶׁגַּם-זֶה הָבֶל
velammah chachamti ani az yoter; vedibbarti velibbi, sheggam-zeh havel
and why was I then more wise?' Then I said in my heart, that this also is vanity.

כִּי אֵין זִכְרוֹן לֶחָכָם עִם-הַכְּסִיל, לְעוֹלָם: בְּשֶׁכְּבָר הַיָּמִים הַבָּאִים
ki ein zichron lechacham im-hakkesil le'olam; beshekkevar hayamim habba'im
For of the wise man, even as of the fool, there is no remembrance for ever; seeing that in the days to come

הַכֹּל נִשְׁכָּח, וְאֵיךְ יָמוּת הֶחָכָם, עִם-הַכְּסִיל
hakkol nishkach, ve'eich yamut hechacham im-hakkesil
all will long ago have been forgotten. And how must the wise man die even as the fool!

וְשָׂנֵאתִי, אֶת-הַחַיִּים--כִּי רַע עָלַי הַמַּעֲשֶׂה, שֶׁנַּעֲשָׂה תַּחַת הַשָּׁמֶשׁ
vesaneti et-hachayim, ki ra alai hamma'aseh, shenna'asah tachat hashamesh
So I hated life; because the work that is wrought under the sun was grievous unto me;

כִּי-הַכֹּל הֶבֶל, וּרְעוּת רוּחַ
ki-hakkol hevel ure'ut ruach
for all is vanity and a striving after wind.

וְשָׂנֵאתִי אֲנִי אֶת-כָּל-עֲמָלִי, שֶׁאֲנִי עָמֵל תַּחַת הַשָּׁמֶשׁ: שֶׁאַנִּיחֶנּוּ, לָאָדָם שֶׁיִּהְיֶה אַחֲרָי
vesaneti ani et-kol-'amali, she'ani amel tachat hashamesh; she'annichennu, la'adam sheyihyeh acharai
And I hated all my labour wherein I laboured under the sun, seeing that I must leave it unto the man that shall be after me.

וּמִי יוֹדֵעַ, הֶחָכָם יִהְיֶה אוֹ סָכָל, וְיִשְׁלַט בְּכָל-עֲמָלִי
umi yodea', hechacham yihyeh o sachal, veyishlat bechol-'amali
And who knoweth whether he will be a wise man or a fool? yet will he have rule over all my labour

שֶׁעָמַלְתִּי וְשֶׁחָכַמְתִּי תַּחַת הַשָּׁמֶשׁ; גַּם-זֶה, הָבֶל
she'amalti veshechachamti tachat hashamesh; gam-zeh havel
wherein I have laboured, and wherein I have shown myself wise under the sun. This also is vanity.

וְסַבּוֹתִי אֲנִי, לְיַאֵשׁ אֶת-לִבִּי--עַל, כָּל-הֶעָמָל, שֶׁעָמַלְתִּי, תַּחַת הַשָּׁמֶשׁ
vesabboti ani leya'esh et-libbi; al kol-he'amal, she'amalti tachat hashamesh
Therefore I turned about to cause my heart to despair concerning all the labour wherein I had laboured under the sun.

כִּי-יֵשׁ אָדָם, שֶׁעֲמָלוֹ בְּחָכְמָה וּבְדַעַת--וּבְכִשְׁרוֹן
ki-yesh adam, she'amalo bechochmah uveda'at uvechishron
For there is a man whose labour is with wisdom, and with knowledge, and with skill;

וּלְאָדָם שֶׁלֹּא עָמַל-בּוֹ, יִתְּנֶנּוּ חֶלְקוֹ--גַּם-זֶה הֶבֶל, וְרָעָה רַבָּה
ule'adam shello amal-bo yittenennu chelko, gam-zeh hevel vera'ah rabbah
yet to a man that hath not laboured therein shall he leave it for his portion. This also is vanity and a great evil.

קֹהֶלֶת

כָּנַסְתִּי לִי גַּם־כֶּסֶף וְזָהָב, וּסְגֻלַּת מְלָכִים וְהַמְּדִינוֹת
kanasti li gam-kesef vezahav, usegullat melachim vehammedinot
I gathered me also silver and gold, and treasure such as kings and the provinces have as their own;

עָשִׂיתִי לִי שָׁרִים וְשָׁרוֹת, וְתַעֲנֻגוֹת בְּנֵי הָאָדָם--שִׁדָּה וְשִׁדּוֹת
asiti li sharim vesharot, veta'anugot benei ha'adam shiddah veshiddot
I got me men-singers and women-singers, and the delights of the sons of men, women very many.

וְגָדַלְתִּי וְהוֹסַפְתִּי, מִכֹּל שֶׁהָיָה לְפָנַי בִּירוּשָׁלִָם; אַף חָכְמָתִי, עָמְדָה לִּי
vegadalti vehosafti, mikkol shehayah lefanai biyerushalayim; af chachemati amedah li
So I was great, and increased more than all that were before me in Jerusalem; also my wisdom stood me in stead.

וְכֹל אֲשֶׁר שָׁאֲלוּ עֵינַי, לֹא אָצַלְתִּי מֵהֶם: לֹא־מָנַעְתִּי אֶת־לִבִּי מִכָּל־שִׂמְחָה
vechol asher sha'alu einai, lo atzalti mehem; lo-mana'ti et-libbi mikkol-simchah
And whatsoever mine eyes desired I kept not from them; I withheld not my heart from any joy,

כִּי־לִבִּי שָׂמֵחַ מִכָּל־עֲמָלִי, וְזֶה־הָיָה חֶלְקִי, מִכָּל־עֲמָלִי
ki-libbi sameach mikkol-'amali, vezeh-hayah chelki mikkol-'amali
for my heart had joy of all my labour; and this was my portion from all my labour.

וּפָנִיתִי אֲנִי, בְּכָל־מַעֲשַׂי שֶׁעָשׂוּ יָדַי, וּבֶעָמָל, שֶׁעָמַלְתִּי לַעֲשׂוֹת
ufaniti ani, bechol-ma'asai she'asu yadai, uve'amal she'amalti la'asot
Then I looked on all the works that my hands had wrought, and on the labour that I had laboured to do;

וְהִנֵּה הַכֹּל הֶבֶל וּרְעוּת רוּחַ, וְאֵין יִתְרוֹן תַּחַת הַשָּׁמֶשׁ
vehinneh hakkol hevel ure'ut ruach, ve'ein yitron tachat hashamesh
and, behold, all was vanity and a striving after wind, and there was no profit under the sun.

וּפָנִיתִי אֲנִי לִרְאוֹת חָכְמָה, וְהוֹלֵלוֹת וְסִכְלוּת
ufaniti ani lir'ot chochmah veholelot vesichlut
And I turned myself to behold wisdom, and madness and folly;

כִּי מֶה הָאָדָם, שֶׁיָּבוֹא אַחֲרֵי הַמֶּלֶךְ, אֵת אֲשֶׁר־כְּבָר, עָשׂוּהוּ
ki meh ha'adam, sheyavo acharei hammelech, et asher-kevar asuhu
for what can the man do that cometh after the king? even that which hath been already done.

וְרָאִיתִי אָנִי, שֶׁיֵּשׁ יִתְרוֹן לַחָכְמָה מִן־הַסִּכְלוּת--כִּיתְרוֹן הָאוֹר, מִן־הַחֹשֶׁךְ
vera'iti ani, sheyesh yitron lachochmah min-hassichlut; kiteron ha'or min-hachoshech
Then I saw that wisdom excelleth folly, as far as light excelleth darkness.

הֶחָכָם עֵינָיו בְּרֹאשׁוֹ, וְהַכְּסִיל בַּחֹשֶׁךְ הוֹלֵךְ
hechacham einav berosho, vehakkesil bachoshech holech
The wise man, his eyes are in his head; but the fool walketh in darkness.

וְיָדַעְתִּי גַם־אָנִי, שֶׁמִּקְרֶה אֶחָד יִקְרֶה אֶת־כֻּלָּם
veyada'ti gam-'ani, shemmikreh echad yikreh et-kullam
And I also perceived that one event happeneth to them all.

קֹהֶלֶת

כִּי בְּרֹב חָכְמָה, רָב-כָּעַס; וְיוֹסִיף דַּעַת, יוֹסִיף מַכְאוֹב

ki berov chochmah rav-ka'as; veyosif da'at yosif mach'ov
For in much wisdom is much vexation; and he that increaseth knowledge increaseth sorrow.

ב

אָמַרְתִּי אֲנִי בְּלִבִּי, לְכָה-נָּא אֲנַסְּכָה בְשִׂמְחָה וּרְאֵה בְטוֹב; וְהִנֵּה גַם-הוּא, הָבֶל

Amarti ani belibbi, lechah-na anassechah vesimchah ure'eh vetov; vehinneh gam-hu havel
I said in my heart: 'Come now, I will try thee with mirth, and enjoy pleasure'; and, behold, this also was vanity.

לִשְׂחוֹק, אָמַרְתִּי מְהוֹלָל; וּלְשִׂמְחָה, מַה-זֹּה עֹשָׂה

lischok amarti meholal; ulesimchah mah-zoh osah
I said of laughter: 'It is mad'; and of mirth: 'What doth it accomplish?'

תַּרְתִּי בְלִבִּי, לִמְשׁוֹךְ בַּיַּיִן אֶת-בְּשָׂרִי; וְלִבִּי נֹהֵג בַּחָכְמָה

tarti velibbi, limshoch bayayin et-besari; velibbi noheg bechochmah
I searched in my heart how to pamper my flesh with wine, and, my heart conducting itself with wisdom,

וְלֶאֱחֹז בְּסִכְלוּת--עַד אֲשֶׁר-אֶרְאֶה אֵי-זֶה טוֹב לִבְנֵי הָאָדָם

vele'echoz besichlut, ad asher-'er'eh, ei-zeh tov livnei ha'adam
how yet to lay hold on folly, till I might see which it was best for the sons of men

אֲשֶׁר יַעֲשׂוּ תַּחַת הַשָּׁמַיִם, מִסְפַּר יְמֵי חַיֵּיהֶם

asher ya'asu tachat hashamayim, mispar yemei chayeihem
that they should do under the heaven the few days of their life.

הִגְדַּלְתִּי, מַעֲשָׂי: בָּנִיתִי לִי בָּתִּים, נָטַעְתִּי לִי כְּרָמִים

higdalti ma'asai; baniti li battim, nata'ti li keramim
I made me great works; I builded me houses; I planted me vineyards;

עָשִׂיתִי לִי, גַּנּוֹת וּפַרְדֵּסִים; וְנָטַעְתִּי בָהֶם, עֵץ כָּל-פֶּרִי

'asiti li, gannot ufardesim; venata'ti vahem etz kol-peri
I made me gardens and parks, and I planted trees in them of all kinds of fruit;

עָשִׂיתִי לִי, בְּרֵכוֹת מָיִם--לְהַשְׁקוֹת מֵהֶם, יַעַר צוֹמֵחַ עֵצִים

'asiti li berechot mayim; lehashkot mehem, ya'ar tzomeach etzim
I made me pools of water, to water therefrom the wood springing up with trees;

קָנִיתִי עֲבָדִים וּשְׁפָחוֹת, וּבְנֵי-בַיִת הָיָה לִי

kaniti avadim ushefachot, uvenei-vayit hayah li
I acquired men-servants and maid-servants, and had servants born in my house;

גַּם מִקְנֶה בָקָר וָצֹאן הַרְבֵּה הָיָה לִי, מִכֹּל שֶׁהָיוּ לְפָנַי בִּירוּשָׁלִָם

gam mikneh vakar vatzon harbeh hayah li, mikkol shehayu lefanai biyerushalayim
also I had great possessions of herds and flocks, above all that were before me in Jerusalem;

קֹהֶלֶת

וּמַה-שֶּׁנַּעֲשָׂה, הוּא שֶׁיֵּעָשֶׂה; וְאֵין כָּל-חָדָשׁ, תַּחַת הַשָּׁמֶשׁ
umah-shenna'asah, hu sheye'aseh; ve'ein kol-chadash tachat hashamesh
and that which hath been done is that which shall be done; and there is nothing new under the sun.

יֵשׁ דָּבָר שֶׁיֹּאמַר רְאֵה-זֶה, חָדָשׁ הוּא: כְּבָר הָיָה לְעֹלָמִים, אֲשֶׁר הָיָה מִלְּפָנֵנוּ
yesh davar sheyomar re'eh-zeh chadash hu; kevar hayah le'olamim, asher hayah millefanenu
Is there a thing whereof it is said: 'See, this is new'?--it hath been already, in the ages which were before us.

אֵין זִכְרוֹן, לָרִאשֹׁנִים
'ein zichron larishonim
There is no remembrance of them of former times;

וְגַם לָאַחֲרֹנִים שֶׁיִּהְיוּ, לֹא-יִהְיֶה לָהֶם זִכָּרוֹן--עִם שֶׁיִּהְיוּ, לָאַחֲרֹנָה
vegam la'acharonim sheyihyu, lo-yihyeh lahem zikkaron, im sheyihyu la'acharonah
neither shall there be any remembrance of them of latter times that are to come, among those that shall come after.

אֲנִי קֹהֶלֶת, הָיִיתִי מֶלֶךְ עַל-יִשְׂרָאֵל--בִּירוּשָׁלִָם
'ani kohelet, hayiti melech al-yisra'el biyerushalayim
I Koheleth have been king over Israel in Jerusalem.

וְנָתַתִּי אֶת-לִבִּי, לִדְרוֹשׁ וְלָתוּר בַּחָכְמָה, עַל כָּל-אֲשֶׁר נַעֲשָׂה, תַּחַת הַשָּׁמָיִם
venatatti et-libbi, lidrosh velatur bachochmah al kol-'asher na'asah tachat hashamayim
And I applied my heart to seek and to search out by wisdom concerning all things that are done under heaven;

הוּא עִנְיַן רָע, נָתַן אֱלֹהִים לִבְנֵי הָאָדָם--לַעֲנוֹת בּוֹ
hu inyan ra', natan elohim livnei ha'adam la'anot bo
it is a sore task that God hath given to the sons of men to be exercised therewith.

רָאִיתִי, אֶת-כָּל-הַמַּעֲשִׂים, שֶׁנַּעֲשׂוּ, תַּחַת הַשָּׁמֶשׁ; וְהִנֵּה הַכֹּל הֶבֶל, וּרְעוּת רוּחַ
ra'iti et-kol-hamma'asim, shenna'asu tachat hashamesh; vehinneh hakkol hevel ure'ut ruach
I have seen all the works that are done under the sun; and, behold, all is vanity and a striving after wind.

מְעֻוָּת, לֹא-יוּכַל לִתְקֹן; וְחֶסְרוֹן, לֹא-יוּכַל לְהִמָּנוֹת
me'uvvat lo-yuchal litkon; vechesron lo-yuchal lehimmanot
That which is crooked cannot be made straight; and that which is wanting cannot be numbered.

דִּבַּרְתִּי אֲנִי עִם-לִבִּי, לֵאמֹר--אֲנִי הִנֵּה הִגְדַּלְתִּי וְהוֹסַפְתִּי חָכְמָה
dibbarti ani im-libbi lemor, ani, hinneh higdalti vehosafti chochmah
I spoke with my own heart, saying: 'Lo, I have gotten great wisdom,

עַל כָּל-אֲשֶׁר-הָיָה לְפָנַי עַל-יְרוּשָׁלִָם; וְלִבִּי רָאָה הַרְבֵּה, חָכְמָה וָדָעַת
al kol-'asher-hayah lefanai al-yerushalayim; velibbi ra'ah harbeh chochmah vada'at
more also than all that were before me over Jerusalem'; yea, my heart hath had great experience of wisdom and knowledge.

וָאֶתְּנָה לִבִּי לָדַעַת חָכְמָה, וְדַעַת הוֹלֵלוֹת וְשִׂכְלוּת: יָדַעְתִּי, שֶׁגַּם-זֶה הוּא רַעְיוֹן רוּחַ.
va'ettenah libbi lada'at chochmah veda'at holelot vesichlut; yada'ti sheggam-zeh hu ra'yon ruach
And I applied my heart to know wisdom, and to know madness and folly--I perceived that this also was a striving after wind.

קֹהֶלֶת

קֹהֶלֶת א

דִּבְרֵי קֹהֶלֶת בֶּן-דָּוִד, מֶלֶךְ בִּירוּשָׁלָ͏ִם
Divrei kohelet ben-david, melech biyerushalayim
The words of Koheleth, the son of David, king in Jerusalem.

הֲבֵל הֲבָלִים אָמַר קֹהֶלֶת, הֲבֵל הֲבָלִים הַכֹּל הָבֶל
havel havalim amar kohelet, havel havalim hakkol havel
Vanity of vanities, saith Koheleth; vanity of vanities, all is vanity.

מַה-יִּתְרוֹן, לָאָדָם: בְּכָל-עֲמָלוֹ--שֶׁיַּעֲמֹל, תַּחַת הַשָּׁמֶשׁ
mah-yitron la'adam; bechol-'amalo, sheya'amol tachat hashamesh
What profit hath man of all his labour wherein he laboureth under the sun?

דּוֹר הֹלֵךְ וְדוֹר בָּא, וְהָאָרֶץ לְעוֹלָם עֹמָדֶת
dor holech vedor ba, veha'aretz le'olam omadet
One generation passeth away, and another generation cometh; and the earth abideth for ever.

וְזָרַח הַשֶּׁמֶשׁ, וּבָא הַשָּׁמֶשׁ; וְאֶל-מְקוֹמוֹ--שׁוֹאֵף זוֹרֵחַ הוּא, שָׁם
vezarach hashemesh uva hashamesh; ve'el-mekomo, sho'ef zoreach hu sham
The sun also ariseth, and the sun goeth down, and hasteth to his place where he ariseth.

הוֹלֵךְ, אֶל-דָּרוֹם, וְסוֹבֵב, אֶל-צָפוֹן
holech el-darom, vesovev el-tzafon
The wind goeth toward the south, and turneth about unto the north;

סוֹבֵב סֹבֵב הוֹלֵךְ הָרוּחַ, וְעַל-סְבִיבֹתָיו שָׁב הָרוּחַ
sovev sovev holech haruach, ve'al-sevivotav shav haruach
it turneth about continually in its circuit, and the wind returneth again to its circuits.

כָּל-הַנְּחָלִים הֹלְכִים אֶל-הַיָּם, וְהַיָּם אֵינֶנּוּ מָלֵא
kol-hannechalim holechim el-hayam, vehayam einennu male
All the rivers run into the sea, yet the sea is not full;

אֶל-מְקוֹם, שֶׁהַנְּחָלִים הֹלְכִים--שָׁם הֵם שָׁבִים, לָלָכֶת
el-mekom, shehannechalim holechim, sham hem shavim lalachet
unto the place whither the rivers go, thither they go again.

כָּל-הַדְּבָרִים יְגֵעִים, לֹא-יוּכַל אִישׁ לְדַבֵּר; לֹא-תִשְׂבַּע עַיִן לִרְאוֹת, וְלֹא-תִמָּלֵא אֹזֶן מִשְּׁמֹעַ
kol-haddevarim yege'im, lo-yuchal ish ledabber; lo-tisba ayin lir'ot, velo-timmalei ozen mishemoa
All things toil to weariness; man cannot utter it, the eye is not satisfied with seeing, nor the ear filled with hearing.

מַה-שֶּׁהָיָה, הוּא שֶׁיִּהְיֶה
mah-shehayah hu sheyihyeh
That which hath been is that which shall be,

אֵיכָה

הֲשִׁיבֵנוּ יְהוָה אֵלֶיךָ וְנָשׁוּבָה, חַדֵּשׁ יָמֵינוּ כְּקֶדֶם
hashivenu hashem eleicha venashuvah, chaddesh yameinu kekedem
Turn Thou us unto Thee, O LORD, and we shall be turned; renew our days as of old.

כִּי אִם־מָאֹס מְאַסְתָּנוּ, קָצַפְתָּ עָלֵינוּ עַד־מְאֹד
ki im-ma'os me'astanu, katzafta aleinu ad-me'od
Thou canst not have utterly rejected us, and be exceeding wroth against us!

אֵיכָה

בְּנַפְשֵׁנוּ נָבִיא לַחְמֵנוּ, מִפְּנֵי חֶרֶב הַמִּדְבָּר

benafshenu navi lachmenu, mippenei cherev hammidbar
We get our bread with the peril of our lives because of the sword of the wilderness.

עוֹרֵנוּ כְּתַנּוּר נִכְמָרוּ, מִפְּנֵי זַלְעֲפוֹת רָעָב

'orenu ketannur nichmaru, mippenei zal'afot ra'av
Our skin is hot like an oven because of the burning heat of famine.

נָשִׁים בְּצִיּוֹן עִנּוּ, בְּתֻלֹת בְּעָרֵי יְהוּדָה

nashim betziyon innu, betulot be'arei yehudah
They have ravished the women in Zion, the maidens in the cities of Judah.

שָׂרִים בְּיָדָם נִתְלוּ, פְּנֵי זְקֵנִים לֹא נֶהְדָּרוּ

sarim beyadam nitlu, penei zekenim lo nehedaru
Princes are hanged up by their hand; the faces of elders are not honoured.

בַּחוּרִים טְחוֹן נָשָׂאוּ, וּנְעָרִים בָּעֵץ כָּשָׁלוּ

bachurim techon nasa'u, une'arim ba'etz kashalu
The young men have borne the mill, and the children have stumbled under the wood.

זְקֵנִים מִשַּׁעַר שָׁבָתוּ, בַּחוּרִים מִנְּגִינָתָם

zekenim misha'ar shavatu, bachurim minneginatam
The elders have ceased from the gate, the young men from their music.

שָׁבַת מְשׂוֹשׂ לִבֵּנוּ, נֶהְפַּךְ לְאֵבֶל מְחֹלֵנוּ

shavat mesos libbenu, nehpach le'evel mecholenu
The joy of our heart is ceased; our dance is turned into mourning.

נָפְלָה עֲטֶרֶת רֹאשֵׁנוּ, אוֹי-נָא לָנוּ כִּי חָטָאנוּ

nafelah ateret roshenu, oy-na lanu ki chatanu
The crown is fallen from our head; woe unto us! for we have sinned.

עַל-זֶה, הָיָה דָוֶה לִבֵּנוּ--עַל-אֵלֶּה, חָשְׁכוּ עֵינֵינוּ

'al-zeh, hayah daveh libbenu, al-'elleh chashechu eineinu
For this our heart is faint, for these things our eyes are dim;

עַל הַר-צִיּוֹן שֶׁשָּׁמֵם, שׁוּעָלִים הִלְּכוּ-בוֹ

'al har-tziyon sheshamem, shu'alim hillechu-vo
For the mountain of Zion, which is desolate, the foxes walk upon it.

אַתָּה יְהוָה לְעוֹלָם תֵּשֵׁב, כִּסְאֲךָ לְדוֹר וָדוֹר

'attah hashem le'olam teshev, kis'acha ledor vador
Thou, O LORD, art enthroned for ever, Thy throne is from generation to generation.

לָמָּה לָנֶצַח תִּשְׁכָּחֵנוּ, תַּעַזְבֵנוּ לְאֹרֶךְ יָמִים

lammah lanetzach tishkachenu, ta'azvenu le'orech yamim
Wherefore dost Thou forget us for ever, and forsake us so long time?

אֵיכָה

גַּם-עָלַיִךְ, תַּעֲבָר-כּוֹס--תִּשְׁכְּרִי, וְתִתְעָרִי
gam-'alayich ta'avor-kos, tishkeri vetit'ari
the cup shall pass over unto thee also; thou shalt be drunken, and shalt make thyself naked.

תַּם-עֲוֹנֵךְ, בַּת-צִיּוֹן--לֹא יוֹסִיף, לְהַגְלוֹתֵךְ
tam-'avonech bat-tziyon, lo yosif lehaglotech
The punishment of thine iniquity is accomplished, O daughter of Zion, He will no more carry thee away into captivity;

פָּקַד עֲוֹנֵךְ בַּת-אֱדוֹם, גִּלָּה עַל-חַטֹּאתָיִךְ
pakad avonech bat-'edom, gillah al-chattotayich
He will punish thine iniquity, O daughter of Edom, He will uncover thy sins.

ה

זְכֹר יְהוָה מֶה-הָיָה לָנוּ, הַבִּיטָה וּרְאֵה אֶת-חֶרְפָּתֵנוּ
Zechor hashem meh-hayah lanu, habbitah ure'eh et-cherpatenu
Remember, O LORD, what is come upon us; behold, and see our reproach.

נַחֲלָתֵנוּ נֶהֶפְכָה לְזָרִים, בָּתֵּינוּ לְנָכְרִים
nachalatenu nehefchah lezarim, batteinu lenochrim
Our inheritance is turned unto strangers, our houses unto aliens.

יְתוֹמִים הָיִינוּ וְאֵין אָב, אִמֹּתֵינוּ כְּאַלְמָנוֹת
yetomim hayinu ve'ein av, immoteinu ke'almanot
We are become orphans and fatherless, our mothers are as widows.

מֵימֵינוּ בְּכֶסֶף שָׁתִינוּ, עֵצֵינוּ בִּמְחִיר יָבֹאוּ
meimeinu bechesef shatinu, etzeinu bimchir yavo'u
We have drunk our water for money; our wood cometh to us for price.

עַל צַוָּארֵנוּ נִרְדָּפְנוּ, יָגַעְנוּ וְלֹא הוּנַח-לָנוּ
'al tzavvarenu nirdafnu, yaga'nu velo hunach-lanu
To our very necks we are pursued; we labour, and have no rest.

מִצְרַיִם נָתַנּוּ יָד, אַשּׁוּר לִשְׂבֹּעַ לָחֶם
mitzrayim natannu yad, ashur lisboa lachem
We have given the hand to Egypt, and to Assyria, to have bread enough;

אֲבֹתֵינוּ חָטְאוּ וְאֵינָם, וַאֲנַחְנוּ עֲוֹנֹתֵיהֶם סָבָלְנוּ
'avoteinu chate'u ve'einam, va'anachnu avonoteihem savalnu
Our fathers have sinned, and are not; and we have borne their iniquities.

עֲבָדִים מָשְׁלוּ בָנוּ, פֹּרֵק אֵין מִיָּדָם
'avadim mashelu vanu, porek ein miyadam
Servants rule over us; there is none to deliver us out of their hand.

אֵיכָה

נָעוּ עִוְרִים בַּחוּצוֹת, נְגֹאֲלוּ בַּדָּם; בְּלֹא יוּכְלוּ, יִגְּעוּ בִּלְבֻשֵׁיהֶם
na'u ivrim bachutzot, nego'alu baddam; belo yuchelu, yigge'u bilvusheihem
They wander as blind men in the streets, they are polluted with blood, so that men cannot touch their garments.

סוּרוּ טָמֵא קָרְאוּ לָמוֹ, סוּרוּ סוּרוּ אַל-תִּגָּעוּ
suru tamei kare'u lamo, suru suru al-tigga'u
'Depart ye! unclean!' men cried unto them, 'Depart, depart, touch not';

כִּי נָצוּ, גַּם-נָעוּ; אָמְרוּ, בַּגּוֹיִם, לֹא יוֹסִפוּ, לָגוּר
ki natzu gam-na'u; ameru baggoyim, lo yosifu lagur
yea, they fled away and wandered; men said among the nations: 'They shall no more sojourn here.'

פְּנֵי יְהוָה חִלְּקָם, לֹא יוֹסִיף לְהַבִּיטָם
penei hashem chillekam, lo yosif lehabbitam
The anger of the LORD hath divided them; He will no more regard them;

פְּנֵי כֹהֲנִים לֹא נָשָׂאוּ, וּזְקֵנִים לֹא חָנָנוּ
penei chohanim lo nasa'u, uzekenim lo chananu
they respected not the persons of the priests, they were not gracious unto the elders.

עוֹדֵינוּ תִּכְלֶינָה עֵינֵינוּ, אֶל-עֶזְרָתֵנוּ הָבֶל; בְּצִפִּיָּתֵנוּ צִפִּינוּ, אֶל-גּוֹי לֹא יוֹשִׁעַ
odeinu tichleinah eineinu, el-'ezratenu havel; betzippiyatenu tzippinu, el-goy lo yoshia
As for us, our eyes do yet fail for our vain help; in our watching we have watched for a nation that could not save.

צָדוּ צְעָדֵינוּ, מִלֶּכֶת בִּרְחֹבֹתֵינוּ; קָרַב קִצֵּנוּ מָלְאוּ יָמֵינוּ, כִּי-בָא קִצֵּנוּ
tzadu tze'adeinu, millechet birchovoteinu; karav kitzeinu male'u yameinu ki-va kitzeinu
They hunt our steps, that we cannot go in our broad places; our end is near, our days are fulfilled; for our end is come.

קַלִּים הָיוּ רֹדְפֵינוּ, מִנִּשְׁרֵי שָׁמָיִם
kallim hayu rodefeinu, minnishrei shamayim
Our pursuers were swifter than the eagles of the heaven;

עַל-הֶהָרִים דְּלָקֻנוּ, בַּמִּדְבָּר אָרְבוּ לָנוּ
al-heharim delakunu, bammidbar arevu lanu
they chased us upon the mountains, they lay in wait for us in the wilderness.

רוּחַ אַפֵּינוּ מְשִׁיחַ יְהוָה, נִלְכַּד בִּשְׁחִיתוֹתָם
ruach appeinu meshiach hashem nilkad bishchitotam; asher amarnu
The breath of our nostrils, the anointed of the LORD, was taken in their pits; of whom we said:

אֲשֶׁר אָמַרְנוּ, בְּצִלּוֹ נִחְיֶה בַגּוֹיִם
betzillo nichyeh vaggoyim
'Under his shadow we shall live among the nations.'

שִׂישִׂי וְשִׂמְחִי בַּת-אֱדוֹם, יוֹשֶׁבֶת בְּאֶרֶץ עוּץ
sisi vesimchi bat-'edom, yoshevet be'eretz utz
Rejoice and be glad, O daughter of Edom, that dwellest in the land of Uz:

אֵיכָה

חָשַׁךְ מִשְּׁחוֹר תָּאֳרָם, לֹא נִכְּרוּ בַּחוּצוֹת
chashach mishechor to'oram, lo nikkeru bachutzot
Their visage is blacker than coal; they are not known in the streets;

צָפַד עוֹרָם עַל-עַצְמָם, יָבֵשׁ הָיָה כָעֵץ
tzafad oram al-'atzmam, yavesh hayah cha'etz
their skin is shrivelled upon their bones; it is withered, it is become like a stick.

טוֹבִים הָיוּ חַלְלֵי-חֶרֶב, מֵחַלְלֵי רָעָב
tovim hayu chalelei-cherev, mechalelei ra'av
They that are slain with the sword are better than they that are slain with hunger;

שֶׁהֵם יָזֻבוּ מְדֻקָּרִים, מִתְּנוּבֹת שָׂדָי
shehem yazuvu medukkarim, mittenuvot sadai
for these pine away, stricken through, for want of the fruits of the field.

יְדֵי, נָשִׁים רַחֲמָנִיּוֹת--בִּשְּׁלוּ, יַלְדֵיהֶן
yedei, nashim rachamaniyot, bishelu yaldeihen
The hands of women full of compassion have sodden their own children;

הָיוּ לְבָרוֹת לָמוֹ, בְּשֶׁבֶר בַּת-עַמִּי
hayu levarot lamo, beshever bat-'ammi
they were their food in the destruction of the daughter of my people.

כִּלָּה יְהוָה אֶת-חֲמָתוֹ, שָׁפַךְ חֲרוֹן אַפּוֹ
killah hashem et-chamato, shafach charon appo
The LORD hath accomplished His fury, He hath poured out His fierce anger;

וַיַּצֶּת-אֵשׁ בְּצִיּוֹן, וַתֹּאכַל יְסֹדֹתֶיהָ
vayatzet-'esh betziyon, vattochal yesodoteiha
and He hath kindled a fire in Zion, which hath devoured the foundations thereof.

לֹא הֶאֱמִינוּ מַלְכֵי-אֶרֶץ, כֹּל יֹשְׁבֵי תֵבֵל
lo he'eminu malchei-'eretz, kol yoshevei tevel
The kings of the earth believed not, neither all the inhabitants of the world,

כִּי יָבֹא צַר וְאוֹיֵב, בְּשַׁעֲרֵי יְרוּשָׁלִָם
ki yavo tzar ve'oyev, besha'arei yerushalayim
that the adversary and the enemy would enter into the gates of Jerusalem.

מֵחַטֹּאות נְבִיאֶיהָ, עֲוֹנֹת כֹּהֲנֶיהָ
mechattot nevi'eiha, avonot kohaneiha
It is because of the sins of her prophets, and the iniquities of her priests,

הַשֹּׁפְכִים בְּקִרְבָּהּ, דַּם צַדִּיקִים
hashofechim bekirbah dam tzaddikim
that have shed the blood of the just in the midst of her.

אֵיכָה

תִּשְׁתַּפֵּכְנָה, אַבְנֵי-קֹדֶשׁ, בְּרֹאשׁ, כָּל-חוּצוֹת
tishtappechenah avnei-kodesh, berosh kol-chutzot
The hallowed stones are poured out at the head of every street.

בְּנֵי צִיּוֹן הַיְקָרִים, הַמְסֻלָּאִים בַּפָּז
benei tziyon hayekarim, hamsulla'im bappaz
The precious sons of Zion, comparable to fine gold,

אֵיכָה נֶחְשְׁבוּ לְנִבְלֵי-חֶרֶשׂ, מַעֲשֵׂה יְדֵי יוֹצֵר
eichah nechshevu lenivlei-cheres, ma'aseh yedei yotzer
how are they esteemed as earthen pitchers, the work of the hands of the potter!

גַּם-תַּנִּים חָלְצוּ שַׁד, הֵינִיקוּ גּוּרֵיהֶן
gam-tannim chaletzu shad, heiniku gureihen
Even the jackals draw out the breast, they give suck to their young ones;

בַּת-עַמִּי לְאַכְזָר, כַּיְעֵנִים בַּמִּדְבָּר
bat-'ammi le'achzar, kay'enim bammidbar
the daughter of my people is become cruel, like the ostriches in the wilderness.

דָּבַק לְשׁוֹן יוֹנֵק אֶל-חִכּוֹ, בַּצָּמָא
davak leshon yonek el-chikko batzama
The tongue of the sucking child cleaveth to the roof of his mouth for thirst;

עוֹלָלִים שָׁאֲלוּ לֶחֶם, פֹּרֵשׂ אֵין לָהֶם
olalim sha'alu lechem, pores ein lahem
the young children ask bread, and none breaketh it unto them.

הָאֹכְלִים, לְמַעֲדַנִּים, נָשַׁמּוּ, בַּחוּצוֹת; הָאֱמֻנִים עֲלֵי תוֹלָע, חִבְּקוּ אַשְׁפַּתּוֹת
ha'ochelim lema'adannim, nashammu bachutzot; ha'emunim alei tola', chibbeku ashpattot
They that did feed on dainties are desolate in the streets; they that were brought up in scarlet embrace dunghills.

וַיִּגְדַּל עֲו‍ֹן בַּת-עַמִּי, מֵחַטַּאת סְדֹם
vayigdal avon bat-'ammi, mechattat sedom
For the iniquity of the daughter of my people is greater than the sin of Sodom,

הַהֲפוּכָה כְמוֹ-רָגַע, וְלֹא-חָלוּ בָהּ יָדָיִם
hahafuchah chemo-raga', velo-chalu vah yadayim
that was overthrown as in a moment, and no hands fell upon her.

זַכּוּ נְזִירֶיהָ מִשֶּׁלֶג, צַחוּ מֵחָלָב
zakku nezireiha misheleg, tzachu mechalav
Her princes were purer than snow, they were whiter than milk,

אָדְמוּ עֶצֶם מִפְּנִינִים, סַפִּיר גִּזְרָתָם
ademu etzem mippeninim, sappir gizratam
they were more ruddy in body than rubies, their polishing was as of sapphire;

אֵיכָה

קָרַבְתָּ בְּיוֹם אֶקְרָאֶךָּ, אָמַרְתָּ אַל-תִּירָא
karavta beyom ekra'eka, amarta al-tira
Thou drewest near in the day that I called upon Thee; Thou saidst: 'Fear not.'

רַבְתָּ אֲדֹנָי רִיבֵי נַפְשִׁי, גָּאַלְתָּ חַיָּי
ravta adonai rivei nafshi ga'alta chayai
O Lord, Thou hast pleaded the causes of my soul; Thou hast redeemed my life.

רָאִיתָה יְהוָה עַוָּתָתִי, שָׁפְטָה מִשְׁפָּטִי
ra'itah hashem avvatati, shafetah mishpati
O LORD, Thou hast seen my wrong; judge Thou my cause.

רָאִיתָה, כָּל-נִקְמָתָם--כָּל-מַחְשְׁבֹתָם, לִי
ra'itah kol-nikmatam, kol-machshevotam li
Thou hast seen all their vengeance and all their devices against me.

שָׁמַעְתָּ חֶרְפָּתָם יְהוָה, כָּל-מַחְשְׁבֹתָם עָלָי
shama'ta cherpatam hashem kol-machshevotam alai
Thou hast heard their taunt, O LORD, and all their devices against me;

שִׂפְתֵי קָמַי וְהֶגְיוֹנָם, עָלַי כָּל-הַיּוֹם
siftei kamai vehegyonam, alai kol-hayom
The lips of those that rose up against me, and their muttering against me all the day.

שִׁבְתָּם וְקִימָתָם הַבִּיטָה, אֲנִי מַנְגִּינָתָם
shivtam vekimatam habbitah, ani manginatam
Behold Thou their sitting down, and their rising up; I am their song.

תָּשִׁיב לָהֶם גְּמוּל יְהוָה, כְּמַעֲשֵׂה יְדֵיהֶם
tashiv lahem gemul hashem kema'aseh yedeihem
Thou wilt render unto them a recompense, O LORD, according to the work of their hands.

תִּתֵּן לָהֶם מְגִנַּת-לֵב, תַּאֲלָתְךָ לָהֶם
titten lahem meginnat-lev, ta'alatecha lahem
Thou wilt give them hardness of heart, Thy curse unto them.

תִּרְדֹּף בְּאַף וְתַשְׁמִידֵם, מִתַּחַת שְׁמֵי יְהוָה
tirdof be'af vetashmidem, mittachat shemei hashem
Thou wilt pursue them in anger, and destroy them from under the heavens of the LORD.

ד

אֵיכָה יוּעַם זָהָב, יִשְׁנֶא הַכֶּתֶם הַטּוֹב
Eichah yu'am zahav, yishnei hakketem hattov
How is the gold become dim! How is the most fine gold changed!

אֵיכָה

סְחִי וּמָאוֹס תְּשִׂימֵנוּ, בְּקֶרֶב הָעַמִּים
sechi uma'os tesimenu bekerev ha'ammim
Thou hast made us as the offscouring and refuse in the midst of the peoples.

פָּצוּ עָלֵינוּ פִּיהֶם, כָּל-אֹיְבֵינוּ
patzu aleinu pihem kol-'oyeveinu
All our enemies have opened their mouth wide against us.

פַּחַד וָפַחַת הָיָה לָנוּ, הַשֵּׁאת וְהַשָּׁבֶר
pachad vafachat hayah lanu hashet vehashaver
Terror and the pit are come upon us, desolation and destruction.

פַּלְגֵי-מַיִם תֵּרַד עֵינִי, עַל-שֶׁבֶר בַּת-עַמִּי
palgei-mayim terad eini, al-shever bat-'ammi
Mine eye runneth down with rivers of water, for the breach of the daughter of my people.

עֵינִי נִגְּרָה וְלֹא תִדְמֶה, מֵאֵין הֲפֻגוֹת
'eini niggerah velo tidmeh me'ein hafugot
Mine eye is poured out, and ceaseth not, without any intermission,

עַד-יַשְׁקִיף וְיֵרֶא, יְהוָה מִשָּׁמָיִם
'ad-yashkif veyere, hashem mishamayim
Till the LORD look forth, and behold from heaven.

עֵינִי עוֹלְלָה לְנַפְשִׁי, מִכֹּל בְּנוֹת עִירִי
'eini olelah lenafshi, mikkol benot iri
Mine eye affected my soul, because of all the daughters of my city.

צוֹד צָדוּנִי כַּצִּפּוֹר, אֹיְבַי חִנָּם
tzod tzaduni katzippor oyevai chinnam
They have chased me sore like a bird, that are mine enemies without cause.

צָמְתוּ בַבּוֹר חַיָּי, וַיַּדּוּ-אֶבֶן בִּי
tzametu vabbor chayai, vayaddu-'even bi
They have cut off my life in the dungeon, and have cast stones upon me.

צָפוּ-מַיִם עַל-רֹאשִׁי, אָמַרְתִּי נִגְזָרְתִּי
tzafu-mayim al-roshi amarti nigzarti
Waters flowed over my head; I said: 'I am cut off.'

קָרָאתִי שִׁמְךָ יְהוָה, מִבּוֹר תַּחְתִּיּוֹת
karati shimcha hashem mibbor tachtiyot
I called upon Thy name, O LORD, Out of the lowest dungeon.

קוֹלִי, שָׁמָעְתָּ: אַל-תַּעְלֵם אָזְנְךָ לְרַוְחָתִי, לְשַׁוְעָתִי
koli shama'eta; al-ta'lem oznecha leravchati leshav'ati
Thou heardest my voice; hide not Thine ear at my sighing, at my cry.

אֵיכָה

כִּי לֹא עִנָּה מִלִּבּוֹ, וַיַּגֶּה בְּנֵי־אִישׁ
ki lo innah millibbo, vayaggeh benei-'ish
For He doth not afflict willingly, nor grieve the children of men.

לְדַכֵּא תַּחַת רַגְלָיו, כֹּל אֲסִירֵי אָרֶץ
ledakkei tachat raglav, kol asirei aretz
To crush under foot all the prisoners of the earth,

לְהַטּוֹת, מִשְׁפַּט־גָּבֶר, נֶגֶד, פְּנֵי עֶלְיוֹן
lehattot mishpat-gaver, neged penei elyon
To turn aside the right of a man before the face of the Most High,

לְעַוֵּת אָדָם בְּרִיבוֹ, אֲדֹנָי לֹא רָאָה
le'avvet adam berivo, adonai lo ra'ah
To subvert a man in his cause, the Lord approveth not.

מִי זֶה אָמַר וַתֶּהִי, אֲדֹנָי לֹא צִוָּה
mi zeh amar vattehi, adonai lo tzivvah
Who is he that saith, and it cometh to pass, when the Lord commandeth it not?

מִפִּי עֶלְיוֹן לֹא תֵצֵא, הָרָעוֹת וְהַטּוֹב
mippi elyon lo tetze, hara'ot vehattov
Out of the mouth of the Most High proceedeth not evil and good?

מַה־יִּתְאוֹנֵן אָדָם חָי, גֶּבֶר עַל־חֲטָאָו
mah-yit'onen adam chai, gever al-chata'av
Wherefore doth a living man complain, a strong man because of his sins?

נַחְפְּשָׂה דְרָכֵינוּ וְנַחְקֹרָה, וְנָשׁוּבָה עַד־יְהוָה
nachpesah deracheinu venachkorah, venashuvah ad-hashem
Let us search and try our ways, and return to the LORD.

נִשָּׂא לְבָבֵנוּ אֶל־כַּפָּיִם, אֶל־אֵל בַּשָּׁמָיִם
nissa levavenu el-kappayim, el-'el bashamayim
Let us lift up our heart with our hands unto God in the heavens.

נַחְנוּ פָשַׁעְנוּ וּמָרִינוּ, אַתָּה לֹא סָלָחְתָּ
nachnu fasha'nu umarinu, attah lo salachta
We have transgressed and have rebelled; Thou hast not pardoned.

סַכֹּתָה בָאַף וַתִּרְדְּפֵנוּ, הָרַגְתָּ לֹא חָמָלְתָּ
sakkotah va'af vattirdefenu, haragta lo chamalta
Thou hast covered with anger and pursued us; Thou hast slain unsparingly.

סַכּוֹתָה בֶעָנָן לָךְ, מֵעֲבוֹר תְּפִלָּה
sakkotah ve'anan lach, me'avor tefillah
Thou hast covered Thyself with a cloud, so that no prayer can pass through.

אֵיכָה

זֹאת אָשִׁיב אֶל-לִבִּי, עַל-כֵּן אוֹחִיל
zot ashiv el-libbi al-ken ochil
This I recall to my mind, therefore have I hope.

חַסְדֵי יְהוָה כִּי לֹא-תָמְנוּ, כִּי לֹא-כָלוּ רַחֲמָיו
chasdei hashem ki lo-tamenu, ki lo-chalu rachamav
Surely the LORD'S mercies are not consumed, surely His compassions fail not.

חֲדָשִׁים, לַבְּקָרִים, רַבָּה, אֱמוּנָתֶךָ
chadashim labbekarim, rabbah emunatecha
They are new every morning; great is Thy faithfulness.

חֶלְקִי יְהוָה אָמְרָה נַפְשִׁי, עַל-כֵּן אוֹחִיל לוֹ
chelki hashem amerah nafshi, al-ken ochil lo
'The LORD is my portion', saith my soul; 'Therefore will I hope in Him.'

טוֹב יְהוָה לְקֹוָו, לְנֶפֶשׁ תִּדְרְשֶׁנּוּ
tov hashem lekovav, lenefesh tidreshennu
The LORD is good unto them that wait for Him, to the soul that seeketh Him.

טוֹב וְיָחִיל וְדוּמָם, לִתְשׁוּעַת יְהוָה
tov veyachil vedumam, litshu'at hashem
It is good that a man should quietly wait for the salvation of the LORD.

טוֹב לַגֶּבֶר, כִּי-יִשָּׂא עֹל בִּנְעוּרָיו
tov laggever, ki-yissa ol bin'urav
It is good for a man that he bear the yoke in his youth.

יֵשֵׁב בָּדָד וְיִדֹּם, כִּי נָטַל עָלָיו
yeshev badad veyiddom, ki natal alav
Let him sit alone and keep silence, because He hath laid it upon him.

יִתֵּן בֶּעָפָר פִּיהוּ, אוּלַי יֵשׁ תִּקְוָה
yitten be'afar pihu, ulai yesh tikvah
Let him put his mouth in the dust, if so be there may be hope.

יִתֵּן לְמַכֵּהוּ לֶחִי, יִשְׂבַּע בְּחֶרְפָּה
yitten lemakkehu lechi yisba becherpah
Let him give his cheek to him that smiteth him, let him be filled full with reproach.

כִּי לֹא יִזְנַח לְעוֹלָם, אֲדֹנָי
ki lo yiznach le'olam adonai
For the Lord will not cast off for ever.

כִּי אִם-הוֹגָה, וְרִחַם כְּרֹב חֲסָדָיו
ki im-hogah, vericham kerov chasadav
For though He cause grief, yet will He have compassion according to the multitude of His mercies.

אֵיכָה

גָּדַר דְּרָכַי בְּגָזִית, נְתִיבֹתַי עִוָּה
gadar derachai begazit, netivotai ivvah
He hath enclosed my ways with hewn stone, He hath made my paths crooked.

דֹּב אֹרֵב הוּא לִי, אֲרִי בְּמִסְתָּרִים
dov orev hu li, ari bemistarim
He is unto me as a bear lying in wait, as a lion in secret places.

דְּרָכַי סוֹרֵר וַיְפַשְּׁחֵנִי, שָׂמַנִי שֹׁמֵם
derachai sorer vayfashecheni samani shomem
He hath turned aside my ways, and pulled me in pieces; He hath made me desolate.

דָּרַךְ קַשְׁתּוֹ וַיַּצִּיבֵנִי, כַּמַּטָּרָא לַחֵץ
darach kashto vayatziveni, kammattara lachetz
He hath bent His bow, and set me as a mark for the arrow.

הֵבִיא, בְּכִלְיוֹתָי, בְּנֵי, אַשְׁפָּתוֹ
hevi bechilyotai, benei ashpato
He hath caused the arrows of His quiver to enter into my reins.

הָיִיתִי שְּׂחֹק לְכָל-עַמִּי, נְגִינָתָם כָּל-הַיּוֹם
hayiti sechok lechol-'ammi, neginatam kol-hayom
I am become a derision to all my people, and their song all the day.

הִשְׂבִּיעַנִי בַמְּרוֹרִים, הִרְוַנִי לַעֲנָה
hisbi'ani vammerorim hirvani la'anah
He hath filled me with bitterness, He hath sated me with wormwood.

וַיַּגְרֵס בֶּחָצָץ שִׁנָּי, הִכְפִּישַׁנִי בָּאֵפֶר
vayagres bechatzatz shinnai, hichpishani ba'efer
He hath also broken my teeth with gravel stones, He hath made me to wallow in ashes.

וַתִּזְנַח מִשָּׁלוֹם נַפְשִׁי, נָשִׁיתִי טוֹבָה
vattiznach mishalom nafshi nashiti tovah
And my soul is removed far off from peace, I forgot prosperity.

וָאֹמַר אָבַד נִצְחִי, וְתוֹחַלְתִּי מֵיְהוָה
va'omar avad nitzchi, vetochalti mehashem
And I said: 'My strength is perished, and mine expectation from the LORD.'

זְכָר-עָנְיִי וּמְרוּדִי, לַעֲנָה וָרֹאשׁ
zechor-'onyi umerudi la'anah varosh
Remember mine affliction and mine anguish, the wormwood and the gall.

זָכוֹר תִּזְכּוֹר, וְתָשׁוֹחַ עָלַי נַפְשִׁי
zachor tizkor, vetashoach alai nafshi
My soul hath them still in remembrance, and is bowed down within me.

אֵיכָה

תִּקְרָא כְיוֹם מוֹעֵד מְגוּרַי מִסָּבִיב
tikra cheyom mo'ed megurai missaviv
Thou hast called, as in the day of a solemn assembly, my terrors on every side,

וְלֹא הָיָה בְּיוֹם אַף־יְהוָה פָּלִיט וְשָׂרִיד
velo hayah beyom af-hashem palit vesarid
and there was none in the day of the LORD'S anger that escaped or remained;

אֲשֶׁר־טִפַּחְתִּי וְרִבִּיתִי, אֹיְבִי כִלָּם
asher-tippachti veribbiti oyevi chillam
those that I have dandled and brought up hath mine enemy consumed.'

ג

אֲנִי הַגֶּבֶר רָאָה עֳנִי, בְּשֵׁבֶט עֶבְרָתוֹ
Ani haggever ra'ah oni, beshevet evrato
I am the man that hath seen affliction by the rod of His wrath.

אוֹתִי נָהַג וַיֹּלַךְ, חֹשֶׁךְ וְלֹא־אוֹר
'oti nahag vayolach choshech velo-'or
He hath led me and caused me to walk in darkness and not in light.

אַךְ בִּי יָשֻׁב יַהֲפֹךְ יָדוֹ, כָּל־הַיּוֹם
'ach bi yashuv yahafoch yado kol-hayom
Surely against me He turneth His hand again and again all the day.

בִּלָּה בְשָׂרִי וְעוֹרִי, שִׁבַּר עַצְמוֹתָי
billah vesari ve'ori, shibbar atzmotai
My flesh and my skin hath He worn out; He hath broken my bones.

בָּנָה עָלַי וַיַּקַּף, רֹאשׁ וּתְלָאָה
banah alai vayakkaf rosh utela'ah
He hath builded against me, and compassed me with gall and travail.

בְּמַחֲשַׁכִּים הוֹשִׁיבַנִי, כְּמֵתֵי עוֹלָם
bemachashakkim hoshivani kemetei olam
He hath made me to dwell in dark places, as those that have been long dead.

גָּדַר בַּעֲדִי וְלֹא אֵצֵא, הִכְבִּיד נְחָשְׁתִּי
gadar ba'adi velo etzei hichbid nechasheti
He hath hedged me about, that I cannot go forth; He hath made my chain heavy.

גַּם כִּי אֶזְעַק וַאֲשַׁוֵּעַ, שָׂתַם תְּפִלָּתִי
gam ki ez'ak va'ashavvea', satam tefillati
Yea, when I cry and call for help, He shutteth out my prayer.

אֵיכָה

בִּלַּעְנוּ; אַךְ זֶה הַיּוֹם שֶׁקִּוִּינֻהוּ, מָצָאנוּ רָאִינוּ
billa'enu; ach zeh hayom shekkivvinuhu matzanu ra'inu
'We have swallowed her up; certainly this is the day that we looked for; we have found, we have seen it.'

עָשָׂה יְהוָה אֲשֶׁר זָמָם, בִּצַּע אֶמְרָתוֹ אֲשֶׁר צִוָּה מִימֵי-קֶדֶם
'asah hashem asher zamam, bitza emrato asher tzivvah miymei-kedem
The LORD hath done that which He devised; He hath performed His word that He commanded in the days of old;

הָרַס, וְלֹא חָמָל; וַיְשַׂמַּח עָלַיִךְ אוֹיֵב
haras velo chamal; vaysammach alayich oyev
He hath thrown down unsparingly; and He hath caused the enemy to rejoice over thee,

הֵרִים קֶרֶן צָרָיִךְ
herim keren tzarayich
He hath exalted the horn of thine adversaries.

צָעַק לִבָּם, אֶל-אֲדֹנָי; חוֹמַת בַּת-צִיּוֹן
tza'ak libbam el-'adonai; chomat bat-tziyon
Their heart cried unto the Lord: 'O wall of the daughter of Zion,

הוֹרִידִי כַנַּחַל דִּמְעָה, יוֹמָם וָלַיְלָה--אַל-תִּתְּנִי פוּגַת לָךְ, אַל-תִּדֹּם בַּת-עֵינֵךְ
horidi channachal dim'ah yomam valaylah, al-titteni fugat lach, al-tiddom bat-'einech
let tears run down like a river day and night; give thyself no respite; let not the apple of thine eye cease.

קוּמִי רֹנִּי בַלַּיְלָה, לְרֹאשׁ אַשְׁמֻרוֹת--שִׁפְכִי כַמַּיִם לִבֵּךְ, נֹכַח פְּנֵי אֲדֹנָי
kumi ronni vallaylah, lerosh ashmurot, shifchi chammayim libbech, nochach penei adonai
Arise, cry out in the night, at the beginning of the watches; pour out thy heart like water before the face of the Lord;

שְׂאִי אֵלָיו כַּפַּיִךְ, עַל-נֶפֶשׁ עוֹלָלַיִךְ--הָעֲטוּפִים בְּרָעָב, בְּרֹאשׁ כָּל-חוּצוֹת
se'i elav kappayich, al-nefesh olalayich, ha'atufim bera'av berosh kol-chutzot
lift up thy hands toward Him for the life of thy young children, that faint for hunger at the head of every street.'

רְאֵה יְהוָה וְהַבִּיטָה, לְמִי עוֹלַלְתָּ כֹּה: אִם-תֹּאכַלְנָה נָשִׁים פִּרְיָם
re'eh hashem vehabbitah, lemi olalta koh; im-tochalnah nashim piryam
'See, O LORD, and consider, to whom Thou hast done thus! Shall the women eat their fruit,

עֹלְלֵי טִפֻּחִים, אִם-יֵהָרֵג בְּמִקְדַּשׁ אֲדֹנָי כֹּהֵן וְנָבִיא
olalei tippuchim, im-yehareg bemikdash adonai kohen venavi
the children that are dandled in the hands? Shall the priest and the prophet be slain in the sanctuary of the Lord?

שָׁכְבוּ לָאָרֶץ חוּצוֹת נַעַר וְזָקֵן, בְּתוּלֹתַי וּבַחוּרַי נָפְלוּ בֶחָרֶב
shachevu la'aretz chutzot na'ar vezaken, betulotai uvachurai nafelu vecharev
The youth and the old man lie on the ground in the streets; my virgins and my young men are fallen by the sword;

הָרַגְתָּ בְּיוֹם אַפֶּךָ, טָבַחְתָּ לֹא חָמָלְתָּ
haragta beyom appecha, tavachta lo chamaleta
Thou hast slain them in the day of Thine anger; Thou hast slaughtered unsparingly.

אֵיכָה

כָּלוּ בַדְּמָעוֹת עֵינַי, חֳמַרְמְרוּ מֵעַי--נִשְׁפַּךְ לָאָרֶץ כְּבֵדִי
kalu vaddema'ot einai chomarmeru me'ai, nishpach la'aretz kevedi
Mine eyes do fail with tears, mine inwards burn, my liver is poured upon the earth,

עַל-שֶׁבֶר בַּת-עַמִּי
al-shever bat-'ammi
for the breach of the daughter of my people;

בֵּעָטֵף עוֹלֵל וְיוֹנֵק, בִּרְחֹבוֹת קִרְיָה
be'atef olel veyonek, birchovot kiryah
because the young children and the sucklings swoon in the broad places of the city.

לְאִמֹּתָם, יֹאמְרוּ, אַיֵּה, דָּגָן וָיָיִן: בְּהִתְעַטְּפָם כֶּחָלָל, בִּרְחֹבוֹת עִיר
le'immotam yomeru, ayeh dagan vayayin; behit'attefam kechalal birchovot ir
They say to their mothers: 'Where is corn and wine?' when they swoon as the wounded in the broad places of the city,

בְּהִשְׁתַּפֵּךְ נַפְשָׁם, אֶל-חֵיק אִמֹּתָם
behishtappech nafsham, el-cheik immotam
when their soul is poured out into their mothers' bosom.

מָה-אֲעִידֵךְ מָה אֲדַמֶּה-לָּךְ, הַבַּת יְרוּשָׁלִַם--מָה אַשְׁוֶה-לָּךְ
mah-'a'idech mah adammeh-lach, habbat yerushalayim, mah ashveh-lach
What shall I take to witness for thee? What shall I liken to thee, O daughter of Jerusalem? What shall I equal to thee,

וַאֲנַחֲמֵךְ, בְּתוּלַת בַּת-צִיּוֹן: כִּי-גָדוֹל כַּיָּם שִׁבְרֵךְ, מִי יִרְפָּא-לָךְ
va'anachamech, betulat bat-tziyon; ki-gadol kayam shivrech mi yirpa-lach
that I may comfort thee, O virgin daughter of Zion? For thy breach is great like the sea; who can heal thee?

נְבִיאַיִךְ, חָזוּ לָךְ שָׁוְא וְתָפֵל, וְלֹא-גִלּוּ עַל-עֲוֺנֵךְ
nevi'ayich, chazu lach shav vetafel, velo-gillu al-'avonech
Thy prophets have seen visions for thee of vanity and delusion; and they have not uncovered thine iniquity,

לְהָשִׁיב שְׁבוּתֵךְ; וַיֶּחֱזוּ לָךְ, מַשְׂאוֹת שָׁוְא וּמַדּוּחִים
lehashiv shevutech; vayechezu lach, mas'ot shav umadduchim
to bring back thy captivity; but have prophesied for thee burdens of vanity and seduction.

סָפְקוּ עָלַיִךְ כַּפַּיִם, כָּל-עֹבְרֵי דֶרֶךְ--שָׁרְקוּ וַיָּנִעוּ רֹאשָׁם, עַל-בַּת יְרוּשָׁלִָם
safeku alayich kappayim kol-'overei derech, shareku vayani'u rosham, al-bat yerushalayim
All that pass by clap their hands at thee; they hiss and wag their head at the daughter of Jerusalem:

הֲזֹאת הָעִיר, שֶׁיֹּאמְרוּ כְּלִילַת יֹפִי--מָשׂוֹשׂ, לְכָל-הָאָרֶץ
hazot ha'ir, sheyomeru kelilat yofi, masos lechol-ha'aretz
'Is this the city that men called the perfection of beauty, the joy of the whole earth?'

פָּצוּ עָלַיִךְ פִּיהֶם, כָּל-אוֹיְבַיִךְ--שָׁרְקוּ וַיַּחַרְקוּ-שֵׁן, אָמְרוּ
patzu alayich pihem kol-'oyevayich, shareku vayacharku-shen, ameru
All thine enemies have opened their mouth wide against thee; they hiss and gnash the teeth; they say:

אֵיכָה

וַיַּחְמֹס כַּגַּן שֻׂכּוֹ, שִׁחֵת מֹעֲדוֹ
vayachmos kaggan sukko, shichet mo'ado
And He hath stripped His tabernacle, as if it were a garden, He hath destroyed His place of assembly;

שִׁכַּח יְהוָה בְּצִיּוֹן מוֹעֵד וְשַׁבָּת
shikkach hashem betziyon mo'ed veshabbat
the LORD hath caused to be forgotten in Zion appointed season and sabbath,

וַיִּנְאַץ בְּזַעַם-אַפּוֹ מֶלֶךְ וְכֹהֵן
vayin'atz beza'am-'appo melech vechohen
and hath rejected in the indignation of His anger the king and the priest.

זָנַח אֲדֹנָי מִזְבְּחוֹ, נִאֵר מִקְדָּשׁוֹ
zanach adonai mizbecho ni'er mikdasho
The Lord hath cast off His altar, He hath abhorred His sanctuary,

הִסְגִּיר בְּיַד-אוֹיֵב, חוֹמֹת אַרְמְנוֹתֶיהָ
hisgir beyad-'oyev, chomot armenoteiha
He hath given up into the hand of the enemy the walls of her palaces;

קוֹל נָתְנוּ בְּבֵית-יְהוָה, כְּיוֹם מוֹעֵד
kol natenu beveit-hashem keyom mo'ed
they have made a noise in the house of the LORD, as in the day of a solemn assembly.

חָשַׁב יְהוָה לְהַשְׁחִית, חוֹמַת בַּת-צִיּוֹן--נָטָה קָו
chashav hashem lehashchit chomat bat-tziyon, natah kav
The LORD hath purposed to destroy the wall of the daughter of Zion; He hath stretched out the line,

לֹא-הֵשִׁיב יָדוֹ מִבַּלֵּעַ; וַיַּאֲבֶל-חֵל וְחוֹמָה, יַחְדָּו אֻמְלָלוּ
lo-heshiv yado mibballea'; vaya'avel-chel vechomah yachdav umlalu
He hath not withdrawn His hand from destroying; but He hath made the rampart and wall to mourn, they languish together.

טָבְעוּ בָאָרֶץ שְׁעָרֶיהָ, אִבַּד וְשִׁבַּר בְּרִיחֶיהָ
tave'u va'aretz she'areiha, ibbad veshibbar bericheiha
Her gates are sunk into the ground; He hath destroyed and broken her bars;

מַלְכָּהּ וְשָׂרֶיהָ בַגּוֹיִם, אֵין תּוֹרָה--גַּם-נְבִיאֶיהָ, לֹא-מָצְאוּ חָזוֹן מֵיְהוָה
malkah vesareiha vaggoyim ein torah, gam-nevi'eiha lo-matze'u chazon mehashem
her king and her princes are among the nations, instruction is no more; yea, her prophets find no vision from the LORD.

יֵשְׁבוּ לָאָרֶץ יִדְּמוּ, זִקְנֵי בַת-צִיּוֹן--הֶעֱלוּ עָפָר עַל-רֹאשָׁם
yeshevu la'aretz yiddemu ziknei vat-tziyon, he'elu afar al-rosham
They sit upon the ground, and keep silence, the elders of the daughter of Zion; they have cast up dust upon their heads,

חָגְרוּ שַׂקִּים; הוֹרִידוּ לָאָרֶץ רֹאשָׁן, בְּתוּלֹת יְרוּשָׁלִָם
chageru sakkim; horidu la'aretz roshan, betulot yerushalayim
they have girded themselves with sackcloth; the virgins of Jerusalem hang down their heads to the ground.

אֵיכָה

ב

אֵיכָה יָעִיב בְּאַפּוֹ אֲדֹנָי, אֶת-בַּת-צִיּוֹן--הִשְׁלִיךְ
Eichah ya'iv be'appo adonai et-bat-tziyon, hishlich
How hath the Lord covered with a cloud the daughter of Zion in His anger! He hath cast down

מִשָּׁמַיִם אֶרֶץ, תִּפְאֶרֶת יִשְׂרָאֵל; וְלֹא-זָכַר הֲדֹם-רַגְלָיו, בְּיוֹם אַפּוֹ
mishamayim eretz, tif'eret yisra'el; velo-zachar hadom-raglav beyom appo
from heaven unto the earth the beauty of Israel, and hath not remembered His footstool in the day of His anger.

בִּלַּע אֲדֹנָי וְלֹא חָמַל, אֵת כָּל-נְאוֹת יַעֲקֹב
billa adonai velo chamal, et kol-ne'ot ya'akov
The Lord hath swallowed up unsparingly all the habitations of Jacob;

הָרַס בְּעֶבְרָתוֹ מִבְצְרֵי בַת-יְהוּדָה
haras be'evrato mivtzerei vat-yehudah
He hath thrown down in His wrath the strongholds of the daughter of Judah;

הִגִּיעַ לָאָרֶץ; חִלֵּל מַמְלָכָה, וְשָׂרֶיהָ
higgia la'aretz; chillel mamlachah vesareiha
He hath brought them down to the ground; He hath profaned the kingdom and the princes thereof.

גָּדַע בָּחֳרִי-אַף, כֹּל קֶרֶן יִשְׂרָאֵל--הֵשִׁיב אָחוֹר יְמִינוֹ, מִפְּנֵי אוֹיֵב
gada bochori-'af, kol keren yisra'el, heshiv achor yemino mippenei oyev
He hath cut off in fierce anger all the horn of Israel; He hath drawn back His right hand from before the enemy;

וַיִּבְעַר בְּיַעֲקֹב כְּאֵשׁ לֶהָבָה, אָכְלָה סָבִיב
vayiv'ar beya'akov ke'esh lehavah, achlah saviv
and He hath burned in Jacob like a flaming fire, which devoureth round about.

דָּרַךְ קַשְׁתּוֹ כְּאוֹיֵב, נִצָּב יְמִינוֹ כְּצָר
darach kashto ke'oyev, nitzav yemino ketzar
He hath bent His bow like an enemy, standing with His right hand as an adversary,

וַיַּהֲרֹג, כֹּל מַחֲמַדֵּי-עָיִן; בְּאֹהֶל, בַּת-צִיּוֹן, שָׁפַךְ כָּאֵשׁ, חֲמָתוֹ
vayaharog, kol machamaddei-'ayin; be'ohel bat-tziyon, shafach ka'esh chamato
and hath slain all that were pleasant to the eye; in the tent of the daughter of Zion He hath poured out His fury like fire.

הָיָה אֲדֹנָי כְּאוֹיֵב, בִּלַּע יִשְׂרָאֵל--בִּלַּע כָּל-אַרְמְנוֹתֶיהָ
hayah adonai ke'oyev billa yisra'el, billa kol-'armenoteiha
The Lord is become as an enemy, He hath swallowed up Israel; He hath swallowed up all her palaces,

שִׁחֵת מִבְצָרָיו; וַיֶּרֶב, בְּבַת-יְהוּדָה, תַּאֲנִיָּה, וַאֲנִיָּה
shichet mivtzarav; vayerev bevat-yehudah, ta'aniyah va'aniyah
He hath destroyed his strongholds; and He hath multiplied in the daughter of Judah mourning and moaning.

אֵיכָה

פֵּרְשָׂה צִיּוֹן בְּיָדֶיהָ, אֵין מְנַחֵם לָהּ--צִוָּה יְהוָה לְיַעֲקֹב
peresah tziyon beyadeiha, ein menachem lah, tzivvah hashem leya'akov
Zion spreadeth forth her hands; there is none to comfort her; the LORD hath commanded concerning Jacob,

סְבִיבָיו צָרָיו; הָיְתָה יְרוּשָׁלִַם לְנִדָּה, בֵּינֵיהֶם
sevivav tzarav; hayetah yerushalayim leniddah beineihem
that they that are round about him should be his adversaries; Jerusalem is among them as one unclean.

צַדִּיק הוּא יְהוָה, כִּי פִיהוּ מָרִיתִי; שִׁמְעוּ-נָא כָל-הָעַמִּים, וּרְאוּ מַכְאֹבִי
tzaddik hu hashem ki fihu mariti; shim'u-na chol-ha'ammim, ure'u mach'ovi
'The LORD is righteous; for I have rebelled against His word; hear, I pray you, all ye peoples, and behold my pain:

בְּתוּלֹתַי וּבַחוּרַי, הָלְכוּ בַשֶּׁבִי
betulotai uvachurai halechu vashevi
my virgins and my young men are gone into captivity.

קָרָאתִי לַמְאַהֲבַי הֵמָּה רִמּוּנִי, כֹּהֲנַי וּזְקֵנַי בָּעִיר גָּוָעוּ
karati lam'ahavai hemmah rimmuni, kohanai uzekenai ba'ir gava'u
I called for my lovers, but they deceived me; my priests and mine elders perished in the city,

כִּי-בִקְשׁוּ אֹכֶל לָמוֹ, וְיָשִׁיבוּ אֶת-נַפְשָׁם
ki-vikshu ochel lamo, veyashivu et-nafsham
while they sought them food to refresh their souls.

רְאֵה יְהוָה כִּי-צַר-לִי, מֵעַי חֳמַרְמָרוּ--נֶהְפַּךְ לִבִּי בְּקִרְבִּי
re'eh hashem ki-tzar-li me'ai chomarmaru, nehpach libbi bekirbi
Behold, O LORD, for I am in distress, mine inwards burn; my heart is turned within me,

כִּי מָרוֹ מָרִיתִי; מִחוּץ שִׁכְּלָה-חֶרֶב, בַּבַּיִת כַּמָּוֶת
ki maro mariti; michutz shikkelah-cherev babbayit kammavet
for I have grievously rebelled. Abroad the sword bereaveth, at home there is the like of death.

שָׁמְעוּ כִּי נֶאֱנָחָה אָנִי, אֵין מְנַחֵם לִי--כָּל-אֹיְבַי שָׁמְעוּ רָעָתִי שָׂשׂוּ
shame'u ki ne'enachah ani, ein menachem li, kol-'oyevai shame'u ra'ati sasu
They have heard that I sigh, there is none to comfort me; all mine enemies have heard of my trouble, and are glad,

כִּי אַתָּה עָשִׂיתָ; הֵבֵאתָ יוֹם-קָרָאתָ, וְיִהְיוּ כָמֹנִי
ki attah asita; heveta yom-karata veyihyu chamoni
for Thou hast done it; Thou wilt bring the day that Thou hast proclaimed, and they shall be like unto me.

תָּבֹא כָל-רָעָתָם לְפָנֶיךָ וְעוֹלֵל לָמוֹ
tavo chol-ra'atam lefaneicha ve'olel lamo
Let all their wickedness come before Thee; and do unto them,

כַּאֲשֶׁר עוֹלַלְתָּ לִי עַל כָּל-פְּשָׁעָי: כִּי-רַבּוֹת אַנְחֹתַי, וְלִבִּי דַוָּי
ka'asher olalta li al kol-pesha'ai; ki-rabbot anchotai velibbi davvai
as Thou hast done unto me for all my transgressions; for my sighs are many and my heart is faint.'

אֵיכָה

כָּל-עַמָּהּ נֶאֱנָחִים מְבַקְשִׁים לֶחֶם, נָתְנוּ מַחֲמַדֵּיהֶם בְּאֹכֶל לְהָשִׁיב נָפֶשׁ
kol-'ammah ne'enachim mevakkeshim lechem, natenu machamaddeihem be'ochel lehashiv nafesh
All her people sigh, they seek bread; they have given their pleasant things for food to refresh the soul.

רְאֵה יְהוָה וְהַבִּיטָה, כִּי הָיִיתִי זוֹלֵלָה
re'eh hashem vehabbitah, ki hayiti zolelah
'See, O LORD, and behold, how abject I am become.'

לוֹא אֲלֵיכֶם, כָּל-עֹבְרֵי דֶרֶךְ--הַבִּיטוּ וּרְאוּ, אִם-יֵשׁ מַכְאוֹב כְּמַכְאֹבִי
lo aleichem kol-'overei derech habbitu ure'u, im-yesh mach'ov kemach'ovi
'Let it not come unto you, all ye that pass by! Behold, and see if there be any pain like unto my pain,

אֲשֶׁר עוֹלַל לִי: אֲשֶׁר הוֹגָה יְהוָה, בְּיוֹם חֲרוֹן אַפּוֹ
asher olal li; asher hogah hashem beyom charon appo
which is done unto me, wherewith the LORD hath afflicted me in the day of His fierce anger.

מִמָּרוֹם שָׁלַח-אֵשׁ בְּעַצְמֹתַי, וַיִּרְדֶּנָּה
mimmarom shalach-'esh be'atzmotai vayirdennah
From on high hath He sent fire into my bones, and it prevaileth against them;

פָּרַשׂ רֶשֶׁת לְרַגְלַי, הֱשִׁיבַנִי אָחוֹר--נְתָנַנִי שֹׁמֵמָה, כָּל-הַיּוֹם דָּוָה
paras reshet leraglai heshivani achor, netanani shomemah, kol-hayom davah
He hath spread a net for my feet, He hath turned me back; He hath made me desolate and faint all the day.

נִשְׂקַד עֹל פְּשָׁעַי בְּיָדוֹ, יִשְׂתָּרְגוּ עָלוּ עַל-צַוָּארִי
niskad ol pesha'ai beyado, yistaregu alu al-tzavvari
The yoke of my transgressions is impressed by His hand; they are knit together, they are come up upon my neck;

הִכְשִׁיל כֹּחִי; נְתָנַנִי אֲדֹנָי, בִּידֵי לֹא-אוּכַל קוּם
hichshil kochi; netanani adonai, biydei lo-'uchal kum
He hath made my strength to fail; the Lord hath delivered me into their hands, against whom I am not able to stand.

סִלָּה כָל-אַבִּירַי אֲדֹנָי בְּקִרְבִּי, קָרָא עָלַי מוֹעֵד
sillah chol-'abbirai adonai bekirbi, kara alai mo'ed
The Lord hath set at nought all my mighty men in the midst of me; He hath called a solemn assembly against me

לִשְׁבֹּר בַּחוּרָי; גַּת דָּרַךְ אֲדֹנָי, לִבְתוּלַת בַּת-יְהוּדָה
lishbor bachurai; gat darach adonai, livtulat bat-yehudah
to crush my young men; the Lord hath trodden as in a winepress the virgin the daughter of Judah.'

עַל-אֵלֶּה אֲנִי בוֹכִיָּה, עֵינִי עֵינִי יֹרְדָה מַּיִם--כִּי-רָחַק מִמֶּנִּי
'al-'elleh ani vochiyah, eini eini yoredah mayim, ki-rachak mimmenni
'For these things I weep; mine eye, mine eye runneth down with water; because the comforter is far from me,

מְנַחֵם, מֵשִׁיב נַפְשִׁי; הָיוּ בָנַי שׁוֹמֵמִים, כִּי גָבַר אוֹיֵב
menachem meshiv nafshi; hayu vanai shomemim, ki gavar oyev
even he that should refresh my soul; my children are desolate, because the enemy hath prevailed.'

אֵיכָה

וַיֵּצֵא מִבַּת-צִיּוֹן, כָּל-הֲדָרָהּ
Vayetzei mibbat-tziyon kol-hadarah
And gone is from the daughter of Zion all her splendour;

הָיוּ שָׂרֶיהָ, כְּאַיָּלִים לֹא-מָצְאוּ מִרְעֶה, וַיֵּלְכוּ בְלֹא-כֹחַ, לִפְנֵי רוֹדֵף
hayu sareiha, ke'ayalim lo-matze'u mir'eh, vayelechu velo-choach lifnei rodef
her princes are become like harts that find no pasture, and they are gone without strength before the pursuer.

זָכְרָה יְרוּשָׁלִַם, יְמֵי עָנְיָהּ וּמְרוּדֶיהָ--כֹּל מַחֲמֻדֶיהָ, אֲשֶׁר הָיוּ מִימֵי קֶדֶם
zacherah yerushalayim, yemei oniyah umerudeiha, kol machamudeiha, asher hayu mimei kedem
Jerusalem remembereth in the days of her affliction and of her anguish all her treasures that she had from the days of old;

בִּנְפֹל עַמָּהּ בְּיַד-צָר
binfol ammah beyad-tzar
now that her people fall by the hand of the adversary,

וְאֵין עוֹזֵר לָהּ--רָאוּהָ צָרִים, שָׂחֲקוּ עַל מִשְׁבַּתֶּהָ
ve'ein ozer lah, ra'uha tzarim, sachaku al mishbatteha
and none doth help her, the adversaries have seen her, they have mocked at her desolations.

חֵטְא חָטְאָה יְרוּשָׁלִַם, עַל-כֵּן לְנִידָה הָיָתָה
chet chate'ah yerushalayim, al-ken lenidah hayatah
Jerusalem hath grievously sinned, therefore she is become as one unclean;

כָּל-מְכַבְּדֶיהָ הִזִּילוּהָ כִּי-רָאוּ עֶרְוָתָהּ
kol-mechabbedeiha hizziluha ki-ra'u ervatah
all that honoured her despise her, because they have seen her nakedness;

גַּם-הִיא נֶאֶנְחָה וַתָּשָׁב אָחוֹר
gam-hi ne'enchah vattashov achor
she herself also sigheth, and turneth backward.

טֻמְאָתָהּ בְּשׁוּלֶיהָ, לֹא זָכְרָה אַחֲרִיתָהּ, וַתֵּרֶד פְּלָאִים
tum'atah beshuleiha, lo zacherah acharitah, vattered pela'im
Her filthiness was in her skirts, she was not mindful of her end; therefore is she come down wonderfully,

אֵין מְנַחֵם לָהּ; רְאֵה יְהוָה אֶת-עָנְיִי, כִּי הִגְדִּיל אוֹיֵב
ein menachem lah; re'eh hashem et-'aneyi, ki higdil oyev
she hath no comforter. 'Behold, O LORD, my affliction, for the enemy hath magnified himself.'

יָדוֹ פָּרַשׂ צָר, עַל כָּל-מַחֲמַדֶּיהָ: כִּי-רָאֲתָה גוֹיִם, בָּאוּ
yado paras tzar, al kol-machamaddeiha; ki-ra'atah goyim ba'u
The adversary hath spread out his hand upon all her treasures; for she hath seen that the heathen are entered

מִקְדָּשָׁהּ--אֲשֶׁר צִוִּיתָה, לֹא-יָבֹאוּ בַקָּהָל לָךְ
mikdashah, asher tzivvitah, lo-yavo'u vakkahal lach
into her sanctuary, concerning whom Thou didst command that they should not enter into Thy congregation.

אֵיכָה

אֵיכָה א

אֵיכָה יָשְׁבָה בָדָד, הָעִיר רַבָּתִי עָם--הָיְתָה, כְּאַלְמָנָה
Eichah yashevah vadad, ha'ir rabbati am, hayetah ke'almanah
How doth the city sit solitary, that was full of people! How is she become as a widow!

רַבָּתִי בַגּוֹיִם, שָׂרָתִי בַּמְּדִינוֹת--הָיְתָה, לָמַס
rabbati vaggoyim, sarati bammedinot, hayetah lamas
She that was great among the nations, and princess among the provinces, how is she become tributary!

בָּכוֹ תִבְכֶּה בַּלַּיְלָה, וְדִמְעָתָהּ עַל לֶחֱיָהּ--אֵין-לָהּ מְנַחֵם, מִכָּל-אֹהֲבֶיהָ
bacho tivkeh ballaylah, vedim'atah al lechyah, ein-lah menachem mikkol-'ohaveiha
She weepeth sore in the night, and her tears are on her cheeks; she hath none to comfort her among all her lovers;

כָּל-רֵעֶיהָ בָּגְדוּ בָהּ, הָיוּ לָהּ לְאֹיְבִים
kol-re'eiha bagedu vah, hayu lah le'oyevim
all her friends have dealt treacherously with her, they are become her enemies.

גָּלְתָה יְהוּדָה מֵעֹנִי, וּמֵרֹב עֲבֹדָה
galetah yehudah me'oni umerov avodah
Judah is gone into exile because of affliction, and because of great servitude;

הִיא יָשְׁבָה בַגּוֹיִם, לֹא מָצְאָה מָנוֹחַ; כָּל-רֹדְפֶיהָ הִשִּׂיגוּהָ, בֵּין הַמְּצָרִים
hi yashevah vaggoyim, lo matze'ah manoach; kol-rodefeiha hissiguha bein hammetzarim
she dwelleth among the nations, she findeth no rest; all her pursuers overtook her within the straits.

דַּרְכֵי צִיּוֹן אֲבֵלוֹת, מִבְּלִי בָּאֵי מוֹעֵד
darchei tziyon avelot, mibbeli ba'ei mo'ed
The ways of Zion do mourn, because none come to the solemn assembly;

כָּל-שְׁעָרֶיהָ שׁוֹמֵמִין, כֹּהֲנֶיהָ נֶאֱנָחִים; בְּתוּלֹתֶיהָ נּוּגוֹת, וְהִיא מַר-לָהּ
kol-she'areiha shomemin, kohaneiha ne'enachim; betuloteiha nugot vehi mar-lah
all her gates are desolate, her priests sigh; her virgins are afflicted, and she herself is in bitterness.

הָיוּ צָרֶיהָ לְרֹאשׁ אֹיְבֶיהָ שָׁלוּ
hayu tzareiha lerosh oyeveiha shalu
Her adversaries are become the head, her enemies are at ease;

כִּי-יְהוָה הוֹגָהּ עַל רֹב-פְּשָׁעֶיהָ
ki-hashem hogah al rov-pesha'eiha
for the LORD hath afflicted her for the multitude of her transgressions;

עוֹלָלֶיהָ הָלְכוּ שְׁבִי, לִפְנֵי-צָר
olaleiha halchu shevi lifnei-tzar
her young children are gone into captivity before the adversary.

רות

וְעֹבֵד הוֹלִיד אֶת-יִשַׁי, וְיִשַׁי הוֹלִיד אֶת-דָּוִד
ve'oved holid et-yishai, veyishai holid et-david
and Obed begot Jesse, and Jesse begot David.

רות

וַיִּקַּח בֹּעַז אֶת-רוּת וַתְּהִי-לוֹ לְאִשָּׁה, וַיָּבֹא אֵלֶיהָ; וַיִּתֵּן יְהוָה לָהּ הֵרָיוֹן, וַתֵּלֶד בֵּן
vayikkach bo'az et-rut vattehi-lo le'ishah, vayavo eleiha; vayitten hashem lah herayon vatteled ben
So Boaz took Ruth, and she became his wife; and he went in unto her, and the LORD gave her conception, and she bore a son.

וַתֹּאמַרְנָה הַנָּשִׁים, אֶל-נָעֳמִי, בָּרוּךְ יְהוָה
vattomarnah hannashim el-no'omi, baruch hashem
And the women said unto Naomi: 'Blessed be the LORD,

אֲשֶׁר לֹא הִשְׁבִּית לָךְ גֹּאֵל הַיּוֹם; וְיִקָּרֵא שְׁמוֹ, בְּיִשְׂרָאֵל
asher lo hishbit lach go'el hayom; veyikkarei shemo beyisra'el
who hath not left thee this day without a near kinsman, and let his name be famous in Israel.

וְהָיָה לָךְ לְמֵשִׁיב נֶפֶשׁ, וּלְכַלְכֵּל אֶת-שֵׂיבָתֵךְ
vehayah loch lemeshiv nefesh, ulechalkel et-seivatech
And he shall be unto thee a restorer of life, and a nourisher of thine old age;

כִּי כַלָּתֵךְ אֲשֶׁר-אֲהֵבַתֶךְ, יְלָדַתּוּ, אֲשֶׁר-הִיא טוֹבָה לָךְ, מִשִּׁבְעָה בָּנִים
ki challatech asher-'ahevatech yeladattu, asher-hi tovah lach, mishiv'ah banim
for thy daughter-in-law, who loveth thee, who is better to thee than seven sons, hath borne him.'

וַתִּקַּח נָעֳמִי אֶת-הַיֶּלֶד וַתְּשִׁתֵהוּ בְחֵיקָהּ, וַתְּהִי-לוֹ לְאֹמֶנֶת
vattikkach no'omi et-hayeled vatteshitehu vecheikah, vattehi-lo le'omenet
And Naomi took the child, and laid it in her bosom, and became nurse unto it.

וַתִּקְרֶאנָה לוֹ הַשְּׁכֵנוֹת שֵׁם לֵאמֹר, יֻלַּד-בֵּן לְנָעֳמִי
vattikrenah lo hashechenot shem lemor, yullad-ben leno'omi
And the women her neighbours gave it a name, saying: 'There is a son born to Naomi';

וַתִּקְרֶאנָה שְׁמוֹ עוֹבֵד, הוּא אֲבִי-יִשַׁי אֲבִי דָוִד
vattikrenah shemo oved, hu avi-yishai avi David
and they called his name Obed; he is the father of Jesse, the father of David.

וְאֵלֶּה תּוֹלְדוֹת פָּרֶץ, פֶּרֶץ הוֹלִיד אֶת-חֶצְרוֹן
ve'elleh toledot paretz, peretz holid et-chetzron
Now these are the generations of Perez: Perez begot Hezron;

וְחֶצְרוֹן הוֹלִיד אֶת-רָם, וְרָם הוֹלִיד אֶת-עַמִּינָדָב
vechetzron holid et-ram, veram holid et-'amminadav
and Hezron begot Ram, and Ram begot Amminadab;

וְעַמִּינָדָב הוֹלִיד אֶת-נַחְשׁוֹן, וְנַחְשׁוֹן הוֹלִיד אֶת-שַׂלְמָה
ve'amminadav holid et-nachshon, venachshon holid et-salmah
and Amminadab begot Nahshon, and Nahshon begot Salmon;

וְשַׂלְמוֹן הוֹלִיד אֶת-בֹּעַז, וּבֹעַז הוֹלִיד אֶת-עוֹבֵד
vesalmon holid et-bo'az, uvo'az holid et-'oved
and Salmon begot Boaz, and Boaz begot Obed;

רות

שָׁלַף אִישׁ נַעֲלוֹ, וְנָתַן לְרֵעֵהוּ; וְזֹאת הַתְּעוּדָה, בְּיִשְׂרָאֵל
shalaf ish na'alo venatan lere'ehu; vezot hatte'udah beyisra'el
a man drew off his shoe, and gave it to his neighbour; and this was the attestation in Israel.--

וַיֹּאמֶר הַגֹּאֵל לְבֹעַז, קְנֵה-לָךְ; וַיִּשְׁלֹף, נַעֲלוֹ
vayomer haggo'el levo'az keneh-lach; vayishlof na'alo
So the near kinsman said unto Boaz: 'Buy it for thyself.' And he drew off his shoe.

וַיֹּאמֶר בֹּעַז לַזְּקֵנִים וְכָל-הָעָם, עֵדִים אַתֶּם הַיּוֹם
vayomer bo'az lazzekenim vechol-ha'am, edim attem hayom
And Boaz said unto the elders, and unto all the people: 'Ye are witnesses this day,

כִּי קָנִיתִי אֶת-כָּל-אֲשֶׁר לֶאֱלִימֶלֶךְ, וְאֵת כָּל-אֲשֶׁר לְכִלְיוֹן וּמַחְלוֹן--מִיַּד, נָעֳמִי
ki kaniti et-kol-'asher le'elimelech, ve'et kol-'asher lechilyon umachlon; miyad no'omi
that I have bought all that was Elimelech's, and all that was Chilion's and Mahlon's, of the hand of Naomi.

וְגַם אֶת-רוּת הַמֹּאֲבִיָּה אֵשֶׁת מַחְלוֹן
vegam et-rut hammo'aviyah eshet machlon
Moreover Ruth the Moabitess, the wife of Mahlon,

קָנִיתִי לִי לְאִשָּׁה, לְהָקִים שֵׁם-הַמֵּת עַל-נַחֲלָתוֹ
kaniti li le'ishah, lehakim shem-hammet al-nachalato
have I acquired to be my wife, to raise up the name of the dead upon his inheritance,

וְלֹא-יִכָּרֵת שֵׁם-הַמֵּת מֵעִם אֶחָיו, וּמִשַּׁעַר מְקוֹמוֹ: עֵדִים אַתֶּם, הַיּוֹם
velo-yikkaret shem-hammet me'im echav umisha'ar mekomo; edim attem hayom
that the name of the dead be not cut off from among his brethren, and from the gate of his place; ye are witnesses this day.'

וַיֹּאמְרוּ כָל-הָעָם אֲשֶׁר-בַּשַּׁעַר, וְהַזְּקֵנִים--עֵדִים
vayomeru kol-ha'am asher-basha'ar vehazzekenim edim
And all the people that were in the gate, and the elders, said: 'We are witnesses.

יִתֵּן יְהוָה אֶת-הָאִשָּׁה הַבָּאָה אֶל-בֵּיתֶךָ, כְּרָחֵל וּכְלֵאָה
yitten hashem et-ha'ishah habba'ah el-beitecha, kerachel uchele'ah
The LORD make the woman that is come into thy house like Rachel and like Leah,

אֲשֶׁר בָּנוּ שְׁתֵּיהֶם אֶת-בֵּית יִשְׂרָאֵל, וַעֲשֵׂה-חַיִל בְּאֶפְרָתָה, וּקְרָא-שֵׁם בְּבֵית לָחֶם
asher banu sheteihem et-beit yisra'el, va'aseh-chayil be'efratah, ukera-shem beveit lachem
which two did build the house of Israel; and do thou worthily in Ephrath, and be famous in Beth-lehem;

וִיהִי בֵיתְךָ כְּבֵית פֶּרֶץ, אֲשֶׁר-יָלְדָה תָמָר לִיהוּדָה
viyhi veitecha keveit peretz, asher-yaledah tamar liyhudah
and let thy house be like the house of Perez, whom Tamar bore unto Judah,

מִן-הַזֶּרַע, אֲשֶׁר יִתֵּן יְהוָה לְךָ, מִן-הַנַּעֲרָה, הַזֹּאת
min-hazzera', asher yitten hashem lecha, min-hanna'arah hazzot
of the seed which the LORD shall give thee of this young woman.'

אֲשֶׁר דִּבֶּר-בֹּעַז, וַיֹּאמֶר סוּרָה שְׁבָה-פֹּה פְּלֹנִי אַלְמֹנִי; וַיָּסַר, וַיֵּשֵׁב
asher dibber-bo'az, vayomer surah shevah-poh peloni almoni; vayasar vayeshev
unto whom he said: 'Ho, such a one! turn aside, sit down here.' And he turned aside, and sat down.

וַיִּקַּח עֲשָׂרָה אֲנָשִׁים, מִזִּקְנֵי הָעִיר--וַיֹּאמֶר שְׁבוּ-פֹה; וַיֵּשֵׁבוּ
vayikkach asarah anashim mizziknei ha'ir vayomer shevu-foh; vayeshevu
And he took ten men of the elders of the city, and said: 'Sit ye down here.' And they sat down.

וַיֹּאמֶר, לַגֹּאֵל
vayomer laggo'el
And he said unto the near kinsman:

חֶלְקַת הַשָּׂדֶה, אֲשֶׁר לְאָחִינוּ לֶאֱלִימֶלֶךְ: מָכְרָה נָעֳמִי, הַשָּׁבָה מִשְּׂדֵה מוֹאָב
chelkat hassadeh, asher le'achinu le'elimelech; macherah no'omi, hashavah missedeh mo'av
'Naomi, that is come back out of the field of Moab, selleth the parcel of land, which was our brother Elimelech's;

וַאֲנִי אָמַרְתִּי אֶגְלֶה אָזְנְךָ לֵאמֹר, קְנֵה נֶגֶד הַיֹּשְׁבִים וְנֶגֶד זִקְנֵי עַמִּי
va'ani amarti egleh oznecha lemor, keneh neged hayoshevim veneged ziknei ammi
and I thought to disclose it unto thee, saying: Buy it before them that sit here, and before the elders of my people.

אִם-תִּגְאַל גְּאָל, וְאִם-לֹא יִגְאַל הַגִּידָה לִּי וְאֵדְעָה
im-tig'al ge'al, ve'im-lo yig'al haggidah li, ve'ede'ah
If thou wilt redeem it, redeem it; but if it will not be redeemed, then tell me, that I may know;

כִּי אֵין זוּלָתְךָ לִגְאוֹל וְאָנֹכִי אַחֲרֶיךָ; וַיֹּאמֶר, אָנֹכִי אֶגְאָל
ki ein zulatecha lig'ol, ve'anochi achareicha; vayomer anochi eg'al
for there is none to redeem it beside thee; and I am after thee.' And he said: 'I will redeem it.'

וַיֹּאמֶר בֹּעַז, בְּיוֹם-קְנוֹתְךָ הַשָּׂדֶה מִיַּד נָעֳמִי; וּמֵאֵת רוּת
vayomer bo'az, beyom-kenotecha hassadeh miyad no'omi; ume'et rut
Then said Boaz: 'What day thou buyest the field of the hand of Naomi--hast thou also bought of Ruth

הַמּוֹאֲבִיָּה אֵשֶׁת-הַמֵּת, קָנִיתִי--לְהָקִים שֵׁם-הַמֵּת, עַל-נַחֲלָתוֹ
hammo'aviyah eshet-hammet kanitah, lehakim shem-hammet al-nachalato
the Moabitess, the wife of the dead, to raise up the name of the dead upon his inheritance?'

וַיֹּאמֶר הַגֹּאֵל, לֹא אוּכַל לִגְאָל-לִי--פֶּן-אַשְׁחִית, אֶת-נַחֲלָתִי
vayomer haggo'el, lo uchal lig'al-li, pen-'ashchit et-nachalati
And the near kinsman said: 'I cannot redeem it for myself, lest I mar mine own inheritance;

גְּאַל-לְךָ אַתָּה אֶת-גְּאֻלָּתִי, כִּי לֹא-אוּכַל לִגְאֹל
ge'al-lecha attah et-ge'ullati, ki lo-'uchal lig'ol
take thou my right of redemption on thee; for I cannot redeem it.'--

וְזֹאת לְפָנִים בְּיִשְׂרָאֵל עַל-הַגְּאֻלָּה וְעַל-הַתְּמוּרָה, לְקַיֵּם כָּל-דָּבָר
vezot lefanim beyisra'el al-hagge'ullah ve'al-hattemurah lekayem kol-davar
Now this was the custom in former time in Israel concerning redeeming and concerning exchanging, to confirm all things:

רות

וּגְאַלְתִּיךְ אָנֹכִי, חַי-יְהוָה; שִׁכְבִי, עַד-הַבֹּקֶר
uge'altich anochi chai-hashem shichvi ad-habboker
then will I do the part of a kinsman to thee, as the LORD liveth; lie down until the morning.'

וַתִּשְׁכַּב מַרְגְּלוֹתָו, עַד-הַבֹּקֶר, וַתָּקָם, בְּטֶרֶם יַכִּיר אִישׁ אֶת-רֵעֵהוּ
vattishkav margelotav margelotav ad-habboker, vattakom beterem yakkir ish et-re'ehu
And she lay at his feet until the morning; and she rose up before one could discern another.

וַיֹּאמֶר, אַל-יִוָּדַע, כִּי-בָאָה הָאִשָּׁה, הַגֹּרֶן
vayomer al-yivvada', ki-va'ah ha'ishah haggoren
For he said: 'Let it not be known that the woman came to the threshing-floor.'

וַיֹּאמֶר, הָבִי הַמִּטְפַּחַת אֲשֶׁר-עָלַיִךְ וְאֶחֳזִי-בָהּ--וַתֹּאחֶז בָּהּ
vayomer, havi hammitpachat asher-'alayich ve'echozi-vah vattochez bah
And he said: 'Bring the mantle that is upon thee, and hold it'; and she held it;

וַיָּמָד שֵׁשׁ-שְׂעֹרִים וַיָּשֶׁת עָלֶיהָ, וַיָּבֹא הָעִיר
vayamod shesh-se'orim vayashet aleiha, vayavo ha'ir
and he measured six measures of barley, and laid it on her; and he went into the city.

וַתָּבוֹא, אֶל-חֲמוֹתָהּ, וַתֹּאמֶר
vattavo el-chamotah, vattomer
And when she came to her mother-in-law, she said:

מִי-אַתְּ בִּתִּי; וַתַּגֶּד-לָהּ--אֵת כָּל-אֲשֶׁר עָשָׂה-לָהּ, הָאִישׁ
mi-'at bitti; vattagged-lah, et kol-'asher asah-lah ha'ish
'Who art thou, my daughter?' And she told her all that the man had done to her.

וַתֹּאמֶר, שֵׁשׁ-הַשְּׂעֹרִים הָאֵלֶּה נָתַן לִי: כִּי אָמַר אֵלַי, אַל-תָּבוֹאִי רֵיקָם אֶל-חֲמוֹתֵךְ
vattomer shesh-hasse'orim ha'elleh natan li; ki amar elai, al-tavo'i reikam el-chamotech
And she said: 'These six measures of barley gave he me; for he said to me: Go not empty unto thy mother-in-law.'

וַתֹּאמֶר, שְׁבִי בִתִּי, עַד אֲשֶׁר תֵּדְעִין, אֵיךְ יִפֹּל דָּבָר
vattomer shevi vitti, ad asher tede'in, eich yippol davar
Then said she: 'Sit still, my daughter, until thou know how the matter will fall;

כִּי לֹא יִשְׁקֹט הָאִישׁ, כִּי-אִם-כִּלָּה הַדָּבָר הַיּוֹם
ki lo yishkot ha'ish, ki-'im-killah haddavar hayom
for the man will not rest, until he have finished the thing this day.'

ד

וּבֹעַז עָלָה הַשַּׁעַר, וַיֵּשֶׁב שָׁם, וְהִנֵּה הַגֹּאֵל עֹבֵר
Uvo'az alah hasha'ar vayeshev sham vehinneh haggo'el over
Now Boaz went up to the gate, and sat him down there; and, behold, the near kinsman of whom Boaz spoke came by;

רות

וַיֹּאכַל בֹּעַז וַיֵּשְׁתְּ, וַיִּיטַב לִבּוֹ, וַיָּבֹא, לִשְׁכַּב בִּקְצֵה הָעֲרֵמָה
vayochal bo'az vayeshet vayitav libbo, vayavo lishkav biktzeh ha'aremah
And when Boaz had eaten and drunk, and his heart was merry, he went to lie down at the end of the heap of corn;

וַתָּבֹא בַלָּט, וַתְּגַל מַרְגְּלֹתָיו וַתִּשְׁכָּב
vattavo vallat, vattegal margelotav vattishkav
and she came softly, and uncovered his feet, and laid her down.

וַיְהִי בַּחֲצִי הַלַּיְלָה, וַיֶּחֱרַד הָאִישׁ וַיִּלָּפֵת; וְהִנֵּה אִשָּׁה, שֹׁכֶבֶת מַרְגְּלֹתָיו
vayhi bachatzi hallaylah, vayecherad ha'ish vayillafet; vehinneh ishah, shochevet margelotav
And it came to pass at midnight, that the man was startled, and turned himself; and, behold, a woman lay at his feet.

וַיֹּאמֶר, מִי-אָתּ; וַתֹּאמֶר, אָנֹכִי רוּת אֲמָתֶךָ
vayomer mi-'at; vattomer, anochi rut amatecha
And he said: 'Who art thou?' And she answered: 'I am Ruth thine handmaid;

וּפָרַשְׂתָּ כְנָפֶךָ עַל-אֲמָתְךָ, כִּי גֹאֵל אָתָּה
ufarasta chenafecha al-'amatecha, ki go'el attah
spread therefore thy skirt over thy handmaid; for thou art a near kinsman.'

וַיֹּאמֶר, בְּרוּכָה אַתְּ לַיהוָה בִּתִּי--הֵיטַבְתְּ חַסְדֵּךְ
vayomer, beruchah at lahashem bitti, heitavt chasdech
And he said: 'Blessed be thou of the LORD, my daughter; thou hast shown more kindness

הָאַחֲרוֹן, מִן-הָרִאשׁוֹן: לְבִלְתִּי-לֶכֶת, אַחֲרֵי הַבַּחוּרִים--אִם-דַּל, וְאִם-עָשִׁיר
ha'acharon min-harishon; levilti-lechet, acharei habbachurim, im-dal ve'im-'ashir
in the end than at the beginning, inasmuch as thou didst not follow the young men, whether poor or rich.

וְעַתָּה, בִּתִּי אַל-תִּירְאִי, כֹּל אֲשֶׁר-תֹּאמְרִי, אֶעֱשֶׂה-לָּךְ
ve'attah, bitti al-tir'i, kol asher-tomeri e'eseh-lach
And now, my daughter, fear not; I will do to thee all that thou sayest;

כִּי יוֹדֵעַ כָּל-שַׁעַר עַמִּי, כִּי אֵשֶׁת חַיִל אָתּ
ki yodea kol-sha'ar ammi, ki eshet chayil at
for all the men in the gate of my people do know that thou art a virtuous woman.

וְעַתָּה כִּי אָמְנָם, כִּי אִם גֹּאֵל אָנֹכִי; וְגַם יֵשׁ גֹּאֵל, קָרוֹב מִמֶּנִּי
ve'attah ki omnam, ki im go'el anochi; vegam yesh go'el karov mimmenni
And now it is true that I am a near kinsman; howbeit there is a kinsman nearer than I.

לִינִי הַלַּיְלָה, וְהָיָה בַבֹּקֶר אִם-יִגְאָלֵךְ
lini hallaylah, vehayah vabboker im-yig'alech
Tarry this night, and it shall be in the morning, that if he will perform unto thee the part of a kinsman,

טוֹב יִגְאָל, וְאִם-לֹא יַחְפֹּץ לְגָאֳלֵךְ
tov yig'al, ve'im-lo yachpotz lego'olech
well; let him do the kinsman's part; but if he be not willing to do the part of a kinsman to thee,

רות

וַתִּדְבַּק בְּנַעֲרוֹת בֹּעַז, לְלַקֵּט--עַד-כְּלוֹת קְצִיר-הַשְּׂעֹרִים, וּקְצִיר הַחִטִּים
vattidbak bena'arot bo'az lelakket, ad-kelot ketzir-hasse'orim uketzir hachittim
So she kept fast by the maidens of Boaz to glean unto the end of barley harvest and of wheat harvest;

וַתֵּשֶׁב, אֶת-חֲמוֹתָהּ
vatteshev et-chamotah
and she dwelt with her mother-in-law.

ג

וַתֹּאמֶר לָהּ, נָעֳמִי חֲמוֹתָהּ: בִּתִּי, הֲלֹא אֲבַקֶּשׁ-לָךְ מָנוֹחַ אֲשֶׁר יִיטַב-לָךְ
Vattomer lah no'omi chamotah; bitti halo avakkesh-lach manoach asher yitav-lach
And Naomi her mother-in-law said unto her: 'My daughter, shall I not seek rest for thee, that it may be well with thee?

וְעַתָּה, הֲלֹא בֹעַז מֹדַעְתָּנוּ, אֲשֶׁר הָיִית, אֶת-נַעֲרוֹתָיו
ve'attah, halo vo'az moda'tanu, asher hayit et-na'arotav
And now is there not Boaz our kinsman, with whose maidens thou wast?

הִנֵּה-הוּא, זֹרֶה אֶת-גֹּרֶן הַשְּׂעֹרִים--הַלָּיְלָה
hinneh-hu, zoreh et-goren hasse'orim hallayelah
Behold, he winnoweth barley to-night in the threshing-floor.

וְרָחַצְתְּ וָסַכְתְּ, וְשַׂמְתְּ שִׂמְלֹתַיִךְ עָלַיִךְ--וְיָרַדְתִּי הַגֹּרֶן
verachatzt vasacht, vesamt simlotayich alayich veyaradt haggoren
Wash thyself therefore, and anoint thee, and put thy raiment upon thee, and get thee down to the threshing-floor;

אַל-תִּוָּדְעִי לָאִישׁ, עַד כַּלֹּתוֹ לֶאֱכֹל וְלִשְׁתּוֹת
al-tivvade'i la'ish, ad kalloto le'echol velishtot
but make not thyself known unto the man, until he shall have done eating and drinking.

וִיהִי בְשָׁכְבוֹ, וְיָדַעַתְּ אֶת-הַמָּקוֹם אֲשֶׁר יִשְׁכַּב-שָׁם
viyhi veshachevo, veyada'at et-hammakom asher yishkav-sham
And it shall be, when he lieth down, that thou shalt mark the place where he shall lie,

וּבָאת וְגִלִּית מַרְגְּלֹתָיו, וְשָׁכָבְתְּ; וְהוּא יַגִּיד לָךְ, אֵת אֲשֶׁר תַּעֲשִׂין
uvat vegillit margelotav veshachavet; vehu yaggid lach, et asher ta'asin
and thou shalt go in, and uncover his feet, and lay thee down; and he will tell thee what thou shalt do.'

וַתֹּאמֶר, אֵלֶיהָ: כֹּל אֲשֶׁר-תֹּאמְרִי אֵלַי, אֶעֱשֶׂה
vattomer eleiha; kol asher-tomeri elai e'eseh
And she said unto her: 'All that thou sayest unto me I will do.'

וַתֵּרֶד, הַגֹּרֶן; וַתַּעַשׂ, כְּכֹל אֲשֶׁר-צִוַּתָּה חֲמוֹתָהּ
vattered haggoren; vatta'as kechol asher-tzivvattah chamotah
And she went down unto the threshing-floor, and did according to all that her mother-in-law bade her.

רות

וַתִּשָּׂא וַתָּבוֹא הָעִיר, וַתֵּרֶא חֲמוֹתָהּ אֵת אֲשֶׁר-לִקֵּטָה
vattissa vattavo ha'ir, vatterei chamotah et asher-likketah
And she took it up, and went into the city; and her mother-in-law saw what she had gleaned;

וַתּוֹצֵא, וַתִּתֶּן-לָהּ, אֵת אֲשֶׁר-הוֹתִרָה, מִשָּׂבְעָהּ
vattotzei vattitten-lah, et asher-hotirah missov'ah
and she brought forth and gave to her that which she had left after she was satisfied.

וַתֹּאמֶר לָהּ חֲמוֹתָהּ אֵיפֹה לִקַּטְתְּ הַיּוֹם, וְאָנָה עָשִׂית
vattomer lah chamotah eifoh likkatt hayom ve'anah asit
And her mother-in-law said unto her: 'Where hast thou gleaned to-day? and where wroughtest thou?

יְהִי מַכִּירֵךְ, בָּרוּךְ; וַתַּגֵּד לַחֲמוֹתָהּ
yehi makkirech baruch; vattagged lachamotah
blessed be he that did take knowledge of thee.' And she told her mother-in-law

אֵת אֲשֶׁר-עָשְׂתָה עִמּוֹ, וַתֹּאמֶר, שֵׁם הָאִישׁ אֲשֶׁר עָשִׂיתִי עִמּוֹ הַיּוֹם, בֹּעַז
et asher-'asetah immo, vattomer, shem ha'ish asher asiti immo hayom bo'az
with whom she had wrought, and said: 'The man's name with whom I wrought to-day is Boaz.'

וַתֹּאמֶר נָעֳמִי לְכַלָּתָהּ
vattomer no'omi lechallatah
And Naomi said unto her daughter-in-law:

בָּרוּךְ הוּא לַיהוָה, אֲשֶׁר לֹא-עָזַב חַסְדּוֹ, אֶת-הַחַיִּים וְאֶת-הַמֵּתִים
baruch hu lahashem asher lo-'azav chasdo, et-hachayim ve'et-hammetim
'Blessed be he of the LORD, who hath not left off His kindness to the living and to the dead.'

וַתֹּאמֶר לָהּ נָעֳמִי, קָרוֹב לָנוּ הָאִישׁ--מִגֹּאֲלֵנוּ, הוּא
vattomer lah no'omi, karov lanu ha'ish, miggo'alenu hu
And Naomi said unto her: 'The man is nigh of kin unto us, one of our near kinsmen.'

וַתֹּאמֶר, רוּת הַמּוֹאֲבִיָּה: גַּם כִּי-אָמַר אֵלַי
vattomer rut hammo'aviyah; gam ki-'amar elai
And Ruth the Moabitess said: 'Yea, he said unto me:

עִם-הַנְּעָרִים אֲשֶׁר-לִי תִּדְבָּקִין, עַד אִם-כִּלּוּ, אֵת כָּל-הַקָּצִיר אֲשֶׁר-לִי
im-hanne'arim asher-li tidbakin, ad im-killu, et kol-hakkatzir asher-li
Thou shalt keep fast by my young men, until they have ended all my harvest.'

וַתֹּאמֶר נָעֳמִי, אֶל-רוּת כַּלָּתָהּ
vattomer no'omi el-rut kallatah
And Naomi said unto Ruth her daughter-in-law:

טוֹב בִּתִּי, כִּי תֵצְאִי עִם-נַעֲרוֹתָיו, וְלֹא יִפְגְּעוּ-בָךְ, בְּשָׂדֶה אַחֵר
tov bitti, ki tetze'i im-na'arotav, velo yifge'u-vach besadeh acher
'It is good, my daughter, that thou go out with his maidens, and that thou be not met in any other field.'

רות

אַחֲרֵי מוֹת אִישֵׁךְ; וַתַּעַזְבִי אָבִיךְ וְאִמֵּךְ, וְאֶרֶץ מוֹלַדְתֵּךְ
acharei mot ishech; vatta'azvi avich ve'immech, ve'eretz moladtech
since the death of thy husband; and how thou hast left thy father and thy mother, and the land of thy nativity,

וַתֵּלְכִי, אֶל-עַם אֲשֶׁר לֹא-יָדַעַתְּ תְּמוֹל שִׁלְשׁוֹם
vattelechi, el-'am asher lo-yada'at temol shilshom
and art come unto a people that thou knewest not heretofore.

יְשַׁלֵּם יְהוָה, פָּעֳלֵךְ; וּתְהִי מַשְׂכֻּרְתֵּךְ שְׁלֵמָה, מֵעִם יְהוָה אֱלֹהֵי יִשְׂרָאֵל
yeshallem hashem po'olech; utehi maskurtech shelemah, me'im hashem elohei yisra'el
The LORD recompense thy work, and be thy reward complete from the LORD, the God of Israel,

אֲשֶׁר-בָּאת, לַחֲסוֹת תַּחַת-כְּנָפָיו
asher-bat lachasot tachat-kenafav
under whose wings thou art come to take refuge.'

וַתֹּאמֶר אֶמְצָא-חֵן בְּעֵינֶיךָ אֲדֹנִי, כִּי נִחַמְתָּנִי
vattomer emtza-chen be'eineicha adoni ki nichamtani
Then she said: 'Let me find favour in thy sight, my lord; for that thou hast comforted me,

וְכִי דִבַּרְתָּ, עַל-לֵב שִׁפְחָתֶךָ; וְאָנֹכִי לֹא אֶהְיֶה, כְּאַחַת שִׁפְחֹתֶיךָ
vechi dibbarta al-lev shifchatecha; ve'anochi lo ehyeh, ke'achat shifchoteicha
and for that thou hast spoken to the heart of thy handmaid, though I be not as one of thy handmaidens.'

וַיֹּאמֶר לָה בֹעַז לְעֵת הָאֹכֶל, גֹּשִׁי הֲלֹם וְאָכַלְתְּ מִן-הַלֶּחֶם, וְטָבַלְתְּ פִּתֵּךְ, בַּחֹמֶץ
vayomer lah vo'az le'et ha'ochel, gshi halom ve'achalt min-hallechem, vetavalt pittech bachometz
And Boaz said unto her at meal-time: 'Come hither, and eat of the bread, and dip thy morsel in the vinegar.'

וַתֵּשֶׁב, מִצַּד הַקֹּצְרִים, וַיִּצְבָּט-לָהּ קָלִי, וַתֹּאכַל וַתִּשְׂבַּע וַתֹּתַר
vatteshev mitzad hakkotzerim, vayitzbot-lah kali, vattochal vattisba vattotar
And she sat beside the reapers; and they reached her parched corn, and she did eat and was satisfied, and left thereof.

וַתָּקָם, לְלַקֵּט; וַיְצַו בֹּעַז אֶת-נְעָרָיו לֵאמֹר
vattakom lelakket; vaytzav bo'az et-ne'arav lemor
And when she was risen up to glean, Boaz commanded his young men, saying:

גַּם בֵּין הָעֳמָרִים תְּלַקֵּט--וְלֹא תַכְלִימוּהָ
gam bein ho'omarim telakket velo tachlimuha
'Let her glean even among the sheaves, and put her not to shame.

וְגַם שֹׁל-תָּשֹׁלּוּ לָהּ, מִן-הַצְּבָתִים; וַעֲזַבְתֶּם וְלִקְּטָה, וְלֹא תִגְעֲרוּ-בָהּ
vegam shol-tashollu lah min-hatzevatim; va'azavtem velikketah velo tig'aru-vah
And also pull out some for her of purpose from the bundles, and leave it, and let her glean, and rebuke her not.'

וַתְּלַקֵּט בַּשָּׂדֶה, עַד-הָעָרֶב; וַתַּחְבֹּט אֵת אֲשֶׁר-לִקֵּטָה, וַיְהִי כְּאֵיפָה שְׂעֹרִים
vattelakket bassadeh ad-ha'arev; vattachbot et asher-likketah, vayhi ke'eifah se'orim
So she gleaned in the field until even; and she beat out that which she had gleaned, and it was about an ephah of barley.

רות

וַיַּעַן, הַנַּעַר הַנִּצָּב עַל-הַקּוֹצְרִים--וַיֹּאמַר
vaya'an, hanna'ar hannitzav al-hakkotzerim vayomar
And the servant that was set over the reapers answered and said:

נַעֲרָה מוֹאֲבִיָּה הִיא, הַשָּׁבָה עִם-נָעֳמִי מִשְּׂדֵי מוֹאָב
na'arah mo'aviyah hi, hashavah im-no'omi missedeh mo'av
'It is a Moabitish damsel that came back with Naomi out of the field of Moab;

וַתֹּאמֶר, אֲלַקֳטָה-נָּא וְאָסַפְתִּי בָעֳמָרִים, אַחֲרֵי, הַקּוֹצְרִים
vattomer, alakotah-na ve'asafti va'omarim, acharei hakkotzerim
and she said: Let me glean, I pray you, and gather after the reapers among the sheaves;

וַתָּבוֹא וַתַּעֲמוֹד, מֵאָז הַבֹּקֶר וְעַד-עַתָּה--זֶה שִׁבְתָּהּ הַבַּיִת, מְעָט
vattavo vatta'amod, me'az habboker ve'ad-'attah, zeh shivtah habbayit me'at
so she came, and hath continued even from the morning until now, save that she tarried a little in the house.'

וַיֹּאמֶר בֹּעַז אֶל-רוּת הֲלוֹא שָׁמַעַתְּ בִּתִּי
vayomer bo'az el-rut halo shama'at bitti
Then said Boaz unto Ruth: 'Hearest thou not, my daughter?

אַל-תֵּלְכִי לִלְקֹט בְּשָׂדֶה אַחֵר, וְגַם לֹא תַעֲבוּרִי, מִזֶּה; וְכֹה תִדְבָּקִין, עִם-נַעֲרֹתָי
al-telechi lilkot besadeh acher, vegam lo ta'avuri mizzeh; vechoh tidbakin im-na'arotai
Go not to glean in another field, neither pass from hence, but abide here fast by my maidens.

עֵינַיִךְ בַּשָּׂדֶה אֲשֶׁר-יִקְצֹרוּן, וְהָלַכְתְּ אַחֲרֵיהֶן
'einayich bassadeh asher-yiktzorun vehalacht achareihen
Let thine eyes be on the field that they do reap, and go thou after them;

הֲלוֹא צִוִּיתִי אֶת-הַנְּעָרִים, לְבִלְתִּי נָגְעֵךְ; וְצָמִת
halo tzivviti et-hanne'arim levilti nage'ech; vetzamit
have I not charged the young men that they shall not touch thee? and when thou art athirst,

וְהָלַכְתְּ אֶל-הַכֵּלִים, וְשָׁתִית, מֵאֲשֶׁר יִשְׁאֲבוּן הַנְּעָרִים
vehalacht el-hakkelim, veshatit me'asher yish'avun hanne'arim
go unto the vessels, and drink of that which the young men have drawn.'

וַתִּפֹּל, עַל-פָּנֶיהָ, וַתִּשְׁתַּחוּ, אָרְצָה; וַתֹּאמֶר אֵלָיו
vattippol al-paneiha, vattishtachu aretzah; vattomer elav
Then she fell on her face, and bowed down to the ground, and said unto him:

מַדּוּעַ מָצָאתִי חֵן בְּעֵינֶיךָ לְהַכִּירֵנִי--וְאָנֹכִי, נָכְרִיָּה
maddua matzati chen be'eineicha lehakkireni, ve'anochi nochriyah
'Why have I found favour in thy sight, that thou shouldest take cognizance of me, seeing I am a foreigner?'

וַיַּעַן בֹּעַז, וַיֹּאמֶר לָהּ--הֻגֵּד הֻגַּד לִי כֹּל אֲשֶׁר-עָשִׂית אֶת-חֲמוֹתֵךְ
vaya'an bo'az vayomer lah, hugged huggad li, kol asher-'asit et-chamotech
And Boaz answered and said unto her: 'It hath fully been told me, all that thou hast done unto thy mother-in-law

רות

וַיהוָה עָנָה בִי, וְשַׁדַּי הֵרַע לִי
vahashem anah vi, veshaddai hera li
seeing the LORD hath testified against me, and the Almighty hath afflicted me?'

וַתָּשָׁב נָעֳמִי, וְרוּת הַמּוֹאֲבִיָּה כַלָּתָהּ עִמָּהּ
vattashov no'omi, verut hammo'aviyah challatah immah
So Naomi returned, and Ruth the Moabitess, her daughter-in-law, with her,

הַשָּׁבָה, מִשְּׂדֵי מוֹאָב; וְהֵמָּה, בָּאוּ בֵּית לֶחֶם, בִּתְחִלַּת, קְצִיר שְׂעֹרִים
hashavah missedei mo'av; vehemmah, ba'u beit lechem, bitchillat ketzir se'orim
who returned out of the field of Moab--and they came to Beth-lehem in the beginning of barley harvest.

ב

וּלְנָעֳמִי מוֹדָע לְאִישָׁהּ, אִישׁ גִּבּוֹר חַיִל--מִמִּשְׁפַּחַת, אֱלִימֶלֶךְ; וּשְׁמוֹ, בֹּעַז
Uleno'omi moda le'ishah, ish gibbor chayil, mimmishpachat elimelech; ushemo bo'az
And Naomi had a kinsman of her husband's, a mighty man of valour, of the family of Elimelech, and his name was Boaz.

וַתֹּאמֶר רוּת הַמּוֹאֲבִיָּה אֶל-נָעֳמִי, אֵלְכָה-נָּא הַשָּׂדֶה וַאֲלַקֳטָה בַשִּׁבֳּלִים
vattomer rut hammo'aviyah el-no'omi, elechah-na hassadeh va'alakotah vashibbolim
And Ruth the Moabitess said unto Naomi: 'Let me now go to the field, and glean among the ears of corn

אַחַר, אֲשֶׁר אֶמְצָא-חֵן בְּעֵינָיו; וַתֹּאמֶר לָהּ, לְכִי בִתִּי
achar asher emtza-chen be'einav; vattomer lah lechi vitti
after him in whose sight I shall find favour.' And she said unto her: 'Go, my daughter.'

וַתֵּלֶךְ וַתָּבוֹא וַתְּלַקֵּט בַּשָּׂדֶה, אַחֲרֵי הַקֹּצְרִים
vattelech vattavo vattelakket bassadeh, acharei hakkotzerim
And she went, and came and gleaned in the field after the reapers;

וַיִּקֶר מִקְרֶהָ--חֶלְקַת הַשָּׂדֶה לְבֹעַז, אֲשֶׁר מִמִּשְׁפַּחַת אֱלִימֶלֶךְ
vayiker mikreha, chelkat hassadeh levo'az, asher mimmishpachat elimelech
and her hap was to light on the portion of the field belonging unto Boaz, who was of the family of Elimelech.

וְהִנֵּה-בֹעַז, בָּא מִבֵּית לֶחֶם, וַיֹּאמֶר לַקּוֹצְרִים
vehinneh-vo'az, ba mibbeit lechem, vayomer lakkotzerim
And, behold, Boaz came from Beth-lehem, and said unto the reapers:

יְהוָה עִמָּכֶם; וַיֹּאמְרוּ לוֹ, יְבָרֶכְךָ יְהוָה
hashem immachem; vayomeru lo yevarechcha hashem
'The LORD be with you.' And they answered him: 'The LORD bless thee.'

וַיֹּאמֶר בֹּעַז לְנַעֲרוֹ, הַנִּצָּב עַל-הַקּוֹצְרִים: לְמִי, הַנַּעֲרָה הַזֹּאת
vayomer bo'az lena'aro, hannitzav al-hakkotzerim; lemi hanna'arah hazzot
Then said Boaz unto his servant that was set over the reapers: 'Whose damsel is this?'

רות

אַל בְּנֹתַי, כִּי-מַר-לִי מְאֹד מִכֶּם--כִּי-יָצְאָה בִי, יַד-יְהוָה
al benotai, ki-mar-li me'od mikkem, ki-yatze'ah vi yad-hashem
nay, my daughters; for it grieveth me much for your sakes, for the hand of the LORD is gone forth against me.'

וַתִּשֶּׂנָה קוֹלָן, וַתִּבְכֶּינָה עוֹד; וַתִּשַּׁק עָרְפָּה לַחֲמוֹתָהּ, וְרוּת דָּבְקָה בָּהּ
vattissenah kolan, vattivkeinah od; vattishak orpah lachamotah, verut davekah bah
And they lifted up their voice, and wept again; and Orpah kissed her mother-in-law; but Ruth cleaved unto her.

וַתֹּאמֶר, הִנֵּה שָׁבָה יְבִמְתֵּךְ, אֶל-עַמָּהּ, וְאֶל-אֱלֹהֶיהָ; שׁוּבִי, אַחֲרֵי יְבִמְתֵּךְ
vattomer, hinneh shavah yevimtech, el-'ammah ve'el-'eloheiha; shuvi acharei yevimtech
And she said: 'Behold, thy sister-in-law is gone back unto her people, and unto her god; return thou after thy sister-in-law.'

וַתֹּאמֶר רוּת אַל-תִּפְגְּעִי-בִי, לְעָזְבֵךְ לָשׁוּב מֵאַחֲרָיִךְ: כִּי אֶל-אֲשֶׁר תֵּלְכִי
vattomer rut al-tifge'i-vi, le'azevech lashuv me'acharayich; ki el-'asher telechi
And Ruth said: 'Entreat me not to leave thee, and to return from following after thee; for whither thou goest,

אֵלֵךְ, וּבַאֲשֶׁר תָּלִינִי אָלִין--עַמֵּךְ עַמִּי, וֵאלֹהַיִךְ אֱלֹהָי
elech, uva'asher talini alin, ammech ammi, velohayich elohai
I will go; and where thou lodgest, I will lodge; thy people shall be my people, and thy God my God;

בַּאֲשֶׁר תָּמוּתִי אָמוּת, וְשָׁם אֶקָּבֵר
ba'asher tamuti amut, vesham ekkaver
where thou diest, will I die, and there will I be buried;

כֹּה יַעֲשֶׂה יְהוָה לִי, וְכֹה יוֹסִיף--כִּי הַמָּוֶת, יַפְרִיד בֵּינִי וּבֵינֵךְ
koh ya'aseh hashem li vechoh yosif, ki hammavet, yafrid beini uveinech
the LORD do so to me, and more also, if aught but death part thee and me.'

וַתֵּרֶא, כִּי-מִתְאַמֶּצֶת הִיא לָלֶכֶת אִתָּהּ; וַתֶּחְדַּל, לְדַבֵּר אֵלֶיהָ
vatterei ki-mit'ammetzet hi lalechet ittah; vattechdal ledabber eleiha
And when she saw that she was stedfastly minded to go with her, she left off speaking unto her.

וַתֵּלַכְנָה שְׁתֵּיהֶם, עַד-בּוֹאָנָה בֵּית לָחֶם; וַיְהִי, כְּבוֹאָנָה בֵּית לֶחֶם
vattelachnah sheteihem, ad-bo'anah beit lachem; vayhi, kevo'anah beit lechem
So they two went until they came to Beth-lehem. And it came to pass, when they were come to Beth-lehem,

וַתֵּהֹם כָּל-הָעִיר עֲלֵיהֶן, וַתֹּאמַרְנָה הֲזֹאת נָעֳמִי
vattehom kol-ha'ir aleihen, vattomarnah hazot no'omi
that all the city was astir concerning them, and the women said: 'Is this Naomi?'

וַתֹּאמֶר אֲלֵיהֶן, אַל-תִּקְרֶאנָה לִי נָעֳמִי: קְרֶאןָ לִי מָרָא, כִּי-הֵמַר שַׁדַּי לִי מְאֹד
vattomer aleihen, al-tikrenah li no'omi; kerena li mara, ki-hemar shaddai li me'od
And she said unto them: 'Call me not Naomi, call me Marah; for the Almighty hath dealt very bitterly with me.

אֲנִי מְלֵאָה הָלַכְתִּי, וְרֵיקָם הֱשִׁיבַנִי יְהוָה; לָמָּה תִקְרֶאנָה לִי, נָעֳמִי
'ani mele'ah halachti, vereikam heshivani hashem lammah tikrenah li no'omi
I went out full, and the LORD hath brought me back home empty; why call ye me Naomi,

רות

וַתֵּצֵא, מִן-הַמָּקוֹם אֲשֶׁר הָיְתָה-שָּׁמָּה, וּשְׁתֵּי כַלּוֹתֶיהָ, עִמָּהּ
vattetze, min-hammakom asher hayetah-shammah, ushetei challoteiha immah
And she went forth out of the place where she was, and her two daughters-in-law with her;

וַתֵּלַכְנָה בַדֶּרֶךְ, לָשׁוּב אֶל-אֶרֶץ יְהוּדָה
vattelachnah vadderech, lashuv el-'eretz yehudah
and they went on the way to return unto the land of Judah.

וַתֹּאמֶר נָעֳמִי, לִשְׁתֵּי כַלֹּתֶיהָ, לֵכְנָה שֹּׁבְנָה, אִשָּׁה לְבֵית אִמָּהּ
vattomer no'omi lishtei challoteiha, lechenah shovenah, ishah leveit immah
And Naomi said unto her two daughters-in-law: 'Go, return each of you to her mother's house;

יַעַשׂ יְהוָה עִמָּכֶם חֶסֶד, כַּאֲשֶׁר עֲשִׂיתֶם עִם-הַמֵּתִים וְעִמָּדִי
ya'as hashem immachem chesed, ka'asher asitem im-hammetim ve'immadi
the LORD deal kindly with you, as ye have dealt with the dead, and with me.

יִתֵּן יְהוָה, לָכֶם, וּמְצֶאןָ מְנוּחָה, אִשָּׁה בֵּית אִישָׁהּ
yitten hashem lachem, umetzena menuchah, ishah beit ishah
The LORD grant you that ye may find rest, each of you in the house of her husband.'

וַתִּשַּׁק לָהֶן, וַתִּשֶּׂאנָה קוֹלָן וַתִּבְכֶּינָה
vattishak lahen, vattissenah kolan vattivkeinah
Then she kissed them; and they lifted up their voice, and wept.

וַתֹּאמַרְנָה-לָּהּ: כִּי-אִתָּךְ נָשׁוּב, לְעַמֵּךְ
vattomarnah-lah; ki-'ittach nashuv le'ammech
And they said unto her: 'Nay, but we will return with thee unto thy people.'

וַתֹּאמֶר נָעֳמִי שֹׁבְנָה בְנֹתַי, לָמָּה תֵלַכְנָה עִמִּי
vattomer no'omi shovenah venotai, lammah telachnah immi
And Naomi said: 'Turn back, my daughters; why will ye go with me?

הַעוֹד-לִי בָנִים בְּמֵעַי, וְהָיוּ לָכֶם לַאֲנָשִׁים.
ha'od-li vanim beme'ai, vehayu lachem la'anashim
have I yet sons in my womb, that they may be your husbands?

שֹׁבְנָה בְנֹתַי לֵכְןָ, כִּי זָקַנְתִּי מִהְיוֹת לְאִישׁ
shovenah venotai lechena, ki zakanti mihyot le'ish
Turn back, my daughters, go your way; for I am too old to have a husband.

כִּי אָמַרְתִּי, יֶשׁ-לִי תִקְוָה--גַּם הָיִיתִי הַלַּיְלָה לְאִישׁ, וְגַם יָלַדְתִּי בָנִים
ki amarti yesh-li tikvah, gam hayiti hallaylah le'ish, vegam yaladti vanim
If I should say: I have hope, should I even have an husband to-night, and also bear sons;

הֲלָהֵן תְּשַׂבֵּרְנָה, עַד אֲשֶׁר יִגְדָּלוּ, הֲלָהֵן תֵּעָגֵנָה, לְבִלְתִּי הֱיוֹת לְאִישׁ
halahen tesabberenah, ad asher yigdalu, halahen te'agenah, levilti heyot le'ish
would ye tarry for them till they were grown? would ye shut yourselves off for them and have no husbands?

רות

רות א

וַיְהִי, בִּימֵי שְׁפֹט הַשֹּׁפְטִים, וַיְהִי רָעָב, בָּאָרֶץ
Vayhi, bimei shefot hashofetim, vayhi ra'av ba'aretz
And it came to pass in the days when the judges judged, that there was a famine in the land.

וַיֵּלֶךְ אִישׁ מִבֵּית לֶחֶם יְהוּדָה, לָגוּר בִּשְׂדֵי מוֹאָב--הוּא וְאִשְׁתּוֹ, וּשְׁנֵי בָנָיו
vayelech ish mibbeit lechem yehudah, lagur bisdei mo'av, hu ve'ishto ushenei vanav
And a certain man of Beth-lehem in Judah went to sojourn in the field of Moab, he, and his wife, and his two sons.

וְשֵׁם הָאִישׁ אֱלִימֶלֶךְ וְשֵׁם אִשְׁתּוֹ נָעֳמִי
veshem ha'ish elimelech veshem ishto no'omi
And the name of the man was Elimelech, and the name of his wife Naomi,

וְשֵׁם שְׁנֵי-בָנָיו מַחְלוֹן וְכִלְיוֹן, אֶפְרָתִים--מִבֵּית לֶחֶם, יְהוּדָה
veshem shenei-vanav machlon vechilyon efratim, mibbeit lechem yehudah
and the name of his two sons Mahlon and Chilion, Ephrathites of Beth-lehem in Judah.

וַיָּבֹאוּ שְׂדֵי-מוֹאָב, וַיִּהְיוּ-שָׁם
vayavo'u sedei-mo'av vayihyu-sham
And they came into the field of Moab, and continued there.

וַיָּמָת אֱלִימֶלֶךְ, אִישׁ נָעֳמִי; וַתִּשָּׁאֵר הִיא, וּשְׁנֵי בָנֶיהָ
vayamot elimelech ish no'omi; vattisha'er hi ushenei vaneiha
And Elimelech Naomi's husband died; and she was left, and her two sons.

וַיִּשְׂאוּ לָהֶם, נָשִׁים מֹאֲבִיּוֹת--שֵׁם הָאַחַת עָרְפָּה
vayis'u lahem, nashim mo'aviyot, shem ha'achat orpah
And they took them wives of the women of Moab: the name of the one was Orpah,

וְשֵׁם הַשֵּׁנִית רוּת; וַיֵּשְׁבוּ שָׁם, כְּעֶשֶׂר שָׁנִים
veshem hashenit rut; vayeshevu sham ke'eser shanim
and the name of the other Ruth; and they dwelt there about ten years.

וַיָּמוּתוּ גַם-שְׁנֵיהֶם, מַחְלוֹן וְכִלְיוֹן; וַתִּשָּׁאֵר, הָאִשָּׁה, מִשְּׁנֵי יְלָדֶיהָ, וּמֵאִישָׁהּ
vayamutu gam-sheneihem machlon vechilyon; vattisha'er ha'ishah, mishenei yeladeiha ume'ishah
And Mahlon and Chilion died both of them; and the woman was left of her two children and of her husband.

וַתָּקָם הִיא וְכַלֹּתֶיהָ, וַתָּשָׁב מִשְּׂדֵי מוֹאָב
vattakom hi vechalloteiha, vattashov missedei mo'av
Then she arose with her daughters-in-law, that she might return from the field of Moab;

כִּי שָׁמְעָה, בִּשְׂדֵה מוֹאָב--כִּי-פָקַד יְהוָה אֶת-עַמּוֹ, לָתֵת לָהֶם לָחֶם
ki shame'ah bisdeh mo'av, ki-fakad hashem et-'ammo, latet lahem lachem
for she had heard in the field of Moab how that the LORD had remembered His people in giving them bread.

שִׁיר הַשִּׁירִים

הַיּוֹשֶׁבֶת בַּגַּנִּים, חֲבֵרִים מַקְשִׁיבִים לְקוֹלֵךְ--הַשְׁמִיעִנִי
hayoshevet baggannim, chaverim makshivim lekolech hashmi'ini
Thou that dwellest in the gardens, the companions hearken for thy voice: 'Cause me to hear it.'

בְּרַח דּוֹדִי, וּדְמֵה-לְךָ לִצְבִי אוֹ לְעֹפֶר הָאַיָּלִים--עַל, הָרֵי בְשָׂמִים
berach dodi, udemeh-lecha litzvi o le'ofer ha'ayalim, al harei vesamim
Make haste, my beloved, and be thou like to a gazelle or to a young hart upon the mountains of spices.

שִׁיר הַשִּׁירִים

שָׁמָּה חִבְּלַתְךָ אִמֶּךָ, שָׁמָּה חִבְּלָה יְלָדַתְךָ
shammah chibbelatcha immecha, shammah chibbelah yeladatcha
there thy mother was in travail with thee; there was she in travail and brought thee forth.

שִׂימֵנִי כַחוֹתָם עַל-לִבֶּךָ, כַּחוֹתָם עַל-זְרוֹעֶךָ--כִּי-עַזָּה כַמָּוֶת אַהֲבָה
simeni chachotam al-libbecha, kachotam al-zero'echa, ki-'azzah chammavet ahavah
Set me as a seal upon thy heart, as a seal upon thine arm; for love is strong as death,

קָשָׁה כִשְׁאוֹל קִנְאָה: רְשָׁפֶיהָ--רִשְׁפֵּי, אֵשׁ שַׁלְהֶבֶתְיָה
kashah chish'ol kin'ah; reshafeiha rishpei esh shalhevetyah
jealousy is cruel as the grave; the flashes thereof are flashes of fire, a very flame of the LORD.

מַיִם רַבִּים, לֹא יוּכְלוּ לְכַבּוֹת אֶת-הָאַהֲבָה, וּנְהָרוֹת, לֹא יִשְׁטְפוּהָ
mayim rabbim, lo yuchelu lechabbot et-ha'ahavah, uneharot lo yishtefuha
Many waters cannot quench love, neither can the floods drown it;

אִם-יִתֵּן אִישׁ אֶת-כָּל-הוֹן בֵּיתוֹ, בָּאַהֲבָה--בּוֹז, יָבוּזוּ לוֹ
im-yitten ish et-kol-hon beito ba'ahavah, boz yavuzu lo
if a man would give all the substance of his house for love, he would utterly be contemned.

אָחוֹת לָנוּ קְטַנָּה, וְשָׁדַיִם אֵין לָהּ; מַה-נַּעֲשֶׂה לַאֲחֹתֵנוּ, בַּיּוֹם שֶׁיְּדֻבַּר-בָּהּ
'achot lanu ketannah, veshadayim ein lah; mah-na'aseh la'achotenu, bayom sheyedubbar-bah
We have a little sister, and she hath no breasts; what shall we do for our sister in the day when she shall be spoken for?

אִם-חוֹמָה הִיא, נִבְנֶה עָלֶיהָ טִירַת כָּסֶף; וְאִם-דֶּלֶת הִיא, נָצוּר עָלֶיהָ לוּחַ אָרֶז
'im-chomah hi, nivneh aleiha tirat kasef; ve'im-delet hi, natzur aleiha luach arez
If she be a wall, we will build upon her a turret of silver; and if she be a door, we will enclose her with boards of cedar.

אֲנִי חוֹמָה, וְשָׁדַי כַּמִּגְדָּלוֹת; אָז הָיִיתִי בְעֵינָיו, כְּמוֹצְאֵת שָׁלוֹם
'ani chomah, veshadai kammigdalot; az hayiti ve'einav kemotze'et shalom
I am a wall, and my breasts like the towers thereof; then was I in his eyes as one that found peace.

כֶּרֶם הָיָה לִשְׁלֹמֹה בְּבַעַל הָמוֹן, נָתַן אֶת-הַכֶּרֶם לַנֹּטְרִים
kerem hayah lishlomoh beva'al hamon, natan et-hakkerem lannoterim
Solomon had a vineyard at Baal-hamon; he gave over the vineyard unto keepers;

אִישׁ יָבִא בְּפִרְיוֹ, אֶלֶף כָּסֶף
ish yavi befiryo elef kasef
every one for the fruit thereof brought in a thousand pieces of silver.

כַּרְמִי שֶׁלִּי, לְפָנָי; הָאֶלֶף לְךָ שְׁלֹמֹה
karmi shelli lefanai; ha'elef lecha shelomoh
My vineyard, which is mine, is before me; thou, O Solomon, shalt have the thousand,

וּמָאתַיִם לְנֹטְרִים אֶת-פִּרְיוֹ
umatayim lenoterim et-piryo
and those that keep the fruit thereof two hundred.

שִׁיר הַשִּׁירִים

נַשְׁכִּימָה, לַכְּרָמִים--נִרְאֶה אִם-פָּרְחָה הַגֶּפֶן
nashkimah lakkeramim, nir'eh im parechah haggefen
Let us get up early to the vineyards; let us see whether the vine hath budded,

פִּתַּח הַסְּמָדַר, הֵנֵצוּ הָרִמּוֹנִים; שָׁם אֶתֵּן אֶת-דֹּדַי, לָךְ
pittach hassemadar, henetzu harimmonim; sham etten et-dodai lach
whether the vine-blossom be opened, and the pomegranates be in flower; there will I give thee my love.

הַדּוּדָאִים נָתְנוּ-רֵיחַ, וְעַל-פְּתָחֵינוּ כָּל-מְגָדִים
hadduda'im natenu-reiach, ve'al-petacheinu kol-megadim
The mandrakes give forth fragrance, and at our doors are all manner of precious fruits,

חֲדָשִׁים, גַּם-יְשָׁנִים; דּוֹדִי, צָפַנְתִּי לָךְ
chadashim gam-yeshanim; dodi tzafanti lach
new and old, which I have laid up for thee, O my beloved.

ח

מִי יִתֶּנְךָ כְּאָח לִי, יוֹנֵק שְׁדֵי אִמִּי
Mi yittencha ke'ach li, yonek shedei immi
Oh that thou wert as my brother, that sucked the breasts of my mother!

אֶמְצָאֲךָ בַחוּץ אֶשָּׁקְךָ, גַּם לֹא-יָבֻזוּ לִי
emtza'acha vachutz eshakecha, gam lo-yavuzu li
When I should find thee without, I would kiss thee; yea, and none would despise me.

אֶנְהָגְךָ, אֲבִיאֲךָ אֶל-בֵּית אִמִּי--תְּלַמְּדֵנִי
'enhagecha, avi'acha el-beit immi telammedeni
I would lead thee, and bring thee into my mother's house, that thou mightest instruct me;

אַשְׁקְךָ מִיַּיִן הָרֶקַח, מֵעֲסִיס רִמֹּנִי
ashkecha miyayin harekach, me'asis rimmoni
I would cause thee to drink of spiced wine, of the juice of my pomegranate.

שְׂמֹאלוֹ תַּחַת רֹאשִׁי, וִימִינוֹ תְּחַבְּקֵנִי.
semolo tachat roshi, viymino techabbekeni
His left hand should be under my head, and his right hand should embrace me.

הִשְׁבַּעְתִּי אֶתְכֶם, בְּנוֹת יְרוּשָׁלִָם: מַה-תָּעִירוּ וּמַה-תְּעֹרְרוּ אֶת-הָאַהֲבָה, עַד שֶׁתֶּחְפָּץ
hishba'ti etchem benot yerushalayim; mah-ta'iru umah-te'oreru et-ha'ahavah ad shettechpatz
'I adjure you, O daughters of Jerusalem: Why should ye awaken, or stir up love, until it please?'

מִי זֹאת, עֹלָה מִן-הַמִּדְבָּר, מִתְרַפֶּקֶת, עַל-דּוֹדָהּ; תַּחַת הַתַּפּוּחַ, עוֹרַרְתִּיךָ
mi zot, olah min-hammidbar, mitrappeket al-dodah; tachat hattappuach orarticha
Who is this that cometh up from the wilderness, leaning upon her beloved? Under the apple-tree I awakened thee;

שִׁיר הַשִׁירִים

שְׁנֵי שָׁדַיִךְ כִּשְׁנֵי עֳפָרִים, תָּאֳמֵי צְבִיָּה
shenei shadayich kishnei ofarim to'omei tzeviyah
Thy two breasts are like two fawns that are twins of a gazelle.

צַוָּארֵךְ, כְּמִגְדַּל הַשֵּׁן; עֵינַיִךְ בְּרֵכוֹת בְּחֶשְׁבּוֹן, עַל-שַׁעַר בַּת-רַבִּים
tzavvarech kemigdal hashen; einayich berechot becheshbon, al-sha'ar bat-rabbim
Thy neck is as a tower of ivory; thine eyes as the pools in Heshbon, by the gate of Bath-rabbim;

אַפֵּךְ כְּמִגְדַּל הַלְּבָנוֹן, צוֹפֶה פְּנֵי דַמָּשֶׂק
appech kemigdal hallevanon, tzofeh penei dammasek
thy nose is like the tower of Lebanon which looketh toward Damascus.

רֹאשֵׁךְ עָלַיִךְ כַּכַּרְמֶל, וְדַלַּת רֹאשֵׁךְ כָּאַרְגָּמָן: מֶלֶךְ, אָסוּר בָּרְהָטִים
roshech alayich kakkarmel, vedallat roshech ka'argaman; melech asur barehatim
Thy head upon thee is like Carmel, and the hair of thy head like purple; the king is held captive in the tresses thereof.

מַה-יָּפִית, וּמַה-נָּעַמְתְּ--אַהֲבָה, בַּתַּעֲנוּגִים
mah-yafit umah-na'amt, ahavah batta'anugim
How fair and how pleasant art thou, O love, for delights!

זֹאת קוֹמָתֵךְ דָּמְתָה לְתָמָר, וְשָׁדַיִךְ לְאַשְׁכֹּלוֹת
zot komatech dametah letamar, veshadayich le'ashkolot
This thy stature is like to a palm-tree, and thy breasts to clusters of grapes.

אָמַרְתִּי אֶעֱלֶה בְתָמָר, אֹחֲזָה בְּסַנְסִנָּיו
'amarti e'eleh vetamar, ochazah besansinnav
I said: 'I will climb up into the palm-tree, I will take hold of the branches thereof;

וְיִהְיוּ-נָא שָׁדַיִךְ כְּאֶשְׁכְּלוֹת הַגֶּפֶן, וְרֵיחַ אַפֵּךְ כַּתַּפּוּחִים
veyihyu-na shadayich ke'eshkelot haggefen, vereiach appech kattappuchim
and let thy breasts be as clusters of the vine, and the smell of thy countenance like apples;

וְחִכֵּךְ, כְּיֵין הַטּוֹב הוֹלֵךְ לְדוֹדִי לְמֵישָׁרִים
vechikkech keyein hattov holech ledodi lemeisharim
And the roof of thy mouth like the best wine, that glideth down smoothly for my beloved,

דּוֹבֵב, שִׂפְתֵי יְשֵׁנִים
dovev siftei yeshenim
moving gently the lips of those that are asleep.'

אֲנִי לְדוֹדִי, וְעָלַי תְּשׁוּקָתוֹ
'ani ledodi, ve'alai teshukato
I am my beloved's, and his desire is toward me.

לְכָה דוֹדִי נֵצֵא הַשָּׂדֶה, נָלִינָה בַּכְּפָרִים
lechah dodi netzei hassadeh, nalinah bakkefarim
Come, my beloved, let us go forth into the field; let us lodge in the villages.

שִׁיר הַשִּׁירִים

רָאוּהָ בָנוֹת וַיְאַשְּׁרוּהָ, מְלָכוֹת וּפִילַגְשִׁים וַיְהַלְלוּהָ
ra'uha vanot vay'asheruha, melachot ufilagshim vayhaleluha
The daughters saw her, and called her happy; yea, the queens and the concubines, and they praised her.

מִי-זֹאת הַנִּשְׁקָפָה, כְּמוֹ-שָׁחַר: יָפָה כַלְּבָנָה, בָּרָה כַּחַמָּה--אֲיֻמָּה, כַּנִּדְגָּלוֹת
mi-zot hannishkafah kemo-shachar; yafah challevanah, barah kachammah, ayummah kannidgalot
Who is she that looketh forth as the dawn, fair as the moon, clear as the sun, terrible as an army with banners?

אֶל-גִּנַּת אֱגוֹז יָרַדְתִּי, לִרְאוֹת בְּאִבֵּי הַנָּחַל
'el-ginnat egoz yaradti, lir'ot be'ibbei hannachal
I went down into the garden of nuts, to look at the green plants of the valley,

לִרְאוֹת הֲפָרְחָה הַגֶּפֶן, הֵנֵצוּ הָרִמֹּנִים
lir'ot hafarechah haggefen, henetzu harimmonim
to see whether the vine budded, and the pomegranates were in flower.

לֹא יָדַעְתִּי--נַפְשִׁי שָׂמַתְנִי, מַרְכְּבוֹת עַמִּי נָדִיב
lo yada'ti, nafshi samatni, markevot ammi-nadiv
Before I was aware, my soul set me upon the chariots of my princely people.

ז

שׁוּבִי שׁוּבִי הַשּׁוּלַמִּית, שׁוּבִי שׁוּבִי וְנֶחֱזֶה-בָּךְ
Shuvi shuvi hashulammit, shuvi shuvi venechezeh-bach
Return, return, O Shulammite; Return, return, that we may look upon thee.

מַה-תֶּחֱזוּ, בַּשּׁוּלַמִּית, כִּמְחֹלַת, הַמַּחֲנָיִם
mah-techezu bashulammit, kimecholat hammachanayim
What will ye see in the Shulammite? As it were a dance of two companies.

מַה-יָּפוּ פְעָמַיִךְ בַּנְּעָלִים, בַּת-נָדִיב
mah-yafu fe'amayich banne'alim bat-nadiv
How beautiful are thy steps in sandals, O prince's daughter!

חַמּוּקֵי יְרֵכַיִךְ--כְּמוֹ חֲלָאִים, מַעֲשֵׂה יְדֵי אָמָּן
chammukei yerechayich, kemo chala'im, ma'aseh yedei omman
The roundings of thy thighs are like the links of a chain, the work of the hands of a skilled workman.

שָׁרְרֵךְ אַגַּן הַסַּהַר, אַל-יֶחְסַר הַמָּזֶג
sharerech aggan hassahar, al-yechsar hammazeg
Thy navel is like a round goblet, wherein no mingled wine is wanting;

בִּטְנֵךְ עֲרֵמַת חִטִּים, סוּגָה בַּשּׁוֹשַׁנִּים
bitnech aremat chittim, sugah bashoshannim
thy belly is like a heap of wheat set about with lilies.

שִׁיר הַשִּׁירִים

I

אָנָה הָלַךְ דּוֹדֵךְ, הַיָּפָה בַּנָּשִׁים
Anah halach dodech, hayafah bannashim
'Whither is thy beloved gone, O thou fairest among women?

אָנָה פָּנָה דוֹדֵךְ, וּנְבַקְשֶׁנּוּ עִמָּךְ
anah panah dodech, unevakshennu immach
Whither hath thy beloved turned him, that we may seek him with thee?'

דּוֹדִי יָרַד לְגַנּוֹ, לַעֲרוּגוֹת הַבֹּשֶׂם--לִרְעוֹת, בַּגַּנִּים, וְלִלְקֹט, שׁוֹשַׁנִּים
dodi yarad leganno, la'arugot habbosem; lir'ot baggannim, velilkot shoshannim
'My beloved is gone down into his garden, to the beds of spices, to feed in the gardens, and to gather lilies.

אֲנִי לְדוֹדִי וְדוֹדִי לִי, הָרֹעֶה בַּשּׁוֹשַׁנִּים
'ani ledodi vedodi li, haro'eh bashoshannim
I am my beloved's, and my beloved is mine, that feedeth among the lilies.'

יָפָה אַתְּ רַעְיָתִי כְּתִרְצָה, נָאוָה כִּירוּשָׁלִָם; אֲיֻמָּה, כַּנִּדְגָּלוֹת
yafah at ra'yati ketirtzah, navah kiyerushalayim; ayummah kannidgalot
Thou art beautiful, O my love, as Tirzah, comely as Jerusalem, terrible as an army with banners.

הָסֵבִּי עֵינַיִךְ מִנֶּגְדִּי, שֶׁהֵם הִרְהִיבֻנִי; שַׂעְרֵךְ כְּעֵדֶר הָעִזִּים, שֶׁגָּלְשׁוּ מִן-הַגִּלְעָד
hasebbi einayich minnegdi, shehem hirhivuni; sa'rech ke'eder ha'izzim, sheggaleshu min-haggil'ad
Turn away thine eyes from me, for they have overcome me. Thy hair is as a flock of goats, that trail down from Gilead.

שִׁנַּיִךְ כְּעֵדֶר הָרְחֵלִים, שֶׁעָלוּ מִן-הָרַחְצָה
shinnayich ke'eder harechelim, she'alu min-harachtzah
Thy teeth are like a flock of ewes, which are come up from the washing;

שֶׁכֻּלָּם, מַתְאִימוֹת, וְשַׁכֻּלָה, אֵין בָּהֶם
shekkullam mat'imot, veshakkulah ein bahem
whereof all are paired, and none faileth among them.

כְּפֶלַח הָרִמּוֹן רַקָּתֵךְ, מִבַּעַד לְצַמָּתֵךְ
kefelach harimmon rakkatech, mibba'ad letzammatech
Thy temples are like a pomegranate split open behind thy veil.

שִׁשִּׁים הֵמָּה מְלָכוֹת, וּשְׁמֹנִים פִּילַגְשִׁים; וַעֲלָמוֹת, אֵין מִסְפָּר
shishim hemmah melachot, ushemonim pilagshim; va'alamot ein mispar
There are threescore queens, and fourscore concubines, and maidens without number.

אַחַת הִיא, יוֹנָתִי תַמָּתִי--אַחַת הִיא לְאִמָּהּ, בָּרָה הִיא לְיוֹלַדְתָּהּ
'achat hi yonati tammati, achat hi le'immah, barah hi leyoladtah
My dove, my undefiled, is but one; she is the only one of her mother; she is the choice one of her that bore her.

שִׁיר הַשִּׁירִים

הִשְׁבַּעְתִּי אֶתְכֶם, בְּנוֹת יְרוּשָׁלִָם: אִם-תִּמְצְאוּ, אֶת-דּוֹדִי--מַה-תַּגִּידוּ לוֹ, שֶׁחוֹלַת אַהֲבָה אָנִי
hishba'ti etchem benot yerushalayim; im-timtze'u et-dodi, mah-taggidu lo, shecholat ahavah ani
'I adjure you, O daughters of Jerusalem, if ye find my beloved, what will ye tell him? that I am love-sick.'

מַה-דּוֹדֵךְ מִדּוֹד, הַיָּפָה בַּנָּשִׁים
mah-dodech middod, hayafah bannashim
'What is thy beloved more than another beloved, O thou fairest among women?

מַה-דּוֹדֵךְ מִדּוֹד, שֶׁכָּכָה הִשְׁבַּעְתָּנוּ
mah-dodech middod, shekkachah hishba'tanu
What is thy beloved more than another beloved, that thou dost so adjure us?'

דּוֹדִי צַח וְאָדוֹם, דָּגוּל מֵרְבָבָה
dodi tzach ve'adom, dagul merevavah
'My beloved is white and ruddy, pre-eminent above ten thousand.

רֹאשׁוֹ, כֶּתֶם פָּז; קְוֻצּוֹתָיו, תַּלְתַּלִּים, שְׁחֹרוֹת, כָּעוֹרֵב
rosho ketem paz; kevvtzotav taltallim, shechorot ka'orev
His head is as the most fine gold, his locks are curled, and black as a raven.

עֵינָיו, כְּיוֹנִים עַל-אֲפִיקֵי מָיִם; רֹחֲצוֹת, בֶּחָלָב--יֹשְׁבוֹת, עַל-מִלֵּאת
'einav keyonim al-'afikei mayim; rochatzot bechalav, yoshevot al-millet
His eyes are like doves beside the water-brooks; washed with milk, and fitly set.

לְחָיָו כַּעֲרוּגַת הַבֹּשֶׂם, מִגְדְּלוֹת מֶרְקָחִים; שִׂפְתוֹתָיו, שׁוֹשַׁנִּים--נֹטְפוֹת, מוֹר עֹבֵר
lechayav ka'arugat habbosem, migdelot merkachim; siftotav shoshannim, notefot mor over
His cheeks are as a bed of spices, as banks of sweet herbs; his lips are as lilies, dropping with flowing myrrh.

יָדָיו גְּלִילֵי זָהָב, מְמֻלָּאִים בַּתַּרְשִׁישׁ; מֵעָיו עֶשֶׁת שֵׁן, מְעֻלֶּפֶת סַפִּירִים
yadav gelilei zahav, memulla'im battarshish; me'av eshet shen, me'ullefet sappirim
His hands are as rods of gold set with beryl; his body is as polished ivory overlaid with sapphires.

שׁוֹקָיו עַמּוּדֵי שֵׁשׁ, מְיֻסָּדִים עַל-אַדְנֵי-פָז; מַרְאֵהוּ, כַּלְּבָנוֹן--בָּחוּר, כָּאֲרָזִים
shokav ammudei shesh, meyussadim al-'adnei-faz; mar'ehu kallevanon, bachur ka'arazim
His legs are as pillars of marble, set upon sockets of fine gold; his aspect is like Lebanon, excellent as the cedars.

חִכּוֹ, מַמְתַקִּים, וְכֻלּוֹ, מַחֲמַדִּים
chikko mamtakkim, vechullo machamaddim
His mouth is most sweet; yea, he is altogether lovely.

זֶה דוֹדִי וְזֶה רֵעִי, בְּנוֹת יְרוּשָׁלִָם
zeh dodi vezeh re'i, benot yerushalayim
This is my beloved, and this is my friend, O daughters of Jerusalem.'

שִׁיר הַשִּׁירִים

אָכַלְתִּי יַעְרִי עִם-דִּבְשִׁי שָׁתִיתִי יֵינִי עִם-חֲלָבִי
achalti ya'ri im-divshi, shatiti yeini im-chalavi
I have eaten my honeycomb with my honey; I have drunk my wine with my milk.

אִכְלוּ רֵעִים, שְׁתוּ וְשִׁכְרוּ דּוֹדִים
ichlu re'im, shetu veshichru dodim
Eat, O friends; drink, yea, drink abundantly, O beloved.

אֲנִי יְשֵׁנָה, וְלִבִּי עֵר; קוֹל דּוֹדִי דוֹפֵק, פִּתְחִי-לִי אֲחֹתִי רַעְיָתִי יוֹנָתִי תַמָּתִי
'ani yeshenah velibbi er; kol dodi dofek, pitchi-li achoti ra'yati yonati tammati
I sleep, but my heart waketh; Hark! my beloved knocketh: 'Open to me, my sister, my love, my dove, my undefiled;

שֶׁרֹּאשִׁי נִמְלָא-טָל, קְוֻצּוֹתַי רְסִיסֵי לָיְלָה
sherroshi nimla-tal, kevvutzotai resisei layelah
for my head is filled with dew, my locks with the drops of the night.'

פָּשַׁטְתִּי, אֶת-כֻּתָּנְתִּי--אֵיכָכָה, אֶלְבָּשֶׁנָּה; רָחַצְתִּי אֶת-רַגְלַי, אֵיכָכָה אֲטַנְּפֵם
pashatti et-kuttonti, eichachah elbashennah; rachatzti et-raglai eichachah atannefem
I have put off my coat; how shall I put it on? I have washed my feet; how shall I defile them?

דּוֹדִי, שָׁלַח יָדוֹ מִן-הַחֹר, וּמֵעַי, הָמוּ עָלָיו
dodi, shalach yado min-hachor, ume'ai hamu alav
My beloved put in his hand by the hole of the door, and my heart was moved for him.

קַמְתִּי אֲנִי, לִפְתֹּחַ לְדוֹדִי; וְיָדַי נָטְפוּ-מוֹר
kamti ani liftoach ledodi; veyadai natefu-mor
I rose up to open to my beloved; and my hands dropped with myrrh,

וְאֶצְבְּעֹתַי מוֹר עֹבֵר, עַל, כַּפּוֹת הַמַּנְעוּל
ve'etzbe'otai mor over, al kappot hamman'ul
and my fingers with flowing myrrh, upon the handles of the bar.

פָּתַחְתִּי אֲנִי לְדוֹדִי, וְדוֹדִי חָמַק עָבָר; נַפְשִׁי, יָצְאָה בְדַבְּרוֹ
patachti ani ledodi, vedodi chamak avar; nafshi yatze'ah vedabbero
I opened to my beloved; but my beloved had turned away, and was gone. My soul failed me when he spoke.

בִּקַּשְׁתִּיהוּ וְלֹא מְצָאתִיהוּ, קְרָאתִיו וְלֹא עָנָנִי
bikkashtihu velo metzatihu, kerativ velo anani
I sought him, but I could not find him; I called him, but he gave me no answer.

מְצָאֻנִי הַשֹּׁמְרִים הַסֹּבְבִים בָּעִיר, הִכּוּנִי פְצָעוּנִי
metza'uni hashomerim hassovevim ba'ir hikkuni fetza'uni
The watchmen that go about the city found me, they smote me, they wounded me;

נָשְׂאוּ אֶת-רְדִידִי מֵעָלַי, שֹׁמְרֵי הַחֹמוֹת
nase'u et-redidi me'alai, shomerei hachomot
the keepers of the walls took away my mantle from me.

שִׁיר הַשִּׁירִים

מַה-יָּפוּ דֹדַיִךְ, אֲחֹתִי כַלָּה; מַה-טֹּבוּ דֹדַיִךְ מִיַּיִן
mah-yafu dodayich achoti challah; mah-tovu dodayich miyayin
How fair is thy love, my sister, my bride! how much better is thy love than wine!

וְרֵיחַ שְׁמָנַיִךְ מִכָּל-בְּשָׂמִים
vereiach shemanayich mikkol-besamim
and the smell of thine ointments than all manner of spices!

נֹפֶת תִּטֹּפְנָה שִׂפְתוֹתַיִךְ, כַּלָּה; דְּבַשׁ וְחָלָב תַּחַת לְשׁוֹנֵךְ
nofet tittofenah siftotayich kallah; devash vechalav tachat leshonech
Thy lips, O my bride, drop honey--honey and milk are under thy tongue;

וְרֵיחַ שַׂלְמֹתַיִךְ כְּרֵיחַ לְבָנוֹן
vereiach salmotayich kereiach levanon
and the smell of thy garments is like the smell of Lebanon.

גַּן נָעוּל, אֲחֹתִי כַלָּה; גַּל נָעוּל, מַעְיָן חָתוּם.
gan na'ul achoti challah; gal na'ul ma'yan chatum
A garden shut up is my sister, my bride; a spring shut up, a fountain sealed.

שְׁלָחַיִךְ פַּרְדֵּס רִמּוֹנִים, עִם פְּרִי מְגָדִים: כְּפָרִים, עִם-נְרָדִים
shelachayich pardes rimmonim, im peri megadim; kefarim im-neradim
Thy shoots are a park of pomegranates, with precious fruits; henna with spikenard plants,

נֵרְדְּ וְכַרְכֹּם, קָנֶה וְקִנָּמוֹן, עִם, כָּל-עֲצֵי לְבוֹנָה; מֹר, וַאֲהָלוֹת, עִם, כָּל-רָאשֵׁי בְשָׂמִים
nerd vecharkom, kaneh vekinnamon, im kol-'atzei levonah; mor va'ahalot, im kol-rashei vesamim
Spikenard and saffron, calamus and cinnamon, with all trees of frankincense; myrrh and aloes, with all the chief spices.

מַעְיַן גַּנִּים, בְּאֵר מַיִם חַיִּים; וְנֹזְלִים, מִן-לְבָנוֹן
ma'yan gannim, be'er mayim chayim; venozelim min-levanon
Thou art a fountain of gardens, a well of living waters, and flowing streams from Lebanon.

עוּרִי צָפוֹן וּבוֹאִי תֵימָן, הָפִיחִי גַנִּי יִזְּלוּ בְשָׂמָיו
'uri tzafon uvo'i teiman, hafichi ganni yizzelu vesamav
Awake, O north wind; and come, thou south; blow upon my garden, that the spices thereof may flow out.

יָבֹא דוֹדִי לְגַנּוֹ, וְיֹאכַל פְּרִי מְגָדָיו
yavo dodi leganno, veyochal peri megadav
Let my beloved come into his garden, and eat his precious fruits.

ה

בָּאתִי לְגַנִּי, אֲחֹתִי כַלָּה--אָרִיתִי מוֹרִי עִם-בְּשָׂמִי
Bati leganni achoti challah ariti mori im-besami
I am come into my garden, my sister, my bride; I have gathered my myrrh with my spice;

שִׁיר הַשִּׁירִים

כְּחוּט הַשָּׁנִי שִׂפְתוֹתַיִךְ, וּמִדְבָּרֵךְ נָאוֶה

kechut hashani siftotayich, umidbareich naveh
Thy lips are like a thread of scarlet, and thy mouth is comely;

כְּפֶלַח הָרִמּוֹן רַקָּתֵךְ, מִבַּעַד לְצַמָּתֵךְ

kefelach harimmon rakkatech, mibba'ad letzammatech
thy temples are like a pomegranate split open behind thy veil.

כְּמִגְדַּל דָּוִיד צַוָּארֵךְ, בָּנוּי לְתַלְפִּיּוֹת

kemigdal david tzavvarech, banui letalpiyot
Thy neck is like the tower of David builded with turrets,

אֶלֶף הַמָּגֵן תָּלוּי עָלָיו, כֹּל שִׁלְטֵי הַגִּבֹּרִים

elef hammagen talui alav, kol shiltei haggibborim
whereon there hang a thousand shields, all the armour of the mighty men.

שְׁנֵי שָׁדַיִךְ כִּשְׁנֵי עֳפָרִים, תְּאוֹמֵי צְבִיָּה, הָרוֹעִים, בַּשּׁוֹשַׁנִּים

shenei shadayich kishnei ofarim te'omei tzeviyah; haro'im bashoshannim
Thy two breasts are like two fawns that are twins of a gazelle, which feed among the lilies.

עַד שֶׁיָּפוּחַ הַיּוֹם, וְנָסוּ הַצְּלָלִים

'ad sheyafuach hayom, venasu hatzelalim
Until the day breathe, and the shadows flee away,

אֵלֶךְ לִי אֶל-הַר הַמּוֹר, וְאֶל-גִּבְעַת הַלְּבוֹנָה

elech li el-har hammor, ve'el-giv'at hallevonah
I will get me to the mountain of myrrh, and to the hill of frankincense.

כֻּלָּךְ יָפָה רַעְיָתִי, וּמוּם אֵין בָּךְ

kullach yafah ra'yati, umum ein bach
Thou art all fair, my love; and there is no spot in thee.

אִתִּי מִלְּבָנוֹן כַּלָּה, אִתִּי מִלְּבָנוֹן תָּבוֹאִי; תָּשׁוּרִי מֵרֹאשׁ אֲמָנָה

'itti millevanon kallah, itti millevanon tavo'i; tashuri merosh amanah
Come with me from Lebanon, my bride, with me from Lebanon; look from the top of Amana,

מֵרֹאשׁ שְׂנִיר וְחֶרְמוֹן, מִמְּעֹנוֹת אֲרָיוֹת, מֵהַרְרֵי נְמֵרִים

merosh senir vechermon, mimme'onot arayot, meharerei nemerim
from the top of Senir and Hermon, from the lions' dens, from the mountains of the leopards.

לִבַּבְתִּנִי, אֲחֹתִי כַלָּה

libbavtini achoti challah
Thou hast ravished my heart, my sister, my bride;

לִבַּבְתִּנִי בְּאַחַת מֵעֵינַיִךְ, בְּאַחַד עֲנָק מִצַּוְּרֹנָיִךְ

libbavtini be'achat me'einayich, be'achad anak mitzavveronayich
thou hast ravished my heart with one of thine eyes, with one bead of thy necklace.

שִׁיר הַשִׁירִים

כֻּלָּם אֲחֻזֵי חֶרֶב, מְלֻמְּדֵי מִלְחָמָה
kullam achuzei cherev, melummedei milchamah
They all handle the sword, and are expert in war;

אִישׁ חַרְבּוֹ עַל-יְרֵכוֹ, מִפַּחַד בַּלֵּילוֹת
ish charbo al-yerecho, mippachad balleilot
every man hath his sword upon his thigh, because of dread in the night.

אַפִּרְיוֹן, עָשָׂה לוֹ הַמֶּלֶךְ שְׁלֹמֹה--מֵעֲצֵי, הַלְּבָנוֹן
'appiryon, asah lo hammelech shelomoh, me'atzei hallevanon
King Solomon made himself a palanquin of the wood of Lebanon.

עַמּוּדָיו, עָשָׂה כֶסֶף, רְפִידָתוֹ זָהָב, מֶרְכָּבוֹ אַרְגָּמָן
'ammudav asah chesef, refidato zahav, merkavo argaman
He made the pillars thereof of silver, the top thereof of gold, the seat of it of purple,

תּוֹכוֹ רָצוּף אַהֲבָה, מִבְּנוֹת יְרוּשָׁלִָם
tocho ratzuf ahavah, mibbenot yerushalayim
the inside thereof being inlaid with love, from the daughters of Jerusalem.

צְאֶנָה וּרְאֶינָה בְּנוֹת צִיּוֹן, בַּמֶּלֶךְ שְׁלֹמֹה--בָּעֲטָרָה,
tze'einah ure'einah benot tziyon bammelech shelomoh ba'atarah
Go forth, O ye daughters of Zion, and gaze upon king Solomon, even upon the crown

שֶׁעִטְּרָה-לּוֹ אִמּוֹ בְּיוֹם חֲתֻנָּתוֹ, וּבְיוֹם, שִׂמְחַת לִבּוֹ
she'itterah-lo immo beyom chatunnato, uveyom simchat libbo
wherewith his mother hath crowned him in the day of his espousals, and in the day of the gladness of his heart.

ד

הִנָּךְ יָפָה רַעְיָתִי, הִנָּךְ יָפָה--עֵינַיִךְ יוֹנִים, מִבַּעַד לְצַמָּתֵךְ
Hinnach yafah ra'yati hinnach yafah, einayich yonim, mibba'ad letzammatech
Behold, thou art fair, my love; behold, thou art fair; thine eyes are as doves behind thy veil;

שַׂעְרֵךְ כְּעֵדֶר הָעִזִּים, שֶׁגָּלְשׁוּ מֵהַר גִּלְעָד
sa'rech ke'eder ha'izzim, sheggaleshu mehar gil'ad
thy hair is as a flock of goats, that trail down from mount Gilead.

שִׁנַּיִךְ כְּעֵדֶר הַקְּצוּבוֹת, שֶׁעָלוּ מִן-הָרַחְצָה
shinnayich ke'eder hakketzuvot, she'alu min-harachtzah
Thy teeth are like a flock of ewes all shaped alike, which are come up from the washing;

שֶׁכֻּלָּם, מַתְאִימוֹת, וְשַׁכֻּלָה, אֵין בָּהֶם
shekkullam mat'imot, veshakkulah ein bahem
whereof all are paired, and none faileth among them.

שִׁיר הַשִּׁירִים

ג

עַל-מִשְׁכָּבִי, בַּלֵּילוֹת, בִּקַּשְׁתִּי, אֵת שֶׁאָהֲבָה נַפְשִׁי; בִּקַּשְׁתִּיו, וְלֹא מְצָאתִיו
Al-mishkavi balleilot, bikkashti et she'ahavah nafshi; bikkashtiv velo metzativ
By night on my bed I sought him whom my soul loveth; I sought him, but I found him not.

אָקוּמָה נָּא וַאֲסוֹבְבָה בָעִיר, בַּשְּׁוָקִים וּבָרְחֹבוֹת
'akumah na va'asovevah va'ir, bashevakim uvarechovot
'I will rise now, and go about the city, in the streets and in the broad ways,

אֲבַקְשָׁה, אֵת שֶׁאָהֲבָה נַפְשִׁי; בִּקַּשְׁתִּיו, וְלֹא מְצָאתִיו
avakshah et she'ahavah nafshi; bikkashtiv velo metzativ
I will seek him whom my soul loveth.' I sought him, but I found him not.

מְצָאוּנִי, הַשֹּׁמְרִים, הַסֹּבְבִים, בָּעִיר: אֵת שֶׁאָהֲבָה נַפְשִׁי, רְאִיתֶם
metza'uni hashomerim, hassovevim ba'ir; et she'ahavah nafshi re'item
The watchmen that go about the city found me: 'Saw ye him whom my soul loveth?'

כִּמְעַט, שֶׁעָבַרְתִּי מֵהֶם, עַד שֶׁמָּצָאתִי, אֵת שֶׁאָהֲבָה נַפְשִׁי; אֲחַזְתִּיו, וְלֹא אַרְפֶּנּוּ
kim'at she'avarti mehem, ad shemmatzati, et she'ahavah nafshi; achaztiv velo arpennu
Scarce had I passed from them, when I found him whom my soul loveth: I held him, and would not let him go,

עַד-שֶׁהֲבֵיאתִיו אֶל-בֵּית אִמִּי, וְאֶל-חֶדֶר הוֹרָתִי
ad-shehaveitiv el-beit immi, ve'el-cheder horati
until I had brought him into my mother's house, and into the chamber of her that conceived me.

הִשְׁבַּעְתִּי אֶתְכֶם בְּנוֹת יְרוּשָׁלִַם, בִּצְבָאוֹת, אוֹ, בְּאַיְלוֹת הַשָּׂדֶה
hishba'ti etchem benot yerushalayim bitzva'ot, o be'aylot hassadeh
'I adjure you, O daughters of Jerusalem, by the gazelles, and by the hinds of the field,

אִם-תָּעִירוּ וְאִם-תְּעוֹרְרוּ אֶת-הָאַהֲבָה, עַד שֶׁתֶּחְפָּץ
im-ta'iru ve'im-te'oreru et-ha'ahavah ad shettechpatz
that ye awaken not, nor stir up love, until it please.'

מִי זֹאת, עֹלָה מִן-הַמִּדְבָּר, כְּתִימְרוֹת, עָשָׁן
mi zot, olah min-hammidbar, ketimrot ashan
Who is this that cometh up out of the wilderness like pillars of smoke,

מְקֻטֶּרֶת מֹר וּלְבוֹנָה, מִכֹּל אַבְקַת רוֹכֵל
mekutteret mor ulevonah, mikkol avkat rochel
perfumed with myrrh and frankincense, with all powders of the merchant?

הִנֵּה, מִטָּתוֹ שֶׁלִּשְׁלֹמֹה--שִׁשִּׁים גִּבֹּרִים, סָבִיב לָהּ: מִגִּבֹּרֵי, יִשְׂרָאֵל
hinneh, mittato shellishlomoh, shishim gibborim saviv lah; miggibborei yisra'el
Behold, it is the litter of Solomon; threescore mighty men are about it, of the mighty men of Israel.

שִׁיר הַשִּׁירִים

מַשְׁגִּיחַ מִן-הַחַלֹּנוֹת, מֵצִיץ מִן-הַחֲרַכִּים
mashgiach min-hachallonot, metzitz min-hacharakkim
he looketh in through the windows, he peereth through the lattice.

עָנָה דוֹדִי, וְאָמַר לִי: קוּמִי לָךְ רַעְיָתִי יָפָתִי, וּלְכִי-לָךְ
'anah dodi ve'amar li; kumi lach ra'yati yafati ulechi-lach
My beloved spoke, and said unto me: 'Rise up, my love, my fair one, and come away.

כִּי-הִנֵּה הַסְּתָו, עָבָר; הַגֶּשֶׁם, חָלַף הָלַךְ לוֹ
ki-hinneh hassetav avar; haggeshem chalaf halach lo
For, lo, the winter is past, the rain is over and gone;

הַנִּצָּנִים נִרְאוּ בָאָרֶץ, עֵת הַזָּמִיר הִגִּיעַ; וְקוֹל הַתּוֹר, נִשְׁמַע בְּאַרְצֵנוּ
hannitzanim nir'u va'aretz, et hazzamir higgia'; vekol hattor nishma be'artzenu
The flowers appear on the earth; the time of singing is come, and the voice of the turtle is heard in our land;

הַתְּאֵנָה חָנְטָה פַגֶּיהָ, וְהַגְּפָנִים סְמָדַר נָתְנוּ רֵיחַ
hatte'enah chanetah faggeiha, vehaggefanim semadar natenu reiach
The fig-tree putteth forth her green figs, and the vines in blossom give forth their fragrance.

קוּמִי לָךְ רַעְיָתִי יָפָתִי, וּלְכִי-לָךְ
kumi lach ra'yati yafati ulechi-lach
Arise, my love, my fair one, and come away.

יוֹנָתִי בְּחַגְוֵי הַסֶּלַע, בְּסֵתֶר הַמַּדְרֵגָה, הַרְאִינִי אֶת-מַרְאַיִךְ
yonati bechagvei hassela', beseter hammadregah, har'ini et-mar'ayich
O my dove, that art in the clefts of the rock, in the covert of the cliff, let me see thy countenance,

הַשְׁמִיעִנִי אֶת-קוֹלֵךְ: כִּי-קוֹלֵךְ עָרֵב, וּמַרְאֵיךְ נָאוֶה
hashmi'ini et-kolech; ki-kolech arev umar'eich naveh
let me hear thy voice; for sweet is thy voice, and thy countenance is comely.'

אֶחֱזוּ-לָנוּ, שֻׁעָלִים--שֻׁעָלִים קְטַנִּים, מְחַבְּלִים כְּרָמִים; וּכְרָמֵינוּ, סְמָדַר.
'echezu-lanu shu'alim, shu'alim ketannim mechabbelim keramim; ucherameinu semadar
'Take us the foxes, the little foxes, that spoil the vineyards; for our vineyards are in blossom.'

דּוֹדִי לִי וַאֲנִי לוֹ, הָרֹעֶה בַּשּׁוֹשַׁנִּים
dodi li va'ani lo, haro'eh bashoshannim
My beloved is mine, and I am his, that feedeth among the lilies.

עַד שֶׁיָּפוּחַ הַיּוֹם, וְנָסוּ הַצְּלָלִים: סֹב דְּמֵה-לְךָ דוֹדִי
'ad sheyafuach hayom, venasu hatzelalim; sov demeh-lecha dodi
Until the day breathe, and the shadows flee away, turn, my beloved,

לִצְבִי, אוֹ לְעֹפֶר הָאַיָּלִים--עַל-הָרֵי בָתֶר
litzvi, o le'ofer ha'ayalim al-harei vater
and be thou like a gazelle or a young hart upon the mountains of spices.

שִׁיר הַשִּׁירִים

ב

אֲנִי חֲבַצֶּלֶת הַשָּׁרוֹן, שׁוֹשַׁנַּת הָעֲמָקִים
Ani chavatzelet hasharon, shoshannat ha'amakim
I am a rose of Sharon, a lily of the valleys.

כְּשׁוֹשַׁנָּה בֵּין הַחוֹחִים, כֵּן רַעְיָתִי בֵּין הַבָּנוֹת
keshoshannah bein hachochim, ken ra'yati bein habbanot
As a lily among thorns, so is my love among the daughters.

כְּתַפּוּחַ בַּעֲצֵי הַיַּעַר, כֵּן דּוֹדִי בֵּין הַבָּנִים
ketappuach ba'atzei haya'ar, ken dodi bein habbanim
As an apple-tree among the trees of the wood, so is my beloved among the sons.

בְּצִלּוֹ חִמַּדְתִּי וְיָשַׁבְתִּי, וּפִרְיוֹ מָתוֹק לְחִכִּי
betzillo chimmadti veyashavti, ufiryo matok lechikki
Under its shadow I delighted to sit, and its fruit was sweet to my taste.

הֱבִיאַנִי אֶל-בֵּית הַיָּיִן, וְדִגְלוֹ עָלַי אַהֲבָה
hevi'ani el-beit hayayin, vediglo alai ahavah
He hath brought me to the banqueting-house, and his banner over me is love.

סַמְּכוּנִי, בָּאֲשִׁישׁוֹת--רַפְּדוּנִי, בַּתַּפּוּחִים: כִּי-חוֹלַת אַהֲבָה, אָנִי
sammechuni ba'ashishot, rappeduni battappuchim; ki-cholat ahavah ani
'Stay ye me with dainties, refresh me with apples; for I am love-sick.'

שְׂמֹאלוֹ תַּחַת לְרֹאשִׁי, וִימִינוֹ תְּחַבְּקֵנִי
semolo tachat leroshi, vimino techabbekeni
Let his left hand be under my head, and his right hand embrace me.

הִשְׁבַּעְתִּי אֶתְכֶם בְּנוֹת יְרוּשָׁלִַם, בִּצְבָאוֹת
hishba'ti etchem benot yerushalayim bitzva'ot
'I adjure you, O daughters of Jerusalem, by the gazelles,

אוֹ, בְּאַיְלוֹת הַשָּׂדֶה: אִם-תָּעִירוּ וְאִם-תְּעוֹרְרוּ אֶת-הָאַהֲבָה, עַד שֶׁתֶּחְפָּץ
o be'aylot hassadeh; im-ta'iru ve'im-te'oreru et-ha'ahavah ad shettechpatz
and by the hinds of the field, that ye awaken not, nor stir up love, until it please.'

קוֹל דּוֹדִי, הִנֵּה-זֶה בָּא; מְדַלֵּג, עַל-הֶהָרִים--מְקַפֵּץ, עַל-הַגְּבָעוֹת
kol dodi, hinneh-zeh ba; medalleg al-heharim, mekappetz al-haggeva'ot
Hark! my beloved! behold, he cometh, leaping upon the mountains, skipping upon the hills.

דּוֹמֶה דוֹדִי לִצְבִי, אוֹ לְעֹפֶר הָאַיָּלִים; הִנֵּה-זֶה עוֹמֵד, אַחַר כָּתְלֵנוּ
domeh dodi litzvi, o le'ofer ha'ayalim; hinneh-zeh omed achar kotlenu
My beloved is like a gazelle or a young hart; behold, he standeth behind our wall,

שִׁיר הַשִּׁירִים

אִם-לֹא תֵדְעִי לָךְ, הַיָּפָה בַּנָּשִׁים
'im-lo tede'i lach, hayafah bannashim
If thou know not, O thou fairest among women,

צְאִי-לָךְ בְּעִקְבֵי הַצֹּאן, וּרְעִי אֶת-גְּדִיֹּתַיִךְ, עַל, מִשְׁכְּנוֹת הָרֹעִים
tze'i-lach be'ikvei hatzon, ure'i et-gediyotayich, al mishkenot haro'im
go thy way forth by the footsteps of the flock and feed thy kids, beside the shepherds' tents.

לְסֻסָתִי בְּרִכְבֵי פַרְעֹה, דִּמִּיתִיךְ רַעְיָתִי
lesusati berichvei far'oh, dimmitich ra'yati
I have compared thee, O my love, to a steed in Pharaoh's chariots.

נָאווּ לְחָיַיִךְ בַּתֹּרִים, צַוָּארֵךְ בַּחֲרוּזִים
navu lechayayich battorim, tzavvarech bacharuzim
Thy cheeks are comely with circlets, thy neck with beads.

תּוֹרֵי זָהָב נַעֲשֶׂה-לָּךְ, עִם נְקֻדּוֹת הַכָּסֶף
torei zahav na'aseh-lach, im nekuddot hakkasef
We will make thee circlets of gold with studs of silver.

עַד-שֶׁהַמֶּלֶךְ, בִּמְסִבּוֹ, נִרְדִּי, נָתַן רֵיחוֹ
'ad-shehammelech bimsibbo, nirdi natan reicho
While the king sat at his table, my spikenard sent forth its fragrance.

צְרוֹר הַמֹּר דּוֹדִי לִי, בֵּין שָׁדַי יָלִין
tzeror hammor dodi li, bein shadai yalin
My beloved is unto me as a bag of myrrh, that lieth betwixt my breasts.

אֶשְׁכֹּל הַכֹּפֶר דּוֹדִי לִי, בְּכַרְמֵי עֵין גֶּדִי
'eshkol hakkofer dodi li, becharmei ein gedi
My beloved is unto me as a cluster of henna in the vineyards of En-gedi.

הִנָּךְ יָפָה רַעְיָתִי, הִנָּךְ יָפָה עֵינַיִךְ יוֹנִים
hinnach yafah ra'yati, hinnach yafah einayich yonim
Behold, thou art fair, my love; behold, thou art fair; thine eyes are as doves.

הִנְּךָ יָפֶה דוֹדִי אַף נָעִים, אַף-עַרְשֵׂנוּ רַעֲנָנָה
hinnecha yafeh dodi af na'im, af-'arsenu ra'ananah
Behold, thou art fair, my beloved, yea, pleasant; also our couch is leafy.

קֹרוֹת בָּתֵּינוּ אֲרָזִים, רַהִיטֵנוּ בְּרוֹתִים
korot batteinu arazim, rahitenu berotim
The beams of our houses are cedars, and our panels are cypresses.

שִׁיר הַשִּׁירִים

*Remember: Hebrew is Read from Right to Left
שִׁיר הַשִּׁירִים א

שִׁיר הַשִּׁירִים, אֲשֶׁר לִשְׁלֹמֹה
Shir hashirim asher lishlomoh
The song of songs, which is Solomon's.

יִשָּׁקֵנִי מִנְּשִׁיקוֹת פִּיהוּ, כִּי-טוֹבִים דֹּדֶיךָ מִיָּיִן
yishakeni minneshikot pihu, ki-tovim dodeicha miyayin
Let him kiss me with the kisses of his mouth--for thy love is better than wine.

לְרֵיחַ שְׁמָנֶיךָ טוֹבִים, שֶׁמֶן תּוּרַק שְׁמֶךָ; עַל-כֵּן, עֲלָמוֹת אֲהֵבוּךָ
lereiach shemaneicha tovim, shemen turak shemecha; al-ken alamot ahevucha
Thine ointments have a goodly fragrance; thy name is as ointment poured forth; therefore do the maidens love thee.

מָשְׁכֵנִי, אַחֲרֶיךָ נָּרוּצָה; הֱבִיאַנִי הַמֶּלֶךְ חֲדָרָיו, נָגִילָה וְנִשְׂמְחָה בָּךְ
mashecheni achareicha narutzah; hevi'ani hammelech chadarav, nagilah venismechah bach
Draw me, we will run after thee; the king hath brought me into his chambers; we will be glad and rejoice in thee,

נַזְכִּירָה דֹדֶיךָ מִיַּיִן, מֵישָׁרִים אֲהֵבוּךָ
nazkirah dodeicha miyayin, meisharim ahevucha
we will find thy love more fragrant than wine! sincerely do they love thee.

שְׁחוֹרָה אֲנִי וְנָאוָה, בְּנוֹת יְרוּשָׁלִָם; כְּאָהֳלֵי קֵדָר, כִּירִיעוֹת שְׁלֹמֹה
shechorah ani venavah, benot yerushalayim; ke'oholei kedar, kiri'ot shelomoh
'I am black, but comely, O ye daughters of Jerusalem, as the tents of Kedar, as the curtains of Solomon.

אַל-תִּרְאוּנִי שֶׁאֲנִי שְׁחַרְחֹרֶת, שֶׁשְּׁזָפַתְנִי הַשָּׁמֶשׁ
'al-tir'uni she'ani shecharchoret, sheshezafatni hashamesh
Look not upon me, that I am swarthy, that the sun hath tanned me;

בְּנֵי אִמִּי נִחֲרוּ-בִי, שָׂמֻנִי נֹטֵרָה אֶת-הַכְּרָמִים
benei immi nicharu-vi, samuni noterah et-hakkeramim
my mother's sons were incensed against me, they made me keeper of the vineyards;

כַּרְמִי שֶׁלִּי, לֹא נָטָרְתִּי
karmi shelli lo natarti
but mine own vineyard have I not kept.'

הַגִּידָה לִּי, שֶׁאָהֲבָה נַפְשִׁי, אֵיכָה תִרְעֶה, אֵיכָה תַּרְבִּיץ בַּצָּהֳרָיִם
haggidah li, she'ahavah nafshi, eichah tir'eh, eichah tarbitz batzohorayim
Tell me, O thou whom my soul loveth, where thou feedest, where thou makest thy flock to rest at noon;

שַׁלָּמָה אֶהְיֶה כְּעֹטְיָה, עַל עֶדְרֵי חֲבֵרֶיךָ
shallamah ehyeh ke'oteyah, al edrei chavereicha
for why should I be as one that veileth herself beside the flocks of thy companions?

שִׁיר הַשִּׁירִים-SHIR HASHIRIM-Song of Songs

רוּת-RUT-Ruth

אֵיכָה-EICHAH-Lamentations

קֹהֶלֶת-KOHELET-Ecclesiastes

אֶסְתֵּר-ESTER-Esther

א	A			א	1
ב	V			ב	2
ב	B	אַ	ah	ג	3
ג	G	אַ	ah	ד	4
ד	D	אֲ	ah	ה	5
ה	H	אָה	ah	ו	6
ו	V	אֵ	ei	ז	7
ז	Z	אֶ	e	ח	8
ח	KH	אֱ	e	ט	9
ט	T	אֵי	ei	י	10
י	Y	אִ	ee	יא	11
כ	KH	אִי	ee	יב	12
כ	K	אֹ	oh		
ל	L	אָ	oh		
מ	M	אֳ	oh		
ם	M	אוֹ	oh		
נ	N	אֻ	oo		
ן	N	אוּ	oo		
ס	S	אְ	e		
ע	A				
פ	F				
פ	P				
צ	TS				
ק	K				
ר	R				
שׁ	SH				
שׂ	S				
ת	T				

hebrew audio available:

at

hebrewaudiobible.com

Made in United States
Orlando, FL
08 July 2022